Collins easy learning

German Grammar

Stell dein Rad neben meines.

Dein Rad steht neben meinem.

Published by Collins
An imprint of HarperCollins Publishers
Westerhill Road
Bishopbriggs
Glasgow G64 2QT

Fourth edition 2016

ISBN 978-0-00-814200-1

10 9 8 7 6 5

www.collinsdictionary.com
www.collins.co.uk/languagesupport

Typeset by Davidson Publishing Solutions, Glasgow

Printed in Italy by GRAFICA VENETA S.p.A.

A catalogue record for this book is available from the British Library.

If you would like to comment on any aspect of this book, please contact us at the given address or online.
E-mail: dictionaries@harpercollins.co.uk
www.facebook.com/collinsdictionary
@collinsdict

Acknowledgements
We would like to thank those authors and publishers who kindly gave permission for copyright material to be used in the Collins Corpus. We would also like to thank Times Newspapers Ltd for providing valuable data.

MANAGING EDITOR
Maree Airlie

CONTRIBUTORS
Val McNulty
Gudrun Pradier

FOR THE PUBLISHER
Gerry Breslin
Craig Balfour
Chloe Osborne

CONTENTS

FOREWORD FOR LANGUAGE TEACHERS

The *Easy Learning German Grammar* is designed to be used with both young and adult learners, as a group reference book to complement your course book during classes, or as a recommended text for self-study and homework/coursework.

The text specifically targets learners from beginner to intermediate or GCSE level, and therefore its structural content and vocabulary have been matched to the relevant specifications up to and including Higher GCSE.

The approach aims to develop knowledge and understanding of grammar and to improve the ability of learners to apply it by:

- defining parts of speech at the start of each major section, with examples in English to clarify concepts
- minimizing the use of grammar terminology and providing clear explanations of terms both within the text and in the **Glossary**
- illustrating all points with examples (and their translations) based on topics and contexts which are relevant to beginner and intermediate course content

The text helps you develop positive attitudes to grammar learning in your classes by:

- giving clear, easy-to-follow explanations
- prioritizing content according to relevant specifications for the levels
- sequencing points to reflect course content, e.g. verb tenses
- highlighting useful **Tips** to deal with common difficulties
- summarizing **Key points** at the end of sections to consolidate learning

In addition to fostering success and building a thorough foundation in German grammar, the optional **Grammar Extra** sections will encourage and challenge your learners to further their studies to higher and advanced levels.

INTRODUCTION FOR STUDENTS

Whether you are starting to learn German for the very first time, brushing up on topics you have studied in class, or revising for your GCSE exams, the *Easy Learning German Grammar* is here to help. This easy-to-use guide takes you through all the basics you will need to speak and understand modern, everyday German.

Newcomers can sometimes struggle with the technical terms they come across when they start to explore the grammar of a new language. The *Easy Learning German Grammar* explains how to get to grips with all the parts of speech you will need to know, using simple language and cutting out jargon.

The text is divided into sections, each dealing with a particular area of grammar. Each section can be studied individually, as numerous cross-references in the text point you to relevant points in other sections of the book for further information.

Every major section begins with an explanation of the area of grammar covered on the following pages. For quick reference, these definitions are also collected together on pages x–xiv in a glossary of essential grammar terms.

What is a verb?
A **verb** is a 'doing' word which describes what someone or something does, what someone or something is, or what happens to them, for example, *be*, *sing*, *live*.

Each grammar point in the text is followed by simple examples of real German, complete with English translations, helping you understand the rules. Underlining has been used in examples throughout the text to highlight the grammatical point being explained.

➤ If you are talking about a part of your body, you usually use a word like *my* or *his* in English, but in German you usually use the definite article.

Er hat sich das Bein gebrochen.	He's broken his leg.
Sie hat sich die Hände schon gewaschen.	She's already washed her hands.

In German, as with any foreign language, there are certain pitfalls which have to be avoided. **Tips** and **Information** notes throughout the text are useful reminders of the things that often trip learners up.

Tip

Use **Sie** in more formal situations for both singular and plural *you*.

Key points sum up all the important facts about a particular area of grammar, to save you time when you are revising and help you focus on the main grammatical points.

Key points

- ✔ With masculine singular nouns in the nominative → use **ein**.
- ✔ With feminine singular nouns in the nominative → use **eine**.
- ✔ With plural nouns → use **die**, **der** or **den**, depending on the case.
- ✔ The indefinite article is not usually used when you say what jobs people do.

If you think you would like to continue with your German studies to a higher level, check out the **Grammar Extra** sections. These are intended for advanced students who are interested in knowing a little more about the structures they will come across beyond GCSE.

Grammar Extra!

Some German adjectives are used as feminine nouns. They have feminine adjective endings which change according to the article which comes before them.

eine Deutsch<u>e</u>	a German woman
die Abgeordnet<u>e</u>	the female MP

➪ *For more information on **Adjectives which can be used as nouns** and for **Feminine adjective endings**, see pages 50 and 42.*

Finally, the supplement at the end of the book contains **Verb Tables**, where 97 important German verbs are conjugated in full. Examples show you how to use these verbs in your own work. If you are unsure of how a verb conjugates in German, you can look up the **Verb Index** on pages 99–103 to find either the conjugation of the verb itself, or a cross-reference to a model verb, which will show you the pattern that verb follows.

We hope that you will enjoy using the *Easy Learning German Grammar* and find it useful in the course of your studies.

Glossary of grammar terms

ABSTRACT NOUN a word used to refer to a quality, idea, feeling or experience, rather than a physical object, for example, *size, reason, happiness*.

ACCUSATIVE CASE the form of nouns, adjectives, pronouns and articles used in German to show the direct object of a verb and after certain prepositions. See **direct object**.

ACTIVE a form of the verb that is used when the subject of the verb is the person or thing that carries out the action described by the verb.

ADJECTIVE a 'describing' word that tells you more about a person or thing, such as their appearance, colour, size or other qualities, for example, *pretty, blue, big*.

ADVERB a word usually used with verbs, adjectives or other adverbs that gives more information about when, where, how or in what circumstances something happens, for example, *quickly, happily, now*.

AGREE (to) to change word endings according to whether you are referring to masculine, feminine, neuter, singular or plural people and things.

AGREEMENT see **agree (to)**.

APOSTROPHE s an ending ('s) added to a noun to show who or what someone or something belongs to, for example, *Danielle's dog, the doctor's husband, the book's cover*.

ARTICLE a word like *the*, *a* and *an*, which is used in front of a noun. See also **definite article** and **indefinite article**.

AUXILIARY VERB a verb such as *be, have* and *do* when used with a main verb to form some tenses, negatives and questions.

BASE FORM the form of the verb without any endings added to it, for example, *walk, have, be, go*. Compare with **infinitive**.

CASE the grammatical function of a noun in a sentence.

CLAUSE a group of words containing a verb.

COMPARATIVE an adjective or adverb with *-er* on the end of it or *more* or *less* in front of it that is used to compare people, things or actions, for example, *slower, less important, more carefully*.

COMPOUND NOUN a word for a living being, thing or idea, which is made up of two or more words, for example, *tin-opener, railway station*.

CONDITIONAL a verb form used to talk about things that would happen or would be true under certain conditions, for example, *I <u>would</u> help you if I could*. It is also used to say what you would like or need, for example, *<u>Could</u> you give me the bill?*

CONJUGATE (to) to give a verb different endings according to whether you are referring to *I, you, they* and so on, and according to whether you are referring to past, present or future, for example, *I have, she had, they will have*.

CONJUGATION a group of verbs which have the same endings as each other or change according to the same pattern.

CONJUNCTION a word such as *and*, *because* or *but* that links two words or phrases of a similar type or two parts of a sentence, for example, *Diane <u>and</u> I have been friends for years.*; *I left <u>because</u> I was bored*. See also **co-ordinating conjunction** and **subordinating conjunction**.

CO-ORDINATING CONJUNCTION a word such as *and*, *but* or *however* that links two words, phrases or clauses.

CONSONANT a letter of the alphabet which is not a vowel, for example, *b*, *f*, *m*, *s*, *v* etc. Compare with **vowel**.

CONSTRUCTION an arrangement of words together in a phrase or sentence.

DATIVE CASE the form of nouns, adjectives, pronouns and articles used in German to show the indirect object of a verb and after certain verbs and prepositions.

DECLENSION German nouns change according to their gender, case and number. This is called declension.

DEFINITE ARTICLE the word *the*. Compare with **indefinite article**.

DEMONSTRATIVE ADJECTIVE one of the words *this*, *that*, *these* and *those* used with a noun to point out a particular person or thing, for example, *this woman*, *that dog*.

DEMONSTRATIVE PRONOUN one of the words *this*, *that*, *these* and *those* used instead of a noun to point out people or things, for example, *That looks fun*.

DIRECT OBJECT a noun referring to the person or thing affected by the action described by a verb, for example, *She wrote her name*.; *I shut the window*. Compare with **indirect object**.

DIRECT OBJECT PRONOUN a word such as *me*, *him*, *us* and *them* which is used instead of a noun to stand in for the person or thing most directly affected by the action described by the verb. Compare with **indirect object pronoun**.

ENDING a form added to a verb stem, for example, ***geh* → *geht***, and to adjectives and nouns depending on whether they refer to masculine, feminine, neuter, singular or plural things.

FEMININE one of three classifications for the gender of German nouns which determines the form of articles, pronouns and adjectives used with the noun and to refer to it. The other two classifications are **masculine** and **neuter**.

FUTURE a verb tense used to talk about something that will happen or will be true.

GENDER whether a noun, article, pronoun or adjective is feminine, masculine or neuter.

GENITIVE CASE the form of nouns, adjectives, pronouns and articles used in German to show that something belongs to someone and after certain prepositions.

IMPERATIVE the form of a verb used when giving orders and instructions, for example, *Shut the door!*; *Sit down!*; *Don't go!*

IMPERFECT one of the verb tenses used to talk about the past, especially in descriptions, and to say what was happening, for example, *It was sunny at the weekend* or what used to happen, for example, *I used to walk to school*. Compare with **perfect**.

IMPERSONAL VERB one which does not refer to a real person or thing and where the subject is represented by *it*, for example, *It's going to rain*; *It's 10 o'clock*.

INDEFINITE ADJECTIVE one of a small group of adjectives used to talk about people or things in a general way, without saying exactly who or what they are, for example, *several*, *all*, *every*.

INDEFINITE ARTICLE the words *a* and *an*. Compare with **definite article**.

INDEFINITE PRONOUN a small group of pronouns such as *everything*, *nobody* and *something*, which are used to refer to people or things in a general way, without saying exactly who or what they are.

INDIRECT OBJECT a noun or pronoun typically used in English with verbs that take two objects. For example, in *I gave the carrot to the rabbit*, *the rabbit* is the indirect object and *carrot* is the direct object. With some German verbs, what is the direct object in English is treated as an indirect object in, for example, **Ich helfe ihr** → *I'm helping her*. Compare with **direct object**.

INDIRECT OBJECT PRONOUN after a verb with two objects (a direct one and an indirect one), used instead of a noun to show the person or the thing the action is intended to benefit or harm, for example, *me* in *He gave me a book* and *Can you get me a towel*? Compare with **direct object pronoun**.

INDIRECT SPEECH the words you use *to* report what someone has said when you aren't using their actual words, for example, *He said that he was going out*.

INFINITIVE the form of the verb with *to* in front of it and without any endings added, for example, *to walk, to have, to be, to go*. Compare with **base form**.

INTERROGATIVE ADJECTIVE a question word used with a noun to ask *who?, what?* or *which?* for example, *What instruments do you play?*; *Which shoes do you like?*

INTERROGATIVE PRONOUN one of the words *who, whose, whom, what* and *which* when they are used instead of a noun to ask questions, for example, *What's happening?*; *Who's coming?*

MASCULINE one of three classifications for the gender of German nouns which determines the form of articles, pronouns and adjectives used with the noun and to refer to it. The other two classifications are **feminine** and **neuter**.

MIXED VERB a German verb whose stem changes its vowel to form the imperfect tense and the past participle, like strong verbs. Its past participle is formed by adding *-t* to the verb stem, like weak verbs. Compare with **strong verb** and **weak verb**.

MODAL VERBS are used to modify or change other verbs to show such things as *ability, permission* or *necessity*. For example, *He can swim*, *May I come?* and *He ought to go*.

NEGATIVE a question or statement which contains a word such as *not*, *never* or *nothing*, and is used to say that something is not happening, or is not true, for example, *I never eat meat*; *Don't you love me?*

NEUTER one of three classifications for the gender of German nouns which determines the form of articles, pronouns and adjectives used with the noun and to refer to it. The other two classifications are **masculine** and **feminine**.

NOMINATIVE CASE the basic form of nouns, pronouns, adjectives and articles used in German and the one you find in the dictionary. It is used for the subject of the sentence. See **subject**.

NOUN a 'naming' word for a living being, thing or idea, for example, *woman, desk, happiness, Andrew*.

OBJECT a noun or pronoun which refers to a person or thing that is affected by the action described by the verb. See also **direct object**, **indirect object** and **subject**.

OBJECT PRONOUN one of the set of pronouns including *me, him* and *them*, which are used instead of the noun as the object of a verb or preposition. Compare with **subject pronoun**.

ORDINAL NUMBER a number used to indicate where something comes in an order or sequence, for example, *first, fifth, sixteenth*.

PART OF SPEECH one of the categories to which all words are assigned and which describe their forms and how they are used in sentences, for example, *noun, verb, adjective, preposition, pronoun*.

PASSIVE a form of the verb that is used when the subject of the verb is the person or thing that is affected by the action, for example, *we were told*.

PAST PARTICIPLE a verb form, for example, *watched, swum* which is used with an auxiliary verb to form perfect and pluperfect tenses and passives. Some past participles are also used as adjectives, for example, *a broken watch*.

PERFECT one of the verb tenses used to talk about the past, especially about actions that took place and were completed in the past. Compare with **imperfect**.

PERSONAL PRONOUN one of the group of words including *I, you* and *they* which are used to refer to yourself, the people you are talking to, or the people or things you are talking about.

PLUPERFECT one of the verb tenses used to describe something that had happened or had been true at a point in the past, for example, *I'd forgotten to finish my homework*.

PLURAL the form of a word which is used to refer to more than one person or thing. Compare with **singular**.

POSSESSIVE ADJECTIVE one of the words *my, your, his, her, its, our* or *their*, used with a noun to show that one person or thing belongs to another.

POSSESSIVE PRONOUN one of the words *mine, yours, hers, his, ours* or *theirs*, used instead of a noun to show that one person or thing belongs to another.

PREPOSITION is a word such as *at, for, with, into* or *from*, which is usually followed by a noun, pronoun or, in English, a word ending in *-ing*. Prepositions show how people and things relate to the rest of the sentence, for example, *She's at home; a tool for cutting grass; It's from David*.

PRESENT a verb form used to talk about what is true at the moment, what happens regularly, and what is happening now, for example, *I'm a student; I travel to college by train; I'm studying languages*.

PRESENT PARTICIPLE a verb form ending in *-ing* which is used in English to form verb tenses, and which may be used as an adjective or a noun, for example, *What are you doing?; the setting sun; Swimming is easy!*

PRONOUN a word which you use instead of a noun, when you do not need or want to name someone or something directly, for example, *it, you, none*.

PROPER NOUN the name of a person, place, organization or thing. Proper nouns are always written with a capital letter, for example, *Kevin, Glasgow, Europe, London Eye*.

QUESTION WORD a word such as *why, where, who, which* or *how* which is used to ask a question.

REFLEXIVE PRONOUN a word ending in *-self* or *-selves*, such as *myself* or *themselves*, which refers back to the subject, for example, *He hurt himself; Take care of yourself*.

REFLEXIVE VERB a verb where the subject and object are the same, and where the action 'reflects back' on the subject. A reflexive verb is used with a reflexive pronoun such as *myself, yourself, herself*, for example, *I washed myself; He cut himself*.

RELATIVE CLAUSE part of the sentence in which the relative pronoun appears.

RELATIVE PRONOUN a word such as *that, who* or *which*, when it is used to link two parts of a sentence together.

SENTENCE a group of words which usually has a verb and a subject. In writing, a sentence has a capital letter at the beginning and a full stop, question mark or exclamation mark at the end.

SINGULAR the form of a word which is used to refer to one person or thing. Compare with **plural**.

STEM the main part of a verb to which endings are added.

STRONG VERB a German verb whose stem changes its vowel to form the imperfect tense and the past participle. Its past participle is not formed by adding *–t* to the verb stem. Also known as irregular verbs. Compare with **weak verb**.

SUBJECT the noun or pronoun used to refer to the person which does the action described by the verb, for example, *My cat doesn't drink milk*. Compare with **object**.

SUBJECT PRONOUN a pronoun such as *I, he, she* and *they* which is used instead of a noun as the subject of a sentence. Pronouns stand in for nouns when it is clear who is being talked about, for example, *My brother isn't here at the moment. He'll be back in an hour*. Compare with **object pronoun**.

SUBJUNCTIVE a verb form used in certain circumstances to express some sort of feeling, or to show doubt about whether something will happen or whether something is true. It is only used occasionally in modern English, for example, *If I were you, I wouldn't bother.; So be it*.

SUBORDINATE CLAUSE a clause which begins with a subordinating conjunction such as *because* or *while* and which must be used with a main clause. In German, the verb always goes to the end of the subordinate clause.

SUBORDINATING CONJUNCTION a word such as *when, because* or *while* that links the subordinate clause and the main clause in a sentence. See also **subordinate clause**.

SUPERLATIVE an adjective or adverb with *-est* on the end of it or *most* or *least* in front of it that is used to compare people, things or actions, for example, *thinnest, most quickly, least interesting*.

SYLLABLE consonant+vowel units that make up the sounds of a word, for example, ca-the-dral (3 syllables), im-po-ssi-ble (4 syllables).

TENSE the form of a verb which shows whether you are referring to the past, present or future.

VERB a 'doing' word which describes what someone or something does, what someone or something is, or what happens to them, for example, *be, sing, live*.

VOWEL one of the letters *a, e, i, o* or *u*. Compare with **consonant**.

WEAK VERB a German verb whose stem does not change its vowel to form the imperfect tense and the past participle. Its past participle is formed by adding *–t* to the verb stem. Also known as regular verbs. Compare with **strong verb**.

Nouns

What is a noun?
A **noun** is a 'naming' word for a living being, thing or idea, for example, *woman*, *happiness*, *Andrew*. German nouns change, according to their gender, case and number. This is called declension.

Using nouns

➤ In German, all nouns are either masculine, feminine or neuter. This is called their gender. In English, we call all things – for example, *table, car, book, apple* – 'it', but in German, even words for things have a gender. It is important to know that the gender of German nouns rarely relates to the sex of the person or thing it refers to. For example, in German, the word for "man" is masculine, but the word for "girl" is neuter and the word for "person" is feminine.

der Mann	man
das Mädchen	girl
die Person	person

Tip
German nouns are always written with a capital letter.

➤ Whenever you are using a noun, you need to know whether it is masculine, feminine or neuter as this affects the form of other words used with it, such as:

- adjectives that describe it
- articles (such as **der** or **ein**) that go before it
- pronouns (such as **er** or **sie**) that replace it

➪ *For more information on **Adjectives**, **Articles** or **Pronouns**, see pages 40, 25 and 69.*

➤ You can find information about gender by looking the word up in a dictionary – in the *Easy Learning German Dictionary*, for example, you will find the definite article (the word for *the*) in front of the word. When you come across a new noun, always learn the word for *the* that goes with it to help you remember its gender.

- **der** before a noun tells you it is masculine
- **die** before a noun tells you it is feminine
- **das** before a noun tells you it is neuter

➪ *For more information on the **Definite article**, see page 25.*

2 Nouns

➤ We refer to something as singular when we are talking about just one, and as plural when we are talking about more than one. The singular is the form of the noun you will usually find when you look a noun up in the dictionary. As in English, nouns in German change their form in the plural.

die Katze cat → **die Katzen** cats

➤ Adjectives, articles and pronouns are also affected by whether a noun is singular or plural.

> *Tip*
>
> Remember that you have to use the right word for *the*, *a* and so on according to the gender and case of the German noun.

For further explanation of grammatical terms, please see pages viii–xii.

Gender

➤ In German a noun can be masculine, feminine or neuter. Gender is quite unpredictable – the best thing is simply to learn each noun with its definite article, that is the word for *the* (**der**, **die** or **das**) which goes with it:

der Teppich	carpet
die Zeit	time
das Bild	picture

However, there are some clues which can help you work out or remember the gender of a noun, as explained below.

1 Masculine nouns

➤ Nouns referring to male people and animals are masculine.

der Mann	man
der Löwe	(male) lion

➤ Seasons, months, days of the week, weather and points of the compass are masculine.

der Sommer	summer
der August	August
der Freitag	Friday
der Wind	wind
der Norden	north

➤ Most nouns referring to things that perform an action are also masculine.

der Wecker	alarm clock
der Computer	computer

Grammar Extra!

German nouns taken from other languages and ending in **-ant**, **-ast**, **-ismus**, and **-or** are masculine:

der Passant	passer-by
der Ballast	ballast
der Kapitalismus	capitalism
der Tresor	safe

➤ Nouns with the following endings are masculine.

Masculine Ending	Example	Meaning
-ich	**der Teppich**	carpet
-ig	**der Essig**	vinegar
-ling	**der Frühling**	spring

Key points

✔ Nouns referring to male people and animals are masculine.
✔ Seasons, months, days of the week, weather and points of the compass are masculine.

2 Feminine nouns

➤ Most nouns ending in **-e** are feminine.

die Falte crease, wrinkle
die Brücke bridge

i Note that male people or animals ending in **-e** are masculine, and, nouns beginning with **Ge-** and ending in **-e** are normally neuter.

der Löwe lion
das Getreide crop

➤ Nouns with the following endings are feminine.

Feminine Ending	Example	Meaning
-heit	**die Schönheit**	beauty
-keit	**die Sehenswürdigkeit**	sight
-schaft	**die Gewerkschaft**	trade union
-ung	**die Zeitung**	newspaper
-ei	**die Bäckerei**	bakery

Grammar Extra!

German nouns taken from other languages and ending in **-anz**, **-enz**, **-ie**, **-ik**, **-ion**, **-tät**, **-ur** are feminine, with some exceptions.

die Distanz distance BUT: **der Kranz** wreath
die Konkurrenz rivalry

die Theorie theory BUT: **das Knie** knee

die Panik panic BUT: **der Pazifik** Pacific

die Union union BUT: **der Spion** spy

die Elektrizität electricity
die Temperatur temperature BUT: **das Abitur** A levels

For further explanation of grammatical terms, please see pages viii–xii.

- Numbers used in counting, for example one, three, fifty are feminine.

  Er hat eine Drei gekriegt. He got a three.

- In German, there are sometimes very different words for male and female, just as in English.

der Mann	man
die Frau	woman
der Vater	father
die Mutter	mother
der Bulle	bull
die Kuh	cow

- Many masculine German nouns can be made feminine by adding **-in** in the singular and **-innen** in the plural.

der Lehrer	(male) teacher
die Lehrerin	(female) teacher
Lehrer und Lehrerinnen	(male and female) teachers
der Leser	(male) reader
die Leserin	(female) reader
unsere Leser und Leserinnen	our readers

Grammar Extra!

Some German adjectives are used as feminine nouns. They have feminine adjective endings which change according to the article which comes before them.

eine Deutsche	a German woman
die Abgeordnete	the female MP

*For more information on **Adjectives which can be used as nouns** and for **Feminine adjective endings**, see pages 50 and 42.*

Key points

- ✔ Most nouns ending in **-e** are feminine.
- ✔ Many feminine nouns end in: **-heit**, **-keit**, **-schaft**, **-ung**, **-ei**.
- ✔ Masculine German words referring to people can be made feminine by adding **-in** in the singular and **-innen** in the plural.
- ✔ Numbers used in counting are feminine.

3 Neuter nouns

➤ Most nouns beginning with **Ge-** are neuter.

das Geschirr	crockery, dishes
das Geschöpf	creature
das Getreide	crop

➤ Nouns ending in **-lein** or **-chen** are also neuter. These are called the diminutive form and refer to small persons or objects.

Endings to form the diminutive	Example	Meaning
-lein	das Tischlein	little table
-chen	das Häuschen	little house

i Note that if these words have one of the vowels **a**, **o** or **u**, an umlaut should be added above the vowel. The final **-e** should also be dropped before these endings

der Bach → Bäch → das Bächlein	(small) stream
die Katze → Kätz → das Kätzchen	kitten

➤ Fractions are also neuter.

ein Drittel davon	a third of it

➤ Nouns which refer to young humans and animals are neuter.

das Baby	baby
das Kind	child
das Kalb	calf
das Lamm	lamb

i Note that the animals themselves can be any gender.

der Hund	dog
die Schlange	snake
das Vieh	cattle

➤ Infinitives (the "to" form of verbs) used as nouns are neuter.

das Schwimmen	swimming
das Spielen	playing
das Radfahren	cycling

➪ *For more information on **Infinitives**, see page 134.*

➤ Nouns with the following endings are <u>neuter</u>.

Neuter Ending	Example	Meaning
-nis	**<u>das</u> Ereig<u>nis</u>**	event
-tum	**<u>das</u> Eigen<u>tum</u>**	property

Grammar Extra!

German nouns taken from other languages and ending in **-at**, **-ett**, **-fon**, **-ma**, **-ment**, **-um** are <u>neuter</u>.

<u>das</u> Reserv<u>at</u>	reservation			
<u>das</u> Tabl<u>ett</u>	tray			
<u>das</u> Tele<u>fon</u>	phone			
<u>das</u> The<u>ma</u>	subject, topic			
<u>das</u> Medika<u>ment</u>	drug			
<u>das</u> Ultimat<u>um</u>	ultimatum	BUT:	**<u>der</u> Reicht<u>um</u>**	wealth
<u>das</u> Studi<u>um</u>	studies			

Key points

- ✔ Most nouns beginning with **Ge-** are neuter.
- ✔ The diminutive form of nouns is neuter.
- ✔ Nouns referring to young humans and animals are neuter.
- ✔ The "to" forms of verbs (called infinitives) used as nouns are neuter.
- ✔ Nouns ending in **-nis** or **-tum** are neuter.

4 <u>Compound nouns</u>

What is a compound noun?
A **compound noun** is a noun made up of two or more words, for example, *tin-opener* and *railway station*.

➤ In German, these words nearly always take their gender from the <u>LAST</u> noun of the compound word.

<u>die</u> Armbanduhr (**Armband** + **<u>die</u> Uhr**)	wristwatch
<u>der</u> Tomatensalat (**Tomaten** + **<u>der</u> Salat**)	tomato salad
<u>der</u> Fußballspieler (**Fußball** + **<u>der</u> Spieler**)	footballer

Grammar Extra!

Some German nouns have more than one gender. A few nouns have two genders and sometimes one of them can only be used in certain regions.

der/das Marzipan	marzipan	(***der Marzipan** is used mostly in Austria*)
der/das Keks	biscuit	(***das Keks** is used mostly in Austria*)
der/das Kaugummi	chewing gum	

Other nouns have two genders and the meaning of the word changes depending on which gender it has.

der Band	volume, book
das Band	ribbon, band, tape; bond
der See	lake
die See	sea
der Leiter	leader, manager
die Leiter	ladder

➤ In German, abbreviations have the same gender as the word they come from.

die BRD	the Federal Republic of Germany (from **die Bundesrepublik Deutschland**)
die DB	the German Railways (from **die Deutsche Bahn**)
das ZDF	German TV channel (from **das Zweite Deutsche Fernsehen**)

Key points

✔ Compound nouns are nouns made up of two or more words and usually take their gender from the last part of the compound word.

✔ Some German nouns have more than one gender and this can affect their meaning.

✔ German abbreviations have the same gender as the words they come from.

The Cases

➤ In German, there are four grammatical cases – nominative, accusative, genitive and dative. The case you should use depends on the grammatical function of the noun in the sentence.

1 The nominative case

➤ The nominative case is the basic form of the noun and is the one you find in the dictionary.

Case	Masculine	Feminine	Neuter
Nominative	**der Wagen** **ein Wagen**	**die Dose** **eine Dose**	**das Lied** **ein Lied**

➪ *For more information on* **Articles**, *see page 25.*

➤ The nominative case is used for:

- the subject of the sentence, that is the person, animal or thing 'doing' the action

  Das Mädchen singt. — The girl is singing.
  Die Katze schläft. — The cat is sleeping.

- after the verbs **sein** (meaning *to be*) and **werden** (meaning *to be, to become*)

  Er ist ein guter Lehrer. — He is a good teacher.
  Das wird ein Pullover. — It's going to be a jumper.

2 The accusative case

➤ The article for feminine and neuter nouns in the accusative case has the same form as in the nominative. **Der** for masculine nouns changes to **den** and **ein** to **einen**.

Case	Masculine	Feminine	Neuter
Nominative	**der Wagen** **ein Wagen**	**die Dose** **eine Dose**	**das Lied** **ein Lied**
Accusative	**den Wagen** **einen Wagen**	**die Dose** **eine Dose**	**das Lied** **ein Lied**

➪ *For more information on* **Articles**, *see page 25.*

➤ The accusative case is used:

- to show the direct object of a verb. This is the person, animal or thing affected by the action of the verb.

He gave me a book. → *What did he give me?* → a book (=*direct object*)

Can you get me a towel? → *What can you get me?* → a towel (=*direct object*)

Ich sehe den Hund. → *What do I see?* → **den Hund** (=*direct object*)

Er hat ein Lied gesungen. → *What did he sing?* → **ein Lied** (=*direct object*)

- after certain prepositions (words in English such as *at*, *for*, *with*, *into* or *from*) which are always used with the accusative.

Es ist für seine Freundin.	It's for his girlfriend.
Es ist schwierig ohne einen Wagen.	It's difficult without a car.
Durch das Rauchen wurde ich krank.	Smoking made me ill.

For more information on ***Prepositions followed by the accusative case****, see page 156.*

- after certain prepositions of place when movement is involved:

an	on, to, at
auf	on, in, to, at
hinter	behind
in	in, into, to
neben	next to, beside
über	over, across, above
unter	under, among
vor	in front of, before
zwischen	between
Stell dein Rad neben mein Auto.	Put your bike next to my car.
Sie legten ein Brett über das Loch.	They put a board over the hole.

i Note that when there is no movement involved after these prepositions, the dative case is used.

Sie geht in die Stadt. (*accusative*)	She's going into town.
Er war in der Stadt. (*dative*)	He was in town.

For more information on ***Prepositions followed by the accusative or the dative case****, see page 158.*

- in many expressions of time and place which do not have a preposition

Das macht sie jeden Donnerstag.	She does that every Thursday.
Die Schule ist einen Kilometer entfernt.	The school is a kilometre away.

- in some set expressions

Guten Abend!	Good evening!
Vielen Dank!	Thank you very much!

3 The genitive case

➤ **Der** for masculine nouns and **das** for neuter nouns change to **des**. **Ein** changes to **eines**. The endings of masculine and neuter singular nouns also change in the genitive case.

➤ **-s** is added to masculine and neuter nouns ending in **-en**, **-el**, **-er**.

der Wagen car → **des Wagens**
das Rauchen smoking → **des Rauchens**
der Esel donkey → **des Esels**
der Computer computer → **des Computers**

Ich mag die Farbe des Wagens.	I like the colour of the car.
Die Größe des Computers ist nicht wichtig.	The size of the computer isn't important.

➤ **-es** is added to most masculine and neuter nouns of one syllable ending in a consonant.

der Freund friend → **des Freundes**
der Mann man → **des Mannes**
der Sitz seat → **des Sitzes**
der Arzt doctor → **des Arztes**
der Tisch table → **des Tisches**
das Schloss castle → **des Schlosses**

Die Schwester des Arztes hilft manchmal in der Sprechstunde.	The doctor's sister helps him in the surgery sometimes.
Das Museum befindet sich in der Nähe des Schlosses.	The museum is near the castle.

➤ **Die** changes to **der** and **eine** to **einer** in the genitive. The endings of feminine singular nouns in the genitive case are the same as in the nominative.

die Ärztin (female) doctor → **der Ärztin**

Case	Masculine	Feminine	Neuter
Nominative	der Wagen ein Wagen	die Dose eine Dose	das Lied ein Lied
Accusative	den Wagen einen Wagen	die Dose eine Dose	das Lied ein Lied
Genitive	des Wagens eines Wagens	der Dose einer Dose	des Lieds eines Lieds

For more information on ***Articles****, see page 25.*

➤ The genitive case is used:

- to show that something belongs to someone

Das Auto der Frau war rot.	The woman's car was red.
Der Hund meiner Mutter ist ganz klein.	My mother's dog is really small.

- after certain prepositions which always take the genitive

Wegen des schlechten Wetters müssen wir nach Hause gehen.	We'll have to go home because of the bad weather.
Trotz ihrer Krankheit geht sie jeden Tag spazieren.	She goes for a walk every day, despite her illness.

- in some expressions of time

eines Tages	one day

4 The dative case

➤ **Der** changes to **dem** and **ein** to **einem** in the dative. Singular nouns in the dative have the same form as in the nominative.

dem Auto	to the car
dem Mädchen	to the girl

➤ **Die** changes to **der** and **eine** to **einer** in the dative. Singular nouns in the dative have the same form as in the nominative.

Case	Masculine	Feminine	Neuter
Nominative	der Wagen ein Wagen	die Dose eine Dose	das Lied ein Lied
Accusative	den Wagen einen Wagen	die Dose eine Dose	das Lied ein Lied
Genitive	des Wagens eines Wagens	der Dose einer Dose	des Lieds eines Lieds
Dative	dem Wagen einem Wagen	der Dose einer Dose	dem Lied einem Lied

➪ *For more information on* ***Articles****, see page 25.*

➤ **-e** is added to some nouns in certain set phrases.

Wir gehen nach Hause.	We're going home.
Er hat sich zu Tode gearbeitet.	He worked himself to death.

Grammar Extra!

-e may also be added to the dative singular of masculine and neuter nouns to make the phrase easier to pronounce

zu welchem Zwecke?	to what purpose?

➤ The dative case is used:

- to show the indirect object of a verb – an indirect object answers the question *who to/for?* or *to/for what?*

  He gave the man the book. → *Who did he give the book to?* → the man (= *noun indirect object*)

  Er gab dem Mann das Buch.

- after certain verbs

Er hilft seiner Mutter im Haushalt.	He helps his mother with the housework.

➪ *For more information on* ***Verbs followed by the dative case****, see page* 148.

- after certain prepositions which always take the dative

Nach dem Essen gingen wir spazieren.	After eating we went for a walk.
Er kam mit einer Freundin.	He came with a friend.

➪ *For more information on* ***Prepositions followed by the dative case****, see page* 153.

- after certain prepositions to show position

an	on, to, at
auf	on, in, to, at
hinter	behind
in	in, into, to
neben	next to, beside
über	over, across, above
unter	under, among
vor	in front of, before
zwischen	between

Ich sitze neben dem Fenster.	I'm sitting next to the window.
Die Katze lag unter dem Tisch.	The cat lay under the table.

i Note that when there is some movement involved after these prepositions, the accusative case is used.

Er war in der Stadt. (*dative*) He was in town.

Sie geht in die Stadt. (*accusative*) She's going into town.

For more information on ***Prepositions followed by the accusative or the dative case****, see page 158.*

- in certain expressions

Mir ist kalt. I'm cold.

- instead of the possessive adjective (*my*, *your*, *his*, *her*, *its*, *our* or *their*) to refer to parts of the body and items of clothing

Ich habe mir die Haare gewaschen. I washed my hair.

Zieh dir die Jacke aus. Take your jacket off.

For more information on ***Possessive adjectives****, see page 37.*

➤ Changes to the definite and indefinite articles **der**, **die** or **das** and **ein**, **eine** or **ein** for each case are summarized in the table below, to help make it easier for you to remember them.

Case	Masculine Singular	Feminine Singular	Neuter Singular
Nominative	**der** **ein**	**die** **eine**	**das** **ein**
Accusative	**den** **einen**	**die** **eine**	**das** **ein**
Genitive	**des** **eines**	**der** **einer**	**des** **eines**
Dative	**dem** **einem**	**der** **einer**	**dem** **einem**

For more information on ***Articles****, see page 25.*

Key points

- ✔ In German, there are four grammatical cases – nominative, accusative, genitive and dative.
- ✔ The case you use depends on the grammatical function of the noun in the sentence.
- ✔ The nominative case is used to show the subject of a sentence and after the verbs, **sein** and **werden**.
- ✔ The accusative case is used to show the direct object of a sentence and after certain prepositions.
- ✔ The genitive case is used to show that something belongs to somebody, and after certain prepositions.
- ✔ The dative case is used to show the indirect object of a sentence, and after certain prepositions and verbs.

Forming plurals

- In English we usually make nouns plural by adding an *-s* to the end (*garden* → *gardens*; *house* → *houses*), although we do have some nouns which are irregular and do not follow this pattern (*mouse* → *mice*; *child* → *children*).
- In German, there are several different ways of making nouns plural.
- The definite article changes in the plural, as shown in the table below:

Case	Masculine Singular	Feminine Singular	Neuter Singular	All Genders Plural
Nominative	der	die	das	die
Accusative	den	die	das	die
Genitive	des	der	des	der
Dative	dem	der	dem	den

For more information on ***Articles****, see page 25.*

Tip

Nouns in the dative plural ALWAYS end in **-n**, except those nouns which come from other languages. Most of their plural forms end in **-s**. For example:

Mit den Autos hatte sie ständig Probleme.	The cars caused her constant problems.

1 Feminine plural nouns ending in -n, -en, -nen

- Most German feminine nouns form their plural by adding **-n**, **-en** or **-nen** to their singular form.

Case	Singular	Plural
Nominative	**die Blume** (flower) **die Frau** (woman) **die Lehrerin** (teacher)	**die Blumen** **die Frauen** **die Lehrerinnen**
Accusative	**die Blume** **die Frau** **die Lehrerin**	**die Blumen** **die Frauen** **die Lehrerinnen**
Genitive	**der Blume** **der Frau** **der Lehrerin**	**der Blumen** **der Frauen** **der Lehrerinnen**
Dative	**der Blume** **der Frau** **der Lehrerin**	**den Blumen** **den Frauen** **den Lehrerinnen**

Die Blumen waren nicht teuer.	The flowers weren't expensive.
Die Lehrerinnen sind ziemlich jung.	The (female) teachers are quite young.
Das Leben der Frauen in vielen Ländern ist schwierig.	In many countries, women's lives are difficult.
Wo gehst du mit den Blumen hin?	Where are you going with the flowers?

2 Nouns with no ending in the plural

➤ Many nouns have no plural ending – these are mostly masculine or neuter nouns ending in **-en**, **-er** or **-el**.

Case	Singular	Plural
Nominative	**der Kuchen** (cake) **der Lehrer** (teacher) **der Onkel** (uncle)	**die Kuchen** **die Lehrer** **die Onkel**
Accusative	**den Kuchen** **den Lehrer** **den Onkel**	**die Kuchen** **die Lehrer** **die Onkel**
Genitive	**des Kuchens** **des Lehrers** **des Onkels**	**der Kuchen** **der Lehrer** **der Onkel**
Dative	**dem Kuchen** **dem Lehrer** **dem Onkel**	**den Kuchen** **den Lehrern** **den Onkeln**

Die Kuchen sehen lecker aus.	The cakes look delicious.
Die Onkel kommen morgen an.	The uncles are coming tomorrow.
Das war die Schuld der Lehrer.	That was the teachers' fault.
Es gibt ein kleines Problem mit den Kuchen.	There's a slight problem with the cakes.

➤ Some of these nouns also have an umlaut added to the first vowel **a**, **o** or **u** in the plural.

Case	Singular	Plural
Nominative	**der Apfel** (apple) **der Garten** (garden)	**die Äpfel** **die Gärten**
Accusative	**den Apfel** **den Garten**	**die Äpfel** **die Gärten**
Genitive	**des Apfels** **des Gartens**	**der Äpfel** **der Gärten**
Dative	**dem Apfel** **dem Garten**	**den Äpfeln** **den Gärten**

Die Äpfel sind nicht reif genug. The apples aren't ripe enough.
Die Gärten waren wunderschön. The gardens were beautiful.
Schau mal die Größe der Äpfel an! Look at the size of the apples!
Den Äpfeln fehlt ein bisschen Sonne. The apples need a bit of sun.

3 Plural nouns ending in ¨-e

➤ Some masculine nouns add an umlaut above the first vowel **a**, **o** or **u** and an **-e** ending to form the plural. A few feminine nouns with **a** in the stem also follow this pattern. Nouns in this group often have one syllable only.

Case	Singular	Plural
Nominative	**der Stuhl** (chair) **die Angst** (fear)	**die Stühle** **die Ängste**
Accusative	**den Stuhl** **die Angst**	**die Stühle** **die Ängste**
Genitive	**des Stuhl(e)s** **der Angst**	**der Stühle** **der Ängste**
Dative	**dem Stuhl** **der Angst**	**den Stühlen** **den Ängsten**

Die Stühle sind neu. The chairs are new.
Die Regierung muss die Ängste der Bevölkerung ernst nehmen. The government has to take the population's fears seriously.
Die Farbe der Stühle. The colour of the chairs.
Der Tischler macht den Stühlen neue Beine. The carpenter is making new legs for the chairs.

4 Masculine and neuter plural nouns ending in -e, -er or ¨-er

➤ Masculine or neuter nouns often add **-e** or **-er** to form the plural.

Case	Singular	Plural
Nominative	**das Geschenk** (present) **der Tisch** (table) **das Kind** (child)	**die Geschenke** **die Tische** **die Kinder**
Accusative	**das Geschenk** **den Tisch** **das Kind**	**die Geschenke** **die Tische** **die Kinder**
Genitive	**des Geschenks** **des Tisches** **des Kindes**	**der Geschenke** **der Tische** **der Kinder**
Dative	**dem Geschenk** **dem Tisch** **dem Kind**	**den Geschenken** **den Tischen** **den Kindern**

For further explanation of grammatical terms, please see pages viii–xii.

Die Geschenke sind auf dem Tisch.	The presents are on the table.
Ich muss die Kinder abholen.	I have to pick up the children.
Die Auswahl der Tische im Laden war groß.	The shop had a large selection of tables.
Sie geht mit den Kindern spazieren.	She's going for a walk with the children.

➤ Some masculine and neuter nouns add an umlaut above the first vowel **a**, **o** or **u** and an **-er** ending in the plural.

Case	Singular	Plural
Nominative	**das Dach** (roof) **der Mann** (man)	**die Dächer** **die Männer**
Accusative	**das Dach** **den Mann**	**die Dächer** **die Männer**
Genitive	**des Dach(e)s** **des Mannes**	**der Dächer** **der Männer**
Dative	**dem Dach** **dem Mann**	**den Dächern** **den Männern**

Die Dächer werden repariert.	The roofs are being repaired.
Man hatte die Männer völlig vergessen.	The men had been completely forgotten.
Was ist die Rolle der Männer in unserer Gesellschaft?	What is the role of men in our society?
Die Frauen sollten den Männern nicht immer recht geben.	Women should not always agree with men.

5 Some unusual plurals

➤ There is another group of German nouns which don't follow any of the rules for forming plurals – you just have to remember them! Here are some of the most common ones. As you will see, many of them are words from other languages, and it is common for such words to form their plural by adding **-s**:

Singular	Meaning	Plural
das Auto	car	**die Autos**
das Hotel	hotel	**die Hotels**
das Restaurant	restaurant	**die Restaurants**
das Baby	baby	**die Babys**
das Thema	theme, topic, subject	**die Themen**
das Drama	drama	**die Dramen**
das Risiko	risk	**die Risiken**
der Park	park	**die Parks**
der Chef	boss, chief, head	**die Chefs**
die Firma	firm	**die Firmen**

Die Hotels in der Stadt sind ziemlich teuer.	The hotels in town are quite expensive.
Die Risiken sind sehr hoch.	The risks are very high.
Die Kinder finden die Babys ganz niedlich.	The children think the babies are really cute.
Was hältst du von den Preisen der Autos?	What do you think of the prices of the cars?
Das ist die Stadt mit den vielen Parks.	That's the town with all the parks.

6 Plural versus singular

➤ Some nouns are always plural in English, but singular in German.

eine Brille	glasses, spectacles
eine Schere	scissors
eine Hose	trousers

➤ These nouns are only used in the plural in German to mean more than one pair.

zwei Hosen	two pairs of trousers

7 Nouns of measurement and quantity

➤ These nouns, used to describe the quantity or size of something, usually remain singular, even if preceded by a plural number.

Möchten Sie zwei Stück?	Would you like two?
Ich wiege fünfzig Kilo.	I weigh eight stone.

➤ The substance which they measure follows in the same case as the noun of quantity, and NOT in the genitive case as in English.

Sie hat drei Tassen Kaffee getrunken.	She drank three cups of coffee.
Er wollte zwei Kilo Kartoffeln.	He wanted two kilos of potatoes.
Drei Glas Weißwein, bitte!	Three glasses of white wine, please.

For further explanation of grammatical terms, please see pages viii–xii.

Key points

- ✔ Most German feminine nouns form their plural by adding **-n**, **-en** or **-nen** to their singular form.
- ✔ Many nouns have no plural ending – these are mostly masculine or neuter singular nouns ending in **-en**, **-er** or **-el**. Some of these nouns also have an umlaut added to the vowel in the plural.
- ✔ Some masculine nouns add an umlaut above the first vowel **a**, **o** or **u** and an **-e** ending to form the plural. A few feminine nouns with **a** in the stem also follow this pattern.
- ✔ Masculine and neuter nouns often add **-e** or **-er** in the plural, and can sometimes add an umlaut above the first vowel **a**, **o** or **u**.
- ✔ There are some unusual plural nouns in German which don't follow any pattern.
- ✔ Some nouns are always plural in English, but singular in German.
- ✔ Nouns of measurement and quantity usually remain singular even if preceded by a plural number.
- ✔ The substance which they measure follows in the same case as the noun of quantity.

Weak nouns

➤ As we have seen, German nouns may change, according to their gender, case and number. This is called declension.

➤ Some masculine nouns have a weak declension – this means that they end in **-en** or, if the word ends in a vowel, in **-n**, in every case EXCEPT in the nominative singular case.

➤ Weak masculine nouns follow the pattern shown:

Case	Singular	Plural
Nominative	**der Junge**	**die Jungen**
Accusative	**den Jungen**	**die Jungen**
Genitive	**des Jungen**	**der Jungen**
Dative	**dem Jungen**	**den Jungen**

➤ Weak masculine nouns include:

- those ending in **-og(e)** referring to men

der Psychologe — the psychologist

Er fragte den Psychologen um Rat. — He asked the psychologist for advice.

- those ending in **-aph** (or **-af**) or **-oph**

der Paragraf — the paragraph
der Philosoph — the philosopher

Der Paragraf umfasste 350 Wörter. — The paragraph was 350 words long.

- those ending in **-ant**

der Elefant — the elephant
der Diamant — the diamond

Der Diamant war sehr viel Geld wert. — The diamond was worth a lot of money.

- those ending in **-t** referring to men

der Astronaut — the astronaut
der Komponist — the composer
der Architekt — the architect

Um Astronaut zu werden, muss man jahrelang trainieren. — You have to train for years to become an astronaut.

For further explanation of grammatical terms, please see pages viii–xii.

- some other common weak masculine nouns:

der Bauer	farmer
der Chirurg	surgeon
der Franzose	Frenchman
der Kollege	colleague
der Mensch	human being
der Ochse	ox
der Spatz	sparrow
Der junge Franzose wollte Schottland besuchen.	The young French guy wanted to visit Scotland.
Ich habe den Franzosen seit einer Woche nicht mehr gesehen.	I haven't seen the French guy for a week.

Grammar Extra!

The noun **der Name** follows the same pattern as **der Junge**, except in the genitive singular, where it adds **-ns** instead of just **-n**. **Der Buchstabe** (meaning *letter* (*of the alphabet*)), **der Funke** (meaning *spark*) and **der Gedanke** (meaning *thought*) also follow this pattern.

Case	Singular	Plural
Nominative	**der Name**	**die Namen**
Accusative	**den Namen**	**die Namen**
Genitive	**des Namens**	**der Namen**
Dative	**dem Namen**	**den Namen**

Das hängt von der Wichtigkeit des Namens ab.	That depends on how important the name is.

Proper nouns

> **What is a proper noun?**
> A **proper noun** is the name of a person, place, organization or thing. Proper nouns are always written with a capital letter, for example, *Kevin*, *Glasgow*, *Europe*, *London Eye*.

➤ In German, names of people and places only change in the genitive singular when they add **-s**, unless they are preceded by the definite article or a demonstrative adjective (in English, *this*, *that*, *these* and *those*).

Annas Buch	Anna's book
Klaras Mantel	Klara's coat
die Werke Goethes	Goethe's works
BUT	
der Untergang der Titanic	the sinking of the Titanic

➩ *For more information on* **Articles** *and* **Demonstrative adjectives**, *see pages 25 and 31.*

Grammar Extra!

Where proper names end in **-s**, **-sch**, **-ss**, **-ß**, **-x**, **-z**, **or -tz**, adding an extra **-s** for the genitive makes them very difficult to pronounce. This is best avoided by using **von** + the dative case.

das Buch von Hans	Hans's book
die Werke von Marx	the works of Marx
die Freundin von Klaus	Klaus's girlfriend

➤ **Herr** (meaning *Mr)* is always declined when it is part of a proper name.

an Herrn Schmidt	to Mr Schmidt
Sehr geehrte Herren	Dear Sirs

➤ Surnames usually form their plurals by adding **-s**, unless they end in **-s**, **-sch**, **-ss**, **-ß**, **-x**, **-z**, or **-tz**, in which case they add **-ens**. They are often preceded by the definite article.

Die Schmidts haben uns zum Abendessen eingeladen.	The Schmidts have invited us to dinner.
Die Schultzens waren nicht zu Hause.	The Schultzes weren't at home.

➩ *For more information on* **Articles**, *see page 25.*

Articles

What is an article?
In English, an **article** is one of the words *the*, *a*, and *an* which is used in front of a noun.

1 Different types of articles

➤ There are two types of article:

- the definite article: *the* in English. This is used to identify a particular thing or person.

  I'm going to the supermarket.
  That's the woman I was talking to.

- the indefinite article: *a* or *an* in English, *some* or *any* (or no word at all) in the plural. This is used to refer to something unspecific, or something that you do not really know about.

  Is there a supermarket near here?
  I need a day off.

2 The definite article

➤ In English the definite article *the* always keeps the same form.

the book
the books
with *the* books

➤ In German, however, the definite article has many forms. All German nouns are either masculine, feminine or neuter and, just as in English, they can be either singular or plural. The word you choose for *the* depends on whether the noun it is used with is masculine, feminine or neuter, singular or plural AND it also depends on the case of the noun. This may sound complicated, but it is not too difficult.

Die Frau ging spazieren.	The woman went for a walk.
Der Mann ist geschieden.	The man is divorced.
Sie fährt mit dem Auto in die Stadt.	She travels into town by car.
Die Farbe der Jacke gefällt mir nicht.	I don't like the colour of the jacket.
Ich muss die Kinder abholen.	I have to pick up the children.
Das will ich mit den Behörden besprechen.	I want to discuss that with the authorities.

*For more information on **Nouns**, see page 1.*

➤ The definite article changes for masculine, feminine and neuter singular nouns.

	Definite Article + Noun	Meaning
Masculine	**der Mann**	the man
Feminine	**die Frau**	the woman
Neuter	**das Mädchen**	the girl

➤ The plural forms of the definite article are the same for all genders.

	Definite Article + Plural Noun	Meaning
Masculine	**die Männer**	the men
Feminine	**die Frauen**	the women
Neuter	**die Mädchen**	the girls

Tip

It is a good idea to learn the article or the gender with the noun when you come across a word for the first time, so that you know whether it is masculine, feminine or neuter. A good dictionary will also give you this information.

➤ The definite article also changes according to the case of the noun in the sentence – nominative, accusative, genitive or dative.

➪ *For more information on **Cases**, see page 9.*

➤ The forms of the definite article in each case are as follows:

Case	Masculine Singular	Feminine Singular	Neuter Singular	All Genders Plural
Nominative	**der**	**die**	**das**	**die**
Accusative	**den**	**die**	**das**	**die**
Genitive	**des**	**der**	**des**	**der**
Dative	**dem**	**der**	**dem**	**den**

<u>Der</u> Mann ging ins Haus.	The man went into the house.
<u>Die</u> Frau geht jeden Abend schwimmen.	The woman goes swimming every night.
Sie wollen <u>das</u> Mädchen adoptieren.	They want to adopt the girl.
<u>Die</u> zwei Frauen nebenan wollen ihr Haus renovieren.	The two women next door want to renovate their house.
<u>Der</u> Mann mit <u>der</u> reichen Frau machte eine Weltreise.	The man with the rich wife travelled around the world.
<u>Die</u> Mädchen gehen morgen ins Kino.	The girls are going to the cinema tomorrow.
Ich will nicht nur mit <u>den</u> Männern arbeiten.	I don't just want to work with the men.

Key points

✔ The definite article changes for masculine, feminine and neuter singular nouns.

✔ The plural forms of the definite article are the same for all genders.

✔ The form of the definite article also changes depending on the case of the noun in the sentence.

3 Using the definite article

➤ The definite article in German (**der**, **die** or **das**) is used in more or less the same way as we use *the* in English, but it is also used in German in a few places where you might not expect it.

➤ The definite article is used with words like *prices*, *life* and *time* that describe qualities, ideas or experiences (called <u>abstract nouns</u>) rather than something that you can touch with your hand. Usually, *the* is missed out in English with this type of word.

<u>Die</u> Preise sind wirklich hoch.	Prices are really high.
<u>Das</u> Leben ist schön.	Life is wonderful.
<u>Die</u> Zeit vergeht schnell.	Time passes quickly.

i Note that these nouns are sometimes used <u>WITHOUT</u> the article.

Es braucht Mut.	It needs (some) courage.
Gibt es dort Leben?	Is there (any) life there?

➤ You also use the definite article with the genitive case to show that something belongs to someone.

die Jacke <u>der</u> Frau	the woman's jacket

ℹ Note that you do not usually use the definite article with the genitive case if the noun is a proper name or is being used as a proper name.
A proper name is the name of a person, place, organization or thing.

Jans Auto — Jan's car

Muttis Auto — Mummy's car

Occasionally, the definite article IS used with proper names:

- to make the sex of the person or the case clearer

  Er hat es der Frau Kekilli gegeben. — He gave it to Frau Kekilli.

- where an adjective is used before the proper name

  Die alte Frau Schnorr ist gestorben. — Old Frau Schnorr has died.

- in certain informal situations or to emphasize something

  Ich habe heute den Kevin gesehen. — I saw Kevin today.

➤ In German, you have to use the definite article in front of masculine and feminine countries and districts, but you don't need it for neuter ones.

Die Schweiz ist auch schön. — Switzerland is also beautiful.

Deutschland ist sehr schön. — Germany is very beautiful.

Grammar Extra!

You also use the definite article when geographical names are preceded by an adjective.

das heutige Deutschland — today's Germany

➤ The definite article is used with names of seasons.

Der Winter kommt bald. — Soon it will be winter.

➤ You often use the definite article with meals.

Im Hotel wird das Abendessen ab acht Uhr serviert. — Dinner is served from eight o'clock in the hotel.

ℹ Note that there are certain expressions with meals when you don't use the definite article.

Um acht Uhr ist Frühstück. — Breakfast is at eight o'clock.

For further explanation of grammatical terms, please see pages viii–xii.

➤ You also use the definite article with the names of roads.

Sie wohnt jetzt in <u>der</u> Geisener Straße.	She lives in Geisener Road now.

➤ The definite article is used with months of the year, except after the prepositions **seit**, **nach** and **vor**.

<u>Der</u> Dezember war ziemlich kalt.	The December was quite cold.
Wir sind seit September hier.	We have been here since September.

➪ *For more information on **Prepositions**, see page 153.*

➤ If you're talking about prices and want to say *each*, *per* or *a*, you use the definite article.

Die kosten fünf Euro <u>das</u> Pfund.	They cost five euros a pound.
Ich habe sechs Euro <u>das</u> Stück bezahlt.	I paid six euros each.

➤ In certain common expressions the definite article is used.

in <u>die</u> Stadt fahren	to go into town
mit <u>der</u> Post	by post
mit <u>dem</u> Zug/Bus/Auto	by train/bus/car

Grammar Extra!

In German, the definite article can be used instead of <u>a demonstrative adjective</u>.

Du willst <u>das</u> Buch lesen!	You want to read <u>that</u> book!

➪ *For more information on **Demonstrative adjectives**, see page 31.*

➤ In German, the definite article is left out of certain set expressions:

von Beruf	by profession
Nachrichten hören	to listen to the news

4 Shortened forms of the definite article

➤ After certain prepositions, the definite article can be shortened, though it is best to avoid using some of these forms in writing:

- **für das → fürs**

  Es ist fürs Baby. It's for the baby.
- **vor dem → vorm**

  Es liegt vorm Haus. It's lying in front of the house.
- **um das → ums**

  Es geht ums Geld. It's a question of money.

➤ The following shortened forms can be used in writing:

- **an dem → am**

  Am 1. Mai fahren wir in die Ferien. We go on holiday on the 1st of May.
- **in dem → im**

  Das Buch liegt im Haus. The book's in the house.
- **zu dem → zum**

  Ich muss zum Bahnhof gehen. I have to go to the station.
- **zu der → zur**

  Sie geht jeden Tag zur Schule. She goes to school every day.

➪ *For more information on* ***Shortened forms of prepositions****, see page 165.*

Key points

✔ The definite article is used in German with:

- abstract nouns
- the genitive case to show possession
- proper names, in certain exceptional cases
- masculine and feminine countries and districts
- names of seasons and months of the year, except after the prepositions **seit**, **nach** and **vor**
- names of roads
- meals and prices

✔ The definite article in German can be used in certain set expressions.

✔ When combined with certain prepositions, the definite article can be shortened.

5 Words declined like the definite article

➤ These words follow the same patterns as the definite article:

	Nominative	Accusative	Genitive	Dative
Plural only	alle	alle	aller	allen
Singular	beides	beides	beides	beiden
Plural	beide	beide	beider	beiden
Singular	dieser, diese, dieses	diesen, diese, dieses	dieses/diesen, dieser, dieses/diesen	diesem, dieser, diesem
Plural	diese	diese	dieser	diesen
Singular	einiger, einige, einiges	einigen, einige, einiges	einiges/einigen, einiger, einiges/einigen	einigem, einiger, einigem
Plural	einige	einige	einiger	einigen
Singular	jeder, jede, jedes	jeden, jede, jedes	jedes/jeden, jeder, jedes/jeden	jedem, jeder, jedem
Plural	jede	jede	jeder	jeden
Singular	jener, jene, jenes	jenen, jene, jenes	jenes/jenen, jener, jenes/jenen	jenem, jener, jenem
Plural	jene	jene	jener	jenen
Singular	mancher, manche, manches	manchen, manche, manches	manches/manchen, mancher, manches/manchen	manchem, mancher, manchem
Plural	manche	manche	mancher	manchen
Singular	solcher, solche, solches	solchen, solche, solches	solches/solchen, solcher, solches/solchen	solchem, solcher, solchem
Plural	solche	solche	solcher	solchen
Singular	welcher, welche, welches	welchen, welche, welches	welches/welchen, welcher, welches/welchen	welchem, welcher, welchem
Plural	welche	welche	welcher	welchen

ℹ Note that **dieser** or **jener** are used to translate the English demonstrative adjectives *this*, *that*, *these* and *those*.

- **alle, aller, allen** (*plural* only) — all, all of them

  Wir haben alle gesehen. — We saw all of them.

  Die Eltern fuhren mit allen Kindern weg. — The parents went off with all their children.

- **beide** (*plural* only) — both
  Ich habe beide Bücher gelesen. — I've read both books.
- **dieser, diese, dieses** — this, this one, these
  Dieser junge Mann ist begabt. — This young man is talented.
  Dieses alte Haus ist wirklich schön. — This old house is really beautiful.
- **einiger, einige, einiges** — some, a few, a little
  Einige von uns gingen spazieren. — Some of us went for a walk.
  Wir haben einiges gesehen. — We saw quite a lot of things.
- **jeder, jede, jedes** — each, each one, every
  Jeder Schüler bekommt ein Zeugnis. — Every pupil receives a report.
  Sie kommt jedes Mal zu spät. — She comes late every time.
- **jener, jene, jenes** — that, that one, those
  Jener Junge hatte seine Brieftasche verloren. — That boy had lost his wallet.
- **mancher, manche, manches** — many a, some
  Mancher Mann bleibt gern mit den Kindern zu Hause. — Some men like staying at home with the children.
  Manches Auto fährt schneller als 220 km/h. — Some cars can go faster than 220 km/h.
- **solcher, solche, solches** — such, such a
  Ein solches Mountainbike hätte ich auch gern. — I'd really like to have a mountain bike like that too.
- **welcher, welche, welches** — which, which one
  Welche Frau hat die Stelle bekommen? — Which woman got the job?

Grammar Extra!

sämtliche and **irgendwelcher** also follow the same pattern as the definite article:

- **sämtliche** — all, entire (*usually plural*)
  Sie besitzt Tolkiens sämtliche Werke. — She owns the complete works of Tolkien.
- **irgendwelcher, -e, -es** — some or other
  Sind noch irgendwelche Reste da? — Is there anything left? *or* Is there still something left?

➤ The words listed above can be used as:

- articles

  Dieser Mann kommt aus Südamerika. — This man comes from South America.
  Sie geht jeden Tag ins Büro. — She goes to the office every day.

For further explanation of grammatical terms, please see pages viii–xii.

- pronouns – a pronoun is a word you use instead of a noun, when you do not need or want to name someone or something directly, for example, *it*, *you*, *none*.

Willst du diesen?	Do you want this one?
Man kann ja nicht alles wissen.	You can't know everything.
Es gibt manche, die keinen Alkohol mögen.	There are some people who don't like alcohol.

➪ *For more information on* **Pronouns**, *see page 69.*

Grammar Extra!

einiger and **irgendwelcher** end in **-en** in the genitive before masculine or neuter nouns ending in **-s**.

Er musste wegziehen wegen irgendwelchen Geredes.	He had to move away because of some gossip.

jeder, **welcher**, **mancher** and **solcher** can also do this or can have the usual **-es** ending.

Das Kind solcher Eltern wird Probleme haben.	The child of such parents will have problems.
Trotz jeden Versuchs scheiterten die Verhandlungen.	Despite all attempts, the negotiations failed.

➤ **solcher**, **beide** and **sämtliche** can be used after another article or possessive adjective (in English, one of the words *my*, *your*, *his*, *her*, *its*, *our* or *their*).

Ein solches Rad habe ich früher auch gehabt.	I used to have a bike like that too.
Diese beiden Männer haben es gesehen.	Both of these men have seen it.

➤ Although **beide** generally has plural forms only, there is one singular form, **beides**. While **beide** is more common and can refer to both people and things, **beides** refers only to things. **Beide** is used for two examples of the same thing or person, while **beides** is used for two different examples.

Es gab zwei Bleistifte und er hat beide genommen.	There were two pencils and he took both.
BUT	
Es gab einen Bleistift und ein Bild und er hat beides genommen.	There was one pencil and one picture and he took both.

ℹ Note that **beides** is singular in German, whereas *both* is plural in English.

Beides ist richtig.	Both are correct.

➤ **dies** often replaces the nominative and accusative **dieses** and **diese** when it is used as a pronoun.

Hast du dies schon gelesen?	Have you already read this?
Dies sind meine neuen Sachen.	These are my new things.

*For more information on **Pronouns**, see page 69.*

➤ **alle** also has a fixed form – **all** – which is used together with other articles or possessive pronouns.

All sein Mut war verschwunden.	All his courage had disappeared.
Was machst du mit all diesem Geld?	What are you doing with all this money?

➤ **ganz** can be used to replace both **alle** and **all** and is declined like an adjective.

Sie ist mit dem ganzen Geld verschwunden.	She disappeared with all the money.

*For more information on **Adjectives**, see page 40.*

➤ **ganz** must be used:

- in time phrases

Es hat den ganzen Tag geschneit.	It snowed the whole day long.

- when talking about geography

Im ganzen Land gab es keinen besseren Wein.	There wasn't a better wine in the whole country.

- with nouns referring to a collection of people or animals (*collective nouns*)

Die ganze Gesellschaft war auf der Versammlung vertreten.	The entire company was represented at the meeting.

Grammar Extra!

derjenige/diejenige/dasjenige (*the one, those*) is declined in the same way as the definite article (**der**) + a weak adjective.

*For more information on **Weak adjectives**, see page 42.*

Case	Masculine	Feminine	Neuter	All Genders Plural
Nominative	derjenige Mann	diejenige Frau	dasjenige Kind	diejenigen Kinder
Accusative	denjenigen Mann	diejenige Frau	dasjenige Kind	diejenigen Kinder
Genitive	desjenigen Mann(e)s	derjenigen Frau	desjenigen Kind(e)s	derjenigen Kinder
Dative	demjenigen Mann	derjenigen Frau	demjenigen Kind	denjenigen Kindern

derselbe/dieselbe/dasselbe (*the same, the same one*) is declined in the same way as **derjenige**. However, after prepositions, the shortened forms of the definite article are used for the appropriate parts of **derselbe**.

zur selben (=zu derselben) Zeit	at the same time
im selben (=in demselben) Zimmer	in the same room

*For more information on **Shortened forms of prepositions**, see page 165.*

Key points

- ✔ There is a group of words which are declined like the definite article **der**.
- ✔ These words can be used as articles or pronouns.
- ✔ **solcher**, **beide** and **sämtliche** can be used after another article or possessive adjective.
- ✔ **beide** generally has plural forms only, but there is one singular form, **beides**.
- ✔ When it is used as a pronoun **dies** often replaces the nominative and accusative **dieses** and **diese**.
- ✔ **alle** also has a fixed form, **all**.
- ✔ **ganz** must be used instead of **alle** in certain situations.

6 The indefinite article

➤ In English we have the indefinite article *a*, which changes to *an* in front of a word that starts with a vowel. In the plural we say either *some*, *any* or nothing at all.

➤ In German the word you choose for *a* depends on whether the noun it is used with is masculine, feminine or neuter, singular or plural AND it also depends on the case of the noun.

Da ist <u>ein</u> Auto.	There's a car.
Sie hat <u>eine</u> Wohnung.	She has a flat.
Er gab es <u>einem</u> Kind.	He gave it to a child.

➤ It has no plural forms.

iPads sind in letzter Zeit billiger geworden.	Recently iPads have become cheaper.

➤ The indefinite article is formed as follows:

Case	Masculine	Feminine	Neuter
Nominative	ein	eine	ein
Accusative	einen	eine	ein
Genitive	eines	einer	eines
Dative	einem	einer	einem

7 Using the indefinite article

➤ The indefinite article is used very much as in English.

Da ist <u>ein</u> Bus.	There's <u>a</u> bus.
Sie hat <u>eine</u> neue Jacke.	She has <u>a</u> new jacket.
Sie gab es <u>einer</u> alten Dame.	She gave it to <u>an</u> old lady.

➤ In certain situations, you do not use the indefinite article:

- when talking about the job someone does

  Sie ist Ärztin. She's a doctor.

- when talking about someone's nationality or religion

  Sie ist Deutsche. She's (a) German.

  Er ist Moslem. He's (a) Muslim.

i Note that the indefinite article IS used when an adjective comes before the noun.

  Sie ist eine sehr begabte Journalistin. She's a very talented journalist.

- in certain fixed expressions

  Es ist Geschmacksache. It's a question of taste.

  Tatsache ist ... It's a fact ...

- after **als** (meaning *as a*)

  Als Lehrerin verdiene ich nicht gut. I don't earn very much as a teacher.

  Als Großmutter darf ich meine Enkel verwöhnen. As a grandmother, I'm allowed to spoil my grandchildren.

8 The indefinite article in negative sentences

➤ In English we use words like *not* and *never* to indicate that something is not happening or is not true. The sentences that these words are used in are called negative sentences.

I don't know him.

I never do my homework on time.

➤ In German, you use a separate negative form of the indefinite article, which is formed exactly like **ein** in the singular, and also has plural forms. It means *no/not a/not one/not any*.

Case	Masculine Singular	Feminine Singular	Neuter Singular	All Genders Plural
Nominative	**kein**	**keine**	**kein**	**keine**
Accusative	**keinen**	**keine**	**kein**	**keine**
Genitive	**keines**	**keiner**	**keines**	**keiner**
Dative	**keinem**	**keiner**	**keinem**	**keinen**

For further explanation of grammatical terms, please see pages viii–xii.

Er hatte keine Geschwister.	He had no brothers or sisters.
Ich sehe keinen Unterschied.	I don't see any difference.
Das ist keine richtige Antwort.	That's no answer.
Kein Mensch hat es gesehen.	Not one person has seen it.

Tip

This negative form of the indefinite article is even used when the *positive* form of the phrase has no article.

Er hatte Angst davor.	He was frightened.
Er hatte keine Angst davor.	He wasn't frightened.

Grammar Extra!

The negative form of the indefinite article is also used in many informal expressions.

Sie hatte kein Geld mehr.	All her money was gone.
Es waren keine drei Monate vergangen, als ...	It was less than three months later that ...
Es hat mich keine zehn Euro gekostet.	It cost me less than ten euros.

If you want to emphasize the **ein** in the sentence, **nicht ein** can be used instead of **kein**.

Nicht ein Kind hat es singen können.	Not one child could sing it.

➪ *For more information on* ***Negatives****, see page 179.*

Key points

✔ The indefinite article is used in German:
- to translate the English *a* and *any* in the singular
- to translate the English *some* or *any* in the plural
- in negative sentences in its separate negative form, **kein**, to translate *not* or *no*

✔ The indefinite article in German is NOT used when:
- talking about someone's job, nationality or religion, unless an adjective is used before the noun
- in certain set expressions or after **als** meaning *as a*

9 Words declined like the indefinite article

➤ The following words are possessive adjectives, one of the words *my*, *your*, *his*, *her*, *its*, *our* or *their* used with a noun to show that one person or thing belongs to another. They follow the same pattern as the indefinite articles **ein** and **kein**.

mein	my
dein	your (*singular familiar*)
sein	his/its
ihr	her/its
unser	our
euer	your (*plural familiar*)
ihr	their
Ihr	your (*polite singular and plural*)

➤ Possessive adjectives are formed in the following way.

	Nominative	Accusative	Genitive	Dative
Singular	mein, meine, mein	meinen, meine, mein	meines, meiner, meines	meinem, meiner, meinem
Plural	meine	meine	meiner	meinen
Singular	dein, deine, dein	deinen, deine, dein	deines, deiner, deines	deinem, deiner, deinem
Plural	deine	deine	deiner	deinen
Singular	sein, seine, sein	seinen, seine, sein	seines, seiner, seines	seinem, seiner, seinem
Plural	seine	seine	seiner	seinen
Singular	ihr, ihre, ihr	ihren, ihre, ihr	ihres, ihrer, ihres	ihrem, ihrer, ihrem
Plural	ihre	ihre	ihrer	ihren
Singular	unser, unsere, unser	unseren, unsere, unser	unseres, unserer, unseres	unserem, unserer, unserem
Plural	unsere	unsere	unserer	unseren
Singular	euer, eure, euer	euren, eure, euer	eures, eurer, eures	eurem, eurer, eurem
Plural	eure	eure	eurer	euren
Singular	ihr, ihre, ihr	ihren, ihre, ihr	ihres, ihrer, ihres	ihrem, ihrer, ihrem
Plural	ihre	ihre	ihrer	ihren
Singular	Ihr, Ihre, Ihr	Ihren, Ihre, Ihr	Ihres, Ihrer, Ihres	Ihrem, Ihrer, Ihrem
Plural	Ihre	Ihre	Ihrer	Ihren

For further explanation of grammatical terms, please see pages viii–xii.

Mein kleiner Bruder will auch mitkommen.	My little brother wants to come too.
Wo steht dein altes Auto?	Where is your old car?
Er spielt Fußball mit seiner Tante.	He is playing football with his aunt.
Was ist mit ihrem Computer los?	What is wrong with her computer?
Ihre Kinder sind wirklich verwöhnt.	Their children are really spoiled.
Wie geht es Ihrer Schwester?	How is your sister?
Ich will meine Kinder regelmäßig sehen.	I want to see my children regularly.

Grammar Extra!

Possessive adjectives are often followed by other adjectives in German sentences. These adjectives then have the same endings as the indefinite article.

Er liebt sein altes Auto.	He loves his old car.
Sie hat ihren neuen Computer verkauft.	She sold her new computer.
Wo ist deine rote Jacke?	Where is your red jacket?

irgendein (meaning *some ... or other*) and its plural form **irgendwelche** also take these endings.

Er ist irgendein bekannter Schauspieler.	He's some famous actor or other.
Sie ist nur irgendeine alte Frau.	She's just some old woman or other.
Sie hat irgendein neues Buch gekauft.	She bought some new book or other.
Ich muss irgendwelche blöden Touristen herumführen.	I have to show some stupid tourists or other round.

Key point

✔ Possessive adjectives, one of the words *my*, *your*, *his*, *her*, *its*, *our* or *their*, are declined like the indefinite articles **ein** and **kein**.

Adjectives

What is an adjective?
An **adjective** is a 'describing' word that tells you more about a person or thing, such as their appearance, colour, size or other qualities, for example, *pretty*, *blue*, *big*.

Using adjectives

➤ Adjectives are words like *clever*, *expensive* and *silly* that tell you more about a noun (a living being, thing or idea). They can also tell you more about a pronoun, such as *he* or *they*. Adjectives are sometimes called 'describing words'. They can be used right next to a noun they are describing, or can be separated from the noun by a verb like *be*, *look*, *feel* and so on.

a clever girl
an expensive coat
a silly idea
He's just being silly.

⇨ *For more information on **Nouns** and **Pronouns**, see pages 1 and 69.*

➤ In English, the only time an adjective changes its form is when you are making a comparison.

She's cleverer than her brother.
That's the silliest idea I ever heard!

➤ In German, however, adjectives usually agree with what they are describing. This means that their endings change depending on whether the person or thing you are referring to is masculine, feminine or neuter, and singular or plural. It also depends on the case of the person or thing you are describing and whether it is preceded by the definite or indefinite article.

Das neue Buch ist da.	The new book has arrived.
Ich wollte es der alten Frau geben.	I wanted to give it to the old woman.
Sie erzählte mir eine langweilige Geschichte.	She told me a boring story.
Die deutschen Traditionen	German traditions

⇨ *For more information on **Cases** and **Articles**, see pages 9 and 25.*

➤ As in English, German adjectives usually come BEFORE the noun they describe, but AFTER the verb in the sentence, unless the noun is the subject of the sentence and is written BEFORE the verb. The only time the adjective does not agree with the word it describes is when it comes AFTER the verb.

eine schwarze Katze	a black cat
Das Buch ist neu.	The book is new.

Key points

✔ Most German adjectives change their form according to the case of the noun they are describing and whether the noun is masculine, feminine or neuter, singular or plural.

✔ In German, as in English, adjectives come before the noun they describe, but AFTER the verb in the sentence.

Making adjectives agree

1 The basic rules

➤ In dictionaries, only the basic form of German adjectives is shown. You need to know how to change it to make it agree with the noun or pronoun the adjective describes.

➤ To make an adjective agree with the noun or pronoun it describes, you simply add one of three sets of different endings:

2 The Weak Declension

➤ The endings used after the definite articles **der**, **die** and **das** and other words declined like them are shown below.

Case	Masculine Singular	Feminine Singular	Neuter Singular	All Genders Plural
Nominative	-e	-e	-e	-en
Accusative	-en	-e	-e	-en
Genitive	-en	-en	-en	-en
Dative	-en	-en	-en	-en

➤ The following table shows you how these different endings are added to the adjective **alt**, meaning *old*, when it is used with the definite article.

Case	Masculine Singular	Feminine Singular	Neuter Singular
Nominative	der alte Mann	die alte Frau	das alte Haus
Accusative	den alten Mann	die alte Frau	das alte Haus
Genitive	des alten Mann(e)s	der alten Frau	des alten Hauses
Dative	dem alten Mann	der alten Frau	dem alten Haus

Nominative:

Der alte Mann wohnt nebenan. — The old man lives next door.

Accusative:

Ich habe die alte Frau in der Bibliothek gesehen. — I saw the old woman in the library.

Genitive:

Die Besitzerin des alten Hauses ist sehr reich. — The owner of the old house is very rich.

Dative:

Er hilft dem alten Mann beim Einkaufen. — He helps the old man to do his shopping.

For further explanation of grammatical terms, please see pages viii–xii.

➤ These are the plural endings of adjectives in the weak declension.

Plural	All Genders
Nominative	**die alten Männer/Frauen/Häuser**
Accusative	**die alten Männer/Frauen/Häuser**
Genitive	**der alten Männer/Frauen/Häuser**
Dative	**den alten Männern/Frauen/Häusern**

3 The Mixed Declension

➤ The endings used after **ein**, **kein**, **irgendein** and the possessive adjectives are shown below.

Note that this declension differs from the weak declension only in the three forms underlined below.

Case	Masculine Singular	Feminine Singular	Neuter Singular	All Genders Plural
Nominative	**-er**	**-e**	**-es**	**-en**
Accusative	**-en**	**-e**	**-es**	**-en**
Genitive	**-en**	**-en**	**-en**	**-en**
Dative	**-en**	**-en**	**-en**	**-en**

*For more information on the **Possessive adjectives**, see page 37.*

➤ The following table shows you how these different endings are added to the adjective **lang**, meaning *long*.

Case	Masculine Singular	Feminine Singular	Neuter Singular
Nominative	**ein langer Weg**	**eine lange Reise**	**ein langes Spiel**
Accusative	**einen langen Weg**	**eine lange Reise**	**ein langes Spiel**
Genitive	**eines langen Weg(e)s**	**einer langen Reise**	**eines langen Spiel(e)s**
Dative	**einem langen Weg**	**einer langen Reise**	**einem langen Spiel**

Nominative:

Eine lange Reise muss geplant werden. You have to plan a long trip.

Accusative:

Ich habe einen langen Weg nach Hause. It takes me a long time to get home.

Genitive:

Die vielen Nachteile einer langen Reise … The many disadvantages of a long journey …

Dative:

Bei einem langen Spiel kann man sich langweilen. You can get bored with a long game.

➤ These are the plural endings of adjectives when they have a mixed declension.

Plural	**All Genders**
Nominative	**ihre langen Wege/Reisen/Spiele**
Accusative	**ihre langen Wege/Reisen/Spiele**
Genitive	**ihrer langen Wege/Reisen/Spiele**
Dative	**ihren langen Wegen/Reisen/Spielen**

4 The Strong Declension

➤ The endings used when there is no article before the noun are shown below.

Case	**Masculine Singular**	**Feminine Singular**	**Neuter Singular**	**All Genders Plural**
Nominative	**-er**	**-e**	**-es**	**-e**
Accusative	**-en**	**-e**	**-es**	**-e**
Genitive	**-en**	**-er**	**-en**	**-er**
Dative	**-em**	**-er**	**-em**	**-en**

➤ The following table shows you how these different endings are added to the adjective **gut**, meaning *good*.

Case	**Masculine Singular**	**Feminine Singular**	**Neuter Singular**
Nominative	**guter Käse**	**gute Marmelade**	**gutes Bier**
Accusative	**guten Käse**	**gute Marmelade**	**gutes Bier**
Genitive	**guten Käses**	**guter Marmelade**	**guten Bier(e)s**
Dative	**gutem Käse**	**guter Marmelade**	**gutem Bier**

For further explanation of grammatical terms, please see pages viii–xii.

Nominative:

Gutes Bier ist sehr wichtig auf einer Party. Good beer is very important at a party.

Accusative:

Wo finde ich guten Käse? Where will I get good cheese?

Genitive:

Das ist ein Zeichen guter Marmelade. That is a sign of good jam.

Dative:

Zu gutem Käse braucht man auch Oliven. You need olives to go with good cheese.

➤ These are the plural endings of adjectives when they have a strong declension.

ℹ Note that the plural form of **Käse** is normally **Käsesorten**.

Plural	All Genders
Nominative	**gute Käsesorten/Marmeladen/Biere**
Accusative	**gute Käsesorten/Marmeladen/Biere**
Genitive	**guter Käsesorten/Marmeladen/Biere**
Dative	**guten Käsesorten/Marmeladen/Bieren**

ℹ Note that these endings allow the adjective to do the work of the missing article by showing the case of the noun and whether it is singular or plural, masculine, feminine or neuter.

➤ The article is omitted more often in German than in English, especially where you have *preposition* + *adjective* + *noun* combinations.

Nach kurzer Fahrt kamen wir in Glasgow an. After a short journey we arrived in Glasgow.

Mit gleichem Gehalt wie du würde ich mir einen Urlaub leisten können. I'd be able to afford a holiday on the same salary as you.

➤ These strong declension endings are also used after any of the following words when the noun they refer to is not preceded by an article.

Word	Meaning
ein bisschen	a little, a bit of
ein wenig	a little
ein paar	a few, a couple
weniger	fewer, less
einige (*plural forms only*)	some
etwas	some, any (*singular*)
mehr	more
lauter	nothing but, sheer, pure
solch	such
was für	what, what kind of
viel	much, many, a lot of
welch ...!	what ...! what a ...!
manch	many a
wenig	little, few, not much
zwei, drei *etc*	two, three *etc*

Morgen hätte ich ein wenig freie Zeit für dich. — I could spare you some time tomorrow.

Sie hat mir ein paar gute Tipps gegeben. — She gave me a few good tips.

Er isst weniger frisches Obst als ich. — He eats less fresh fruit than me.

Heutzutage wollen mehr junge Frauen Ingenieurinnen werden. — Nowadays, more young women want to be engineers.

Solche leckere Schokolade habe ich schon lange nicht mehr gegessen. — I haven't had such good chocolate for a long time.

Wir haben viel kostbare Zeit verschwendet. — We have wasted a lot of valuable time.

Welch herrliches Wetter! — What wonderful weather!

➤ With **wenig** and numbers from **zwei** onwards, adjectives behave as follows:

- Strong, when there is no article:

  Es gab damals nur wenig frisches Obst. There was little fresh fruit at that time.

  Zwei kleine Jungen kamen die Straße entlang. Two small boys came along the street.

- Weak, when the definite article comes first:

  Das wenige frische Obst, das es damals gab, war teuer. The little fresh fruit that was available then, was expensive.

  Die zwei kleinen Jungen, die die Straße entlangkamen. The two small boys who came along the street.

- Mixed, when a possessive adjective comes first:

  Meine zwei kleinen Jungen sind manchmal frech. My two small sons are cheeky sometimes.

➤ These strong declension endings also need to be used after possessives where no other word shows the case of the following noun and whether it's masculine, feminine or neuter, singular or plural.

Sebastians altes Buch lag auf dem Tisch. Sebastian's old book was lying on the table.

Mutters neuer Computer sieht toll aus. Mother's new computer looks great.

Tip

When these various endings are added to adjectives, you have to watch out for some spelling changes.

When endings are added to the adjective **hoch**, meaning *high*, the simple form changes to **hoh**.

Das Gebäude ist hoch. The building is high.

Das ist ein hohes Gebäude. That is a high building.

Adjectives ending in **-el** lose the **-e** when endings are added.

Das Zimmer ist dunkel. The room is dark.

Man sieht nichts in dem dunklen Zimmer. You can't see anything in the dark room.

Adjectives ending in **-er** often lose the **-e** when endings are added.

Das Auto war teuer. The car was expensive.

Sie kaufte ein teures Auto. She bought an expensive car.

Key points

✔ To make an adjective agree with the noun it is describing, you simply add one of three sets of endings: weak, mixed or strong.

✔ Strong endings are also used after particular words when not preceded by an article, for example, **ein bisschen**, **ein paar**, **wenig** and after possessive adjectives.

5 Participles as adjectives

➤ In English, the present participle is a verb form ending in *-ing*, which may be used as an adjective or a noun. In German, you simply add **-d** to the infinitive of the verb to form the present participle, which may then be used as an adjective with all the usual endings.

Auf dem Tisch stand ein Foto von einem lachenden Kind.	There was a photo of a laughing child on the table.

ℹ Note that the present participles of **sein** and **haben** cannot be used like this.

➤ The past participle of a verb can also be used as an adjective.

Meine Mutter hat meine verlorenen Sachen gefunden.	My mother found my lost things.

⇨ *For more information on **Past participles**, see page 113.*

6 Adjectives preceded by the dative case

➤ With many adjectives you use the dative case, for example:

- **ähnlich** similar to
  Er ist seinem Vater sehr ähnlich. — He's very like his father.
- **bekannt** familiar to
  Sie kommt mir bekannt vor. — She seems familiar to me.
- **dankbar** grateful to
  Ich bin dir sehr dankbar. — I'm very grateful to you.
- **fremd** strange, alien to
  Das ist mir fremd. — That's alien to me.
- **gleich** all the same to/like
  Es ist mir gleich. — It's all the same to me.

- **leicht** easy for

  Du machst es dir wirklich zu leicht. You really make things too easy for yourself.

- **nah(e)** close to

  Unser Haus ist nahe der Universität. Our house is near the university.

- **peinlich** embarrassing for

  Das war ihr aber peinlich. She was really embarrassed.

- **unbekannt** unknown to

  Das war mir unbekannt. I didn't know that.

Key points

✔ In German, both present and past participles can also be used as adjectives.

✔ With many German adjectives you use the dative case.

Adjectives used as nouns

➤ All adjectives in German, and participles used as adjectives, can also be used as nouns. These are often called adjectival nouns.

➤ Adjectives and participles used as nouns have:

- a capital letter like other nouns

Der neue Angestellte ist früh angekommen.	The new employee arrived early.

- weak, strong or mixed endings, depending on which article, if any, comes before them

Sie ist die neue Angestellte.	She is the new employee.
Das Gute daran ist, dass ich mehr verdiene.	The good thing about it is that I'm earning more.
Es bleibt beim Alten.	Things remain as they were.

Key points

✔ Adjectives in German, and participles used as adjectives, can also be used as nouns. These are often called adjectival nouns.

✔ Adjectival nouns begin with a capital letter and take the same endings as normal adjectives.

Some other points about adjectives

1 Adjectives describing nationality

➤ These are not spelt with a capital letter in German except in public or official names.

Die deutsche Sprache ist schön.	The German language is beautiful.
Das französische Volk war entsetzt.	The people of France were horrified.
BUT:	
Die Deutsche Bahn hat Erfolg.	The German railways are successful.

➤ However, when these adjectives are used as nouns to refer to a language, a capital letter is used.

Sie sprechen kein Englisch.	They don't speak English.

➤ In German, for expressions like *he is English/he is German etc* a noun or adjectival noun is used instead of an adjective.

Er ist Deutscher.	He is German.
Sie ist Deutsche.	She is German.

2 Adjectives taken from place names

➤ These are formed by adding **-er** to names of towns. They never change by adding endings to show case.

Kölner, Frankfurter, Berliner *etc*	from Cologne, Frankfurt, Berlin *etc*
Der Kölner Dom ist wirklich beeindruckend.	Cologne cathedral is really impressive.
Ich möchte ein Frankfurter Würstchen.	I'd like a frankfurter sausage.

➤ Adjectives from **die Schweiz**, meaning Switzerland, and some other regions can also be formed in this way.

Schweizer Käse mag ich gern.	I really like Swiss cheese.

➤ Adjectives like these can be used as nouns denoting the inhabitants of a town, in which case they take the same endings as normal nouns.

Die Sprache des Kölners heißt Kölsch.	People from Cologne speak Kölsch.
Die Entscheidung wurde von den Frankfurtern begrüßt.	People from Frankfurt welcomed the decision.

i Note that the feminine form of such nouns is formed by adding **-in** in the singular and **-innen** in the plural.

Christine, die Londonerin war, wollte nach Glasgow ziehen.	Christine, who was from London, wanted to move to Glasgow.

Adjectives

Key points

- ✔ Adjectives describing nationality are not spelt with a capital letter in German except in public or official names, BUT when they are used as nouns to refer to a language, they do have a capital letter.
- ✔ Adjectives taken from place names are formed by adding **-er** to the name of the town and never change by adding endings to show case.
- ✔ They can also be used as nouns denoting the inhabitants of a place.

For further explanation of grammatical terms, please see pages viii–xii.

Comparatives of adjectives

What is a comparative adjective?
A **comparative adjective** in English is one with *-er* added to it or *more* or *less* in front of it, that is used to compare people or things, for example, *slower*, *more beautiful*.

➤ In German, to say that something is *easier*, *more expensive* and so on, you add **-er** to the simple form of most adjectives.

einfach → einfach<u>er</u>

Das war viel einfacher für dich. That was much easier for you.

i Note that adjectives whose simple form ends in **-en** or **-er** may drop the final **-e** to form the comparative, as in **teurer**.

teuer → teurer

Diese Jacke ist teur<u>er</u>. This jacket is more expensive.

➤ To introduce the person or thing you are making the comparison with, use **als** (meaning *than*).

Er ist kleiner <u>als</u> seine Schwester. He is smaller than his sister.

Diese Frage ist einfacher <u>als</u> die erste. This question is easier than the first one.

➤ To say that something or someone is *as ... as* something or someone else, you use **so ... wie** or **genauso ... wie**, if you want to make it more emphatic. To say *not as ... as*, you use **nicht so ... wie**.

Sie ist <u>so</u> gut <u>wie</u> ihr Bruder. She is as good as her brother.

Er war <u>genauso</u> glücklich <u>wie</u> ich. He was just as happy as I was.

Sie ist <u>nicht so</u> alt <u>wie</u> du. She is not as old as you.

➤ Here are some examples of commonly used adjectives which have a vowel change in the comparative form:

Adjective	Meaning	Comparative	Meaning
alt	old	**älter**	older
stark	strong	**stärker**	stronger
schwach	weak	**schwächer**	weaker
scharf	sharp	**schärfer**	sharper
lang	long	**länger**	longer
kurz	short	**kürzer**	shorter
warm	warm	**wärmer**	warmer
kalt	cold	**kälter**	colder
hart	hard	**härter**	harder
groß	big	**größer**	bigger

➤ Adjectives whose simple form ends in **-el** lose the **-e** before adding the comparative ending **-er**.

eitel → eitler	vain → vainer
Er ist eitler als ich.	He is vainer than me.
dunkel → dunkler	dark → darker
Deine Haare sind dunkler als ihre.	Your hair is darker than hers.

➤ When used before the noun, comparative forms of adjectives take the same weak, strong or mixed endings as their simple forms.

Die jüngere Schwester ist größer als die ältere.	The younger sister is bigger than the older one.
Mein jüngerer Bruder geht jetzt zur Schule.	My younger brother goes to school now.

⇨ *For more information on **Making adjectives agree**, see page 42.*

Grammar Extra!

➤ With a few adjectives, comparative forms may also be used to translate the idea of *-ish* or *rather ...*

Comparative	Meaning
älter	elderly
dünner	thinnish
dicker	fattish
größer	largish
jünger	youngish
kleiner	smallish
kürzer	shortish
neuer	newish

Eine ältere Frau kam die Straße entlang.	An elderly woman was coming along the street.
Er war von jüngerem Aussehen.	He was of youngish appearance.

Key points

- ✔ In German, to form the comparative you add **-er** to the simple form of most adjectives.
- ✔ To compare people or things in German, you use **so ... wie**, **genauso ... wie**, if you want to make it more emphatic, or **nicht so ... wie**.
- ✔ *Than* in comparatives corresponds to **als**.
- ✔ There is a change in the vowel in many of the simple forms of German adjectives when forming their comparatives.
- ✔ Adjectives whose simple form ends in **-el**, such as **dunkel**, lose the **-e** before adding the comparative ending **-er**.

Superlatives of adjectives

What is a superlative adjective?
A **superlative adjective** in English is one with *-est* on the end of it or *most* or *least* in front of it, that is used to compare people or things, for example, *thinnest*, *most beautiful*.

➤ In German, to say that something or someone is *easiest*, *youngest*, *most expensive* and so on, you add **-st** to the simple form of the adjective. As with comparative forms, the vowel in the simple form can change. Superlative forms are generally used with the definite article and take the same weak endings as their simple forms.

Deine Hausaufgaben waren die einfachsten.	Your homework was easiest.
Sie ist die Jüngste in der Familie.	She is the youngest in the family.
Ich wollte die teuerste Jacke im Laden kaufen.	I wanted to buy the most expensive jacket in the shop.

➤ Adjectives ending in **-t**, **-tz**, **-z**, **-sch**, **-ss** or **-ß** form the superlative by adding **-est** instead of **-st**.

der/die/das schlechteste	the worst
Das war der schlechteste Film seit Jahren.	That was the worst film in years.
der/die/das schmerzhafteste	the most painful
Das war ihre schmerzhafteste Verletzung.	That was her most painful injury.
der/die/das süßeste	the sweetest
Ich möchte den süßesten Nachtisch.	I would like the sweetest dessert.
der/die/das stolzeste	the proudest
Sie war die stolzeste Mutter in der Gegend.	She was the proudest mother in the area.
der/die/das frischeste	the freshest
Für dieses Rezept braucht man das frischeste Obst.	You need the freshest fruit for this recipe.

➤ Adjectives ending in **-eu** and **-au** also add **-est** to form the superlative.

der/die/das neueste	the newest, the latest
Ich brauche die neueste Ausgabe des Wörterbuchs.	I need the latest edition of the dictionary.
der/die/das schlaueste	the cleverest
Sie ist die schlaueste Schülerin in der Klasse.	She is the cleverest student in the class.

➤ The English superlative *most*, meaning *very*, can be expressed in German by any of the following words.

Superlative	Meaning
äußerst	extremely
sehr	very
besonders	especially
außerordentlich	exceptionally
höchst	extremely (not used with words of one syllable)
furchtbar	terribly (used only in conversation)
richtig	really/most (used only in conversation)

Sie ist ein äußerst begabter Mensch. She is a most gifted person.
Das Essen war besonders schlecht. The food was really dreadful.
Der Wein war furchtbar teuer. The wine was terribly expensive.
Das sieht richtig komisch aus. That looks really funny.

Tip

Just as English has some irregular comparative and superlative forms – *better* instead of '*more good*', and *worst* instead of '*most bad*' – German also has a few irregular forms.

Adjective	Meaning	Comparative	Meaning	Superlative	Meaning
gut	good	**besser**	better	**der beste**	the best
hoch	high	**höher**	higher	**der höchste**	the highest
viel	much/a lot	**mehr**	more	**der meiste**	the most
nah	near	**näher**	nearer	**der nächste**	the nearest

Ich habe eine bessere Idee. I have a better idea.
Wo liegt der nächste Bahnhof? Where is the nearest station?

Key points

✔ Most German superlatives are formed by adding **-st** to the simple form of the adjective.

✔ Adjectives ending in **-t**, **-tz**, **-z**, **-sch**, **-ss**, **-ß**, **-eu** or **-au**, form the superlative by adding **-est** instead of **-st**.

✔ **Gut**, **hoch**, **viel** and **nah** have irregular comparative and superlative forms: **gut/besser/der beste**, **hoch/höher/der höchste**, **viel/mehr/der meiste**, **nah/näher/der nächste**.

Adverbs

What is an adverb?
An **adverb** is a word usually used with verbs, adjectives or other adverbs that gives more information about when, how, where, or in what circumstances something happens: *quickly, happily, now* are all adverbs.

How adverbs are used

➤ In general, adverbs are used together with:

- verbs (*act quickly, speak strangely, smile cheerfully*)
- adjectives (*rather ill, a lot better, deeply sorry*)
- other adverbs (*really fast, too quickly, very well*)

➤ Adverbs can also relate to the whole sentence; they often tell you what the speaker is thinking or feeling.

Fortunately, Jan had already left.
Actually, I don't think I'll come.

How adverbs are formed

The basic rules

➤ Many English adverbs end in *-ly*, which is added to the end of the adjective (*quick* → *quickly*; *sad* → *sadly*; *frequent* → *frequently*).

➤ In contrast, most German adverbs used to comment on verbs are simply adjectives used as adverbs. And the good news is that unlike adjectives, they do not change by adding different endings.

Habe ich das richtig gehört?	Did I hear that correctly?
Er war schick angezogen.	He was stylishly dressed.

➤ A small number of German adverbs which do not directly comment on the verb are formed by adding **-weise** or **-sweise** to a noun.

Noun	Meaning	Adverb	Meaning
das Beispiel	example	**beispielsweise**	for example
die Beziehung	relation, connection	**beziehungsweise**	or/or rather/ that is to say
der Schritt	step	**schrittweise**	step by step
die Zeit	time	**zeitweise**	at times
der Zwang	compulsion	**zwangsweise**	compulsorily

Grammar Extra!

Some German adverbs are also formed by adding **-erweise** to an uninflected adjective. These adverbs are mainly used by the person speaking to express an opinion.

Adjective	Meaning	Adverb	Meaning
erstaunlich	astonishing	**erstaunlicherweise**	astonishingly enough
glücklich	happy, fortunate	**glücklicherweise**	fortunately
komisch	strange, funny	**komischerweise**	strangely enough

➤ There is another important group of adverbs which are NOT formed from adjectives or nouns, for example, words like **unten**, **oben** and **leider**.

Das beste Buch lag <u>unten</u> auf dem Stapel.	The best book was at the bottom of the pile.
Die Schlafzimmer sind <u>oben</u>.	The bedrooms are upstairs.
Ich kann <u>leider</u> nicht kommen.	Unfortunately I can't come.

➤ Adverbs of time fit into this category and the following are some common ones:

Adverb of time	Meaning
endlich	finally
heute	today
immer	always
morgen	tomorrow
morgens	in the mornings
sofort	at once

Sie kann erst <u>morgen</u> kommen.	She can't come till tomorrow.
Priska hat <u>immer</u> Hunger.	Priska is always hungry.
Ja, ich mache das <u>sofort</u>.	Yes, I'll do it at once.

For further explanation of grammatical terms, please see pages viii–xii.

➤ Adverbs often express the idea of 'to what extent', for example, words in English like *extremely* and *especially*. These are sometimes called adverbs of degree. Some common adverbs of this type in German are:

Adverb of degree	Meaning
äußerst	extremely
besonders	especially
beträchtlich	considerably
fast	almost
kaum	hardly, scarcely
ziemlich	fairly

Es hat mir nicht besonders gefallen. — I didn't particularly like it.
Ich bin fast fertig. — I'm almost finished.
Er war ziemlich sauer. — He was quite angry.

Adverbs of place

➤ Adverbs of place are words such as *where?*, *there*, *up*, *nowhere*. German adverbs of place behave very differently from their English counterparts in the following ways:

- Where there is no movement involved and the adverb is simply referring to a location, you use the form of the adverb you find in the dictionary.

  Wo ist sie? — Where is she?
  Sie sind nicht da. — They're not there.
  Hier darf man nicht parken. — You can't park here.

- To show some movement AWAY from the person speaking, you use the adverb **hin**.

  Oliver und Andrea geben heute eine Party. Gehen wir hin? — Oliver and Andrea are having a party today. Shall we go?

  In German, **hin** is often added to another adverb to create what are called compound adverbs, which show there is some movement involved. In English, we would just use adverbs in this case.

Compound adverb	Meaning
dahin	(to) there
dorthin	there
hierhin	here
irgendwohin	(to) somewhere or other
überallhin	everywhere
wohin?	where (to)?

  Wohin fährst du? — Where are you going?
  Sie liefen überallhin. — They ran everywhere.

- To show some movement TOWARDS the person speaking, you use the adverb **her**. As with **hin**, this is often added to another adverb.

Compound adverb	Meaning
daher	from there
hierher	here
irgendwoher	from somewhere or other
überallher	from all over
woher?	where from?

  Woher kommst du? — Where do you come from?
  Woher hast du das? — Where did you get that from?
  Das habe ich irgendwoher gekriegt. — I got that from somewhere or other.

For further explanation of grammatical terms, please see pages viii–xii.

Key points

- ✔ Many German adverbs are simply adjectives used as adverbs, but they are not declined, unlike adjectives.
- ✔ In German, some adverbs are formed by adding **-weise** or **-sweise** to a noun.
- ✔ Compound adverbs formed by adding **hin** or **her** are often used to show movement away from or towards the person speaking (or writing).

Comparatives and superlatives of adverbs

1 Comparative adverbs

What is a comparative adverb?
A **comparative adverb** is one which, in English, has *-er* on the end of it or *more* or *less* in front of it, for example, *earlier, later, sooner, more/less frequently*.

➤ Adverbs can be used to make comparisons in German, just as they can in English. The comparative of adverbs is formed in exactly the same way as that of adjectives, that is by adding **-er** to the basic form. **Als** is used for *than*.

Sie läuft schneller als ihr Bruder.	She runs faster than her brother.
Ich sehe ihn seltener als früher.	I see him less often than before.

➤ To make *as ... as* or *not as ... as* comparisons with adverbs, you use the same phrases as with adjectives.

- **so ... wie** as ... as

Er läuft so schnell wie sein Bruder.	He runs as fast as his brother.

- **nicht so ... wie** not as ... as

Sie kann nicht so gut schwimmen wie du.	She can't swim as well as you.

➤ The idea of *more and more ...* is expressed in German by using **immer** and the comparative form.

Die Männer sprachen immer lauter.	The men were talking louder and louder.

➤ *the more ... the more ...* is expressed in German by **je ... desto ...** or **je ... umso ...**

Je eher, desto besser.	The sooner the better.
Je schneller sie fährt, umso mehr Angst habe ich!	The faster she drives, the more frightened I am!

➪ *For more information on* ***Comparative adjectives****, see page* 53.

2 Superlative adverbs

What is a superlative adverb?
A **superlative adverb** is one which, in English, has *-est* on the end of it or *most* or *least* in front of it, for example, *soonest*, *fastest*, *most/least frequently*.

➤ The superlative of adverbs in German is formed in the following way and, unlike adjectives, is not declined:

am + *adverb* + **-sten**

Wer von ihnen arbeitet am schnellsten?	Which of them works fastest?
Er hat es am langsamsten gemacht.	He did it slowest.

➤ Adverbs ending in **-d**, **-t**, **-tz**, **-z**, **-sch**, **-ss**, or **-ß** form the superlative by adding **-esten**. This makes pronunciation easier.

Das Erdbeereis war bei den Kindern am beliebtesten.	The strawberry ice cream was the most popular one with the kids.
Am heißesten war es im Südspanien.	It was hottest in southern Spain.

➪ *For more information on* ***Superlative adjectives****, see page* 55.

ℹ Note that some superlative adverbs are used to show the extent of a quality rather than a comparison. The following adverbs are used in this way:

Adverb	Meaning
bestens	very well
höchstens	at the most/at best
meistens	mostly/most often
spätestens	at the latest
wenigstens	at least

Die Geschäfte gehen bestens.	Business is going very well.
Er kommt meistens zu spät an.	He usually arrives late.
Wenigstens bekomme ich mehr Geld dafür.	At least I'm getting more money for it.

3 Adverbs with irregular comparatives and superlatives

➤ A few German adverbs have irregular comparative and superlative forms.

Adverb	Meaning	Comparative	Meaning	Superlative	Meaning
gern	well	**lieber**	better	**am liebsten**	best
bald	soon	**eher**	sooner	**am ehesten**	soonest
viel	much, a lot	**mehr**	more	**am meisten**	most

Am liebsten lese ich Kriminalromane. — I like detective stories best.
Sie hat am meisten gewonnen. — She won the most.

Key points

- ✔ Comparatives of adverbs are formed in the same way as comparatives of adjectives, adding **-er** to the basic form.
- ✔ To compare people or things, you use **so ... wie**, **ebenso ... wie** or **nicht so ... wie**.
- ✔ *Than* in comparatives of adverbs corresponds to **als**.
- ✔ Superlatives of adverbs are formed by using the formula **am** + *adverb* + **-sten/-esten**.
- ✔ Unlike adjectives, adverbs do not change their form to agree with the verb, adjective or other adverb they relate to.

For further explanation of grammatical terms, please see pages viii–xii.

Word order with adverbs

➤ In English, adverbs can come in different places in a sentence.

I'm never coming back.

See you soon!

Suddenly the phone rang.

I'd really like to come.

➤ This is also true of adverbs in German, but as a general rule they are placed close to the word to which they refer.

- Adverbs of time often come first in the sentence, but this is not fixed.

Morgen gehen wir ins Theater OR:	
Wir gehen morgen ins Theater.	We're going to the theatre tomorrow.

- Adverbs of place can be put at the beginning of a sentence to provide emphasis.

Dort haben sie Fußball gespielt OR:	
Sie haben dort Fußball gespielt	They played football there.

- Adverbs of manner are adverbs which comment on verbs. These are likely to come after the verb to which they refer, but in tenses which are made up of **haben** or **sein** + the past participle of the main verb, they come immediately before the past participle.

Sie spielen gut.	They play well.
Sie haben heute gut gespielt.	They played well today.
Du benimmst dich immer schlecht.	You always behave badly.
Du hast dich schlecht benommen.	You have behaved badly.

➪ *For more information on **Forming the past participle**, see page 114.*

➤ Where there is more than one adverb in a sentence, it's useful to remember the following rule:

"time, manner, place"

Wir haben gestern gut dorthin gefunden.	We found our way there all right yesterday.

gestern = adverb of time

gut = adverb of manner

dorthin = adverb of place

➤ Where there is a pronoun object (a word like *her*, *it*, *me* or *them*) in a sentence, it comes before all adverbs.

Sie haben <u>es gestern sehr billig</u> gekauft.	They bought it very cheaply yesterday.

es = pronoun object

gestern = adverb of time

billig = adverb of manner

➪ *For more information on **Pronoun objects**, see page 74.*

Key points

✔ In German, the position of adverbs in a sentence is not fixed, but they generally come close to the words they refer to.

✔ Where there is more than one adverb in a sentence, it is useful to remember the rule: time, manner, place.

✔ Where there is a pronoun object in a sentence, it comes before all adverbs.

Emphasizers

What is an emphasizer?
An **emphasizer** is a type of word commonly used in both German and English, especially in the spoken language, to emphasize or change the meaning of a sentence.

➤ The following words are the most common emphasizers.

- **aber** is used to add emphasis to a statement

Das ist <u>aber</u> schön!	Oh, that's pretty!
Diese Jacke ist <u>aber</u> teuer!	This jacket is really expensive!

- **denn** is also used as a conjunction, but here it is used as an adverb to emphasize the meaning.

Was ist <u>denn</u> hier los?	What's going on here then?
Wo <u>denn</u>?	Where?

Tip
You can't always translate emphasizers directly, especially **denn** and **aber**.

➪ *For more information on **Conjunctions**, see page 168.*

- **doch** is used in one of three ways:

  As a positive reply to a negative statement or question:

Hat es dir nicht gefallen? – <u>Doch</u>!	Didn't you like it? – Oh yes, I did!

  To strengthen an imperative, that is the form of a verb used when giving instructions:

Lass ihn <u>doch</u>!	Just leave him.

  To make a question out of a statement:

Das schaffst du <u>doch</u>?	You'll manage it, won't you?

➪ *For more information on **Imperatives**, see page 105.*

- **mal** can be used in one of two ways:

  With imperatives:

Komm <u>mal</u> her!	Come here!
Moment <u>mal</u>, bitte!	Just a minute!

In informal language:

Mal sehen.	We'll see.
Hören Sie mal ...	Look here now ...
Er soll es nur mal versuchen!	Just let him try it!

- **Ja** can also be used in one of two ways.

  To strengthen a statement:

Er sieht ja wie seine Mutter aus.	He looks like his mother.
Das kann ja sein.	That may well be.

In informal language:

Ja und?	So what?/What then?
Das ist ja lächerlich.	That's ridiculous.
Das ist es ja.	That's just it.

- **Schon** also has more than one use.

  It is used informally with an imperative:

Mach schon!	Get on with it!

It is also used in other informal statements:

Da kommt sie schon wieder!	Here she comes again!
Schon gut. Ich habe verstanden.	Okay, I get the message.

Key points

✔ There are lots of little adverbs used in both English and German to emphasize or soften the meaning of a sentence in some way.

✔ The most common of these are **aber**, **denn**, **doch**, **mal**, **ja** and **schon**.

For further explanation of grammatical terms, please see pages viii–xii.

Pronouns

What is a pronoun?
A **pronoun** is a word you use instead of a noun, when you do not need or want to name someone or something directly, for example, *it*, *you*, *none*.

➤ There are several different types of pronoun:

- Personal pronouns such as *I*, *you*, *he*, *her* and *they*, which are used to refer to yourself, the person you are talking to, or other people and things. They can be either subject pronouns (*I*, *you*, *he* and so on) or object pronouns (*him*, *her*, *them* and so on).
- Possessive pronouns like *mine* and *yours*, which show who someone or something belongs to.
- Indefinite pronouns like *someone* or *nothing*, which refer to people or things in a general way without saying exactly who or what they are.
- Relative pronouns like *who*, *which* or *that*, which link two parts of a sentence together.
- Demonstrative pronouns like *this* or *those*, which point things or people out.
- Reflexive pronouns – a type of object pronoun that forms part of German reflexive verbs like **sich setzen** (meaning *to sit down*) or **sich waschen** (meaning *to wash*).

➪ *For more information on* **Reflexive verbs**, *see page 102.*

- The pronouns **wer?** (meaning *who?*) and **was?** (meaning *what?*) and their different forms, which are used to ask questions.

➤ Pronouns often stand in for a noun to save repeating it.

I finished my homework and gave it to my teacher.

Do you remember Jack? I saw him at the weekend.

➤ Word order with personal pronouns is usually different in German and English.

Personal pronouns: subject

What is a subject pronoun?
A **subject pronoun** is a word such as *I*, *he*, *she* and *they*. It refers to the person or thing which performs the action expressed by the verb. Pronouns stand in for nouns when it is clear who is being talked about, for example: *My brother isn't here at the moment. He'll be back in an hour.*

1 Using subject pronouns

➤ Here are the German subject pronouns or personal pronouns in the nominative case:

Subject Pronoun (Nominative Case)	Meaning
ich	I
du	you *(familiar)*
er	he/it
sie	she/it
es	it/he/she
man	one
wir	we
ihr	you *(plural)*
sie	they
Sie	you *(polite)*

Ich fahre nächste Woche nach Italien. — I'm going to Italy next week.
Wir wohnen in Frankfurt. — We live in Frankfurt.

⇨ *For more information on the **Nominative case**, see page 9.*

2 du, ihr or Sie?

➤ In English we have only one way of saying *you*. In German, there are three words: **du**, **ihr** and **Sie**. The word you use depends on:

- whether you are talking to one person or more than one person
- whether you are talking to a friend or family member, or someone else

➤ Use the familiar **du** if talking to one person you know well, such as a friend, someone younger than you or a relative

Kommst du mit ins Kino? — Are you coming to the cinema?

➤ Use the formal or polite **Sie** if talking to one person you do not know so well, such as your teacher, your boss or a stranger.

Was haben Sie gesagt?	What did you say?

> ## *Tip*
> If you are in doubt as to which form of *you* to use, it is safest to use **Sie** and you will not offend anybody. However, once a colleague or acquaintance has suggested you call each other **du**, starting to use **Sie** again may be considered insulting.

➤ Use the familiar **ihr** if talking to more than one person you know well or relatives.

Also, was wollt ihr heute Abend essen?	So, what do you want to eat tonight?

➤ Use **Sie** if talking to more than one person you do not know so well.

Wo fahren Sie hin?	Where are you going to?

> ## *Tip*
> Use **Sie** in more formal situations for both the singular and plural *you*.

> ## *Tip*
> All of the subject pronouns only have a capital letter when they begin a sentence, except for the polite form of *you*, **Sie**, which always has a capital letter.

Ich gebe dir das Buch zurück, wenn ich es zu Ende gelesen habe.	I'll give you the book back when I've finished reading it.
Du kannst mich morgen besuchen, wenn du Zeit hast.	You can come and visit me tomorrow, if you have time.
Wir wären Ihnen sehr dankbar, wenn Sie uns telefonisch benachrichtigen würden.	We'd be very grateful if you could phone and let us know.

3 Er/sie/es

➤ In English we generally refer to things (such as *table*, *book*, *car*) only as *it*. In German, **er** (meaning *he*), **sie** (meaning *she*) and **es** (meaning *it*) are used to talk about a thing, as well as about a person or an animal. You use **er** for masculine nouns, **sie** for feminine nouns and **es** for neuter nouns.

Der Tisch ist groß	→	**Er ist groß**
The table is large	→	It is large
Die Jacke ist blau	→	**Sie ist blau**
The jacket is blue	→	It is blue
Das Kind stand auf	→	**Es stand auf**
The child stood up	→	He/she stood up

ℹ Note that English speakers often make the mistake of calling all objects **es**.

➤ The subject pronoun **sie** (meaning *they*) is used in the plural to talk about things, as well as people or animals. Use **sie** for masculine, feminine and neuter nouns.

'Wo sind Michael und Sebastian?' –	'Where are Michael and Sebastian?' –
'Sie sind im Garten.'	'They're in the garden.'
'Hast du die Karten gekauft?' –	'Did you buy the tickets?' –
'Nein, sie waren ausverkauft.'	'No, they were sold out.'
'Nimmst du die Hunde mit?' –	'Are you taking the dogs with you?' –
'Nein, die Nachbarin passt auf sie auf.'	'No, the next-door neighbour is looking after them.'

4 Man

➤ This is often used in German in the same way as we use *you* in English to mean people in general.

Wie schreibt man das?	How do you spell that?
Man kann nie wissen.	You never know.

➤ **Man** can also mean *they* used in a vague way.

Man sagt, dass das Wetter immer schlecht ist.	They say the weather is always bad.

For further explanation of grammatical terms, please see pages viii–xii.

Tip

Man is often used to avoid a passive construction in German.

Man hat das schon oft im Fernsehen gezeigt.	It's already been shown a lot on TV.

➪ *For more information on the **Passive**, see page 150.*

The form of the verb you use with **man** is the same as the **er/sie/es** form.

➪ *For more information on **Verbs**, see pages 91-152.*

Key points

- ✔ The German subject pronouns are: **ich**, **du**, **er**, **sie**, **es**, **Sie** and **man** in the singular, and **wir**, **ihr**, **sie** and **Sie** in the plural.
- ✔ To say *you* in German, use **du** if you are talking to one person you know well or to someone younger than you; use **ihr** if you are talking to more than one person you know well and use **Sie** if you are talking to one or more people you do not know well.
- ✔ **Er/sie/es** (masculine/feminine/neuter singular) and **sie** (masculine or feminine or neuter plural) are used to refer to things, as well as to people or animals.
- ✔ **Man** can mean *you*, *they* or people in general. It is often used instead of a passive construction.

Personal pronouns: direct object

What is a direct object pronoun?
A **direct object pronoun** is a word such as *me, him, us* and *them* which is used instead of the noun to stand in for the person or thing most directly affected by the action expressed by the verb.

1 Using direct object pronouns

➤ Direct object pronouns stand in for nouns when it is clear who or what is being talked about, and save having to repeat the noun.

I've lost my glasses. Have you seen them?
'Have you met Jo?' – 'Yes, I really like her!'

➤ Here are the German direct object pronouns or personal pronouns in the accusative case:

Direct Object Pronoun (Accusative Case)	Meaning
mich	me
dich	you *(familiar)*
ihn	him/it
sie	her/it
es	it/him/her
einen	one
uns	us
euch	you *(plural)*
sie	them
Sie	you *(polite)*

Ich lade dich zum Essen ein. — I'll invite you for a meal.
Sie hat ihn letztes Jahr kennengelernt. — She met him last year.

2 Word order with direct object pronouns

➤ In tenses consisting of one verb part only, for example the present and the simple past, the direct object pronoun usually comes directly AFTER the verb.

Sie bringen ihn nach Hause. — They'll take him home.

➤ In tenses such as the perfect that are formed with **haben** or **sein** and the past participle, the direct object pronoun comes AFTER the part of the verb that comes from **haben** or **sein** and BEFORE the past participle.

Er hat mich durchs Fenster gesehen. — He saw me through the window.

For further explanation of grammatical terms, please see pages viii–xii.

➤ When a modal verb like **wollen** (meaning *to want*) or **können** (meaning *to be able to, can*) is followed by another verb in the infinitive (the '*to*' form of the verb), the direct object pronoun comes directly AFTER the modal verb.

Wir wollen Sie nicht mehr sehen. We don't want to see you anymore.

➪ *For more information on **Modal verbs**, see page 136.*

Key points

✔ The German direct object pronouns are: **mich**, **dich**, **ihn**, **sie**, **es**, **Sie** and **einen** in the singular, and **uns**, **euch**, **sie** and **Sie** in the plural.

✔ The direct object pronoun usually comes directly after the verb, but in tenses like the perfect comes after the part of the verb that comes from **haben** or **sein** and before the past participle.

✔ When a modal verb such as **wollen** is followed by the infinitive of another verb, the direct object pronoun comes directly after the modal verb.

Personal pronouns: indirect object

What is an indirect object pronoun?
When a verb has two objects (a direct one and an indirect one), the **indirect object pronoun** is used instead of a noun to show the person or thing the action is intended to benefit or harm, for example, *me* in *He gave me a book; Can you get me a towel?*

1 Using indirect object pronouns

➤ It is important to understand the difference between direct and indirect object pronouns, as they have different forms in German:

- an indirect object answers the question *who to?* or *who for?* and *to what?* or *for what?*
  He gave me a book. → *Who did he give the book to?* → me (=*indirect object pronoun*)
  Can you get me a towel? → *Who can you get a towel for?* → me (=*indirect object pronoun*)

- if something answers the question *what?* or *who?*, then it is the direct object and NOT the indirect object
  He gave me a book → *What did he give me?* → a book (=*direct object*)
  Can you get me a towel? → *What can you get me?* → a towel (=*direct object*)

➤ Here are the German indirect object pronouns in the dative case:

Indirect Object Pronoun (Dative Case)	**Meaning**
mir	to/for me
dir	to/for you (*familiar*)
ihm	to/for him/it
ihr	to/for her/it
ihm	to/for it/him/her
einem	to/for one
uns	to/for us
euch	to/for you (*plural*)
ihnen	to/for them
Ihnen	to/for you (*polite*)

Er hat mir das geschenkt. He gave me that as a present.
Sie haben ihnen eine tolle Geschichte erzählt. They told them a great story.

For further explanation of grammatical terms, please see pages viii–xii.

2 Word order with indirect object pronouns

➤ Word order for indirect object pronouns is the same as for direct object pronouns. The pronoun usually comes directly after the verb, except with tenses like the perfect and modal verbs such as **wollen**.

Sie bringt mir das Schwimmen bei.	She's teaching me how to swim.
Sie hat es ihm gegeben.	She gave it to him.
Ich will dir etwas sagen.	I want to tell you something.

➤ When you have both a direct object pronoun AND an indirect object pronoun in the same sentence, the direct object pronoun or personal pronoun in the accusative always comes first. A good way of remembering this is to think of the following:

PAD = Pronoun Accusative Dative

Sie haben es ihm verziehen.	They forgave him for it.
Ich bringe es dir schon bei.	I'll teach you.

Key points

- ✔ The German indirect object pronouns are: **mir**, **dir**, **ihm**, **ihr**, **ihm**, **Ihnen** and **einem** in the singular, and **uns**, **euch**, **ihnen** and **Ihnen** in the plural.
- ✔ The indirect object pronoun comes after the verb, except with tenses like the perfect and when used with modal verbs such as **wollen**.
- ✔ The indirect object pronoun always comes after the direct object pronoun.

Personal pronouns: after prepositions

➤ When a personal pronoun is used after a preposition and refers to a person, the personal pronoun is in the case required by the preposition. For example, the preposition **mit** is always followed by the dative case.

Ich bin mit ihm spazieren gegangen. I went for a walk with him.

➤ When a thing rather than a person is referred to, **da-** is added at the beginning of the preposition:

Manuela hatte ein Messer geholt und wollte damit den Kuchen schneiden. Manuela had brought a knife and was about to cut the cake with it.

ℹ Note that before a preposition beginning with a vowel, the form **dar-** + preposition is used.

Lege es bitte darauf. Put it there please.

➤ The following prepositions are affected in this way:

Preposition	Preposition + da or dar
an	daran
auf	darauf
aus	daraus
bei	dabei
durch	dadurch
für	dafür
in	darin
mit	damit
nach	danach
neben	daneben
über	darüber
unter	darunter
zwischen	dazwischen

➪ *For more information on* ***Prepositions****, see page* 153.

ℹ Note that these combined forms are also used after verbs followed by prepositions.

sich erinnern an + accusative case = to remember
Ich erinnere mich nicht daran. I don't remember (it).

Grammar Extra!

After certain prepositions used to express movement, that is **aus** (meaning *out* or *from*), **auf** (meaning *on*) and **in** (meaning *in* or *into*), combined forms with **hin** and **her** are used to give more emphasis to the action being carried out.

Preposition	hin or her + Preposition
aus	hinaus/heraus
auf	hinauf/herauf
in	hinein/herein

Er ging die Treppe leise hinauf. He went up the stairs quietly.
Endlich fand sie unser Zelt und kam herein. She finally found our tent and came inside.
Sie öffnete die Reisetasche und legte die Hose hinein. She opened the bag and put in her trousers.

Key points

- ✔ When a personal pronoun referring to a person is used after a preposition, the personal pronoun is in the case required by the preposition.
- ✔ When a personal pronoun referring to a thing is used after a preposition, the construction **da(r)-** + preposition is used.

Possessive pronouns

What is a possessive pronoun?
In English you can say *This is my car* or *This car is mine*. In the first sentence *my* is a possessive adjective. In the second, *mine* is a possessive pronoun.

A **possessive pronoun** is one of the words *mine, yours, hers, his, ours* or *theirs*, which are used instead of a noun to show that one thing or person belongs to another, for example, *Ask Carol if this pen is hers.*

➤ German possessive pronouns are the same words as the possessive adjectives **mein**, **dein**, **sein**, **ihr**, **unser**, **euer**, **ihr**, **Ihr**, with the same endings, EXCEPT in the masculine nominative singular, the neuter nominative singular and the neuter accusative singular, as shown below.

	Possessive Adjective	Meaning	Possessive Pronoun	Meaning
Masculine Nominative Singular	**Das ist mein Wagen**	That is my car	**Dieser Wagen ist meiner**	That car is mine
Neuter Nominative Singular	**Das ist mein Buch**	That is my book	**Dieses Buch ist meins**	That book is mine
Neuter Accusative Singular	**Sie hat mein Buch genommen**	She has taken my book	**Sie hat meins genommen**	She has taken mine

➤ Here is the German possessive pronoun **meiner**, meaning *mine*, in all its forms:

Case	Masculine Singular	Feminine Singular	Neuter Singular	All Genders Plural
Nominative	**meiner**	**meine**	**mein(e)s**	**meine**
Accusative	**meinen**	**meine**	**mein(e)s**	**meine**
Genitive	**meines**	**meiner**	**meines**	**meiner**
Dative	**meinem**	**meiner**	**meinem**	**meinen**

i Note that the nominative and accusative neuter forms only of all the possessive pronouns are often pronounced without the last **-e**, for example **meins** instead of **meines**.

Der Wagen da drüben ist meiner.	The car over there is mine.
Er ist kleiner als deiner.	It is smaller than yours.
Das ist besser als meins!	That's better than mine!
Das Haus nebenan ist schöner als seins.	The house next door is nicer than his.
Meine Jacke war teurer als ihre.	My jacket was more expensive than hers.

For further explanation of grammatical terms, please see pages viii–xii.

Note that **deiner**, meaning *yours (familiar)*, **seiner**, meaning *his/its*, **ihrer**, meaning *hers/its/theirs*, **Ihrer**, meaning *yours (polite)*, **unserer**, meaning *ours* and **euerer**, meaning *yours (plural familiar)* have the same endings as **meiner**.

Tip

Unserer, meaning *ours* is often pronounced **unsrer** and **euerer**, meaning *yours (plural familiar)* is often pronounced **eurer**. This pronunciation is occasionally reflected in writing.

Case	Masculine Singular	Feminine Singular	Neuter Singular	All Genders Plural
Nominative	uns(e)rer	uns(e)re	uns(e)res	uns(e)re
Accusative	uns(e)ren	uns(e)re	uns(e)res	uns(e)re
Genitive	uns(e)res	uns(e)rer	uns(e)res	uns(e)rer
Dative	uns(e)rem	uns(e)rer	uns(e)rem	uns(e)ren

Case	Masculine Singular	Feminine Singular	Neuter Singular	All Genders Plural
Nominative	eu(e)rer	eu(e)re	eu(e)res	eu(e)re
Accusative	eu(e)ren	eu(e)re	eu(e)res	eu(e)re
Genitive	eu(e)res	eu(e)rer	eu(e)res	eu(e)rer
Dative	eu(e)rem	eu(e)rer	eu(e)rem	eu(e)ren

War euer Urlaub billiger als unsrer? Was your holiday cheaper than ours?

Note the translation of *of mine, of yours* etc, where the personal pronoun in the dative is used:

Er ist ein Freund von mir. He is a friend of mine.

Ich habe eine CD von dir bei mir zu Hause. I have a CD of yours at home.

Key points

- ✔ German possessive pronouns have the same form and endings as the possessive adjectives **mein**, **dein**, **sein**, **ihr**, **unser**, **euer**, **ihr**, **Ihr**, except in the masculine nominative singular, the neuter nominative singular and the neuter accusative singular.
- ✔ The nominative and accusative neuter forms of all the possessive pronouns are often pronounced without the last **-e**, for example **meins** instead of **meines**.
- ✔ **Unserer**, meaning *ours* is often pronounced **unsrer** and **euerer**, meaning *yours (plural familiar)* is often pronounced **eurer**. This pronunciation is occasionally reflected in writing.

Indefinite pronouns

What is an indefinite pronoun?
An **indefinite pronoun** is one of a small group of pronouns such as *everything*, *nobody* and *something* which are used to refer to people or things in a general way without saying exactly who or what they are.

➤ In German, the indefinite pronouns **jemand** (meaning *someone, somebody*) and **niemand** (meaning *no-one, nobody*) are often used in speech without any endings. In written German, the endings are added.

Case	Indefinite Pronoun
Nominative	jemand/niemand
Accusative	jemanden/niemanden
Genitive	jemand(e)s/niemand(e)s
Dative	jemandem/niemandem

Ich habe es jemandem gegeben. I gave it to someone.
Jemand hat es genommen. Someone has stolen it.
Sie hat niemanden gesehen. She didn't see anyone.
Ich bin unterwegs niemandem begegnet. I didn't meet anyone on the way.

Tip
If you want to express the sense of *somebody or other*, use **irgendjemand** which is declined like **jemand**.

Ich habe es irgendjemandem gegeben. I gave it to somebody or other.

➤ The indefinite pronoun **keiner** has the same endings as the article **kein**, **keine**, **kein** except in the nominative masculine and nominative and accusative neuter forms, and can be used to refer to people or things. When referring to people it means *nobody*, *not ... anybody* or *none* and when referring to things, it means *not ... any* or *none*.

Case	Masculine Singular	Feminine Singular	Neuter Singular	All Genders Plural
Nominative	keiner	keine	keins	keine
Accusative	keinen	keine	keins	keine
Genitive	keines	keiner	keines	keiner
Dative	keinem	keiner	keinem	keinen

For further explanation of grammatical terms, please see pages viii–xii.

Ich kenne hier keinen. — I don't know anybody here.

Keiner weiß Bescheid über ihn. — Nobody knows about him.

Das trifft auf keinen zu. — That does not apply to anybody here.

Er wollte ein Stück Schokolade, aber ich hatte keine. — He wanted a piece of chocolate, but I didn't have any.

„Hast du Geld?" – „Nein, gar keins." — "Have you got any money?" – "No, none at all."

➤ The indefinite pronoun **einer** (meaning *one*) only has a singular form and can also be used to refer to people or things.

Case	Masculine Singular	Feminine Singular	Neuter Singular
Nominative	**einer**	**eine**	**ein(e)s**
Accusative	**einen**	**eine**	**ein(e)s**
Genitive	**eines**	**einer**	**eines**
Dative	**einem**	**einer**	**einem**

Sie trifft sich mit einem ihrer alten Studienfreunde. — She's meeting one of her old friends from university.

Ich brauche nur einen (e.g. **einen Wagen, einen Pullover** etc) OR:
Ich brauche nur eine (e.g. **eine Blume, eine Tasche** etc) OR:
Ich brauche nur eins (e.g. **ein Buch, ein Notizbuch** etc) I only need one.

Key points

✔ **Jemand** and **niemand** can be used without endings in spoken German but have endings added in written German.

✔ **Keiner** has the same endings as the article **kein**, **keine**, **kein** except in the nominative masculine and nominative and accusative neuter forms, and refers to people or things.

✔ **Einer** only has a singular form and refers to people or things.

Reflexive pronouns

What is a reflexive pronoun?
A **reflexive pronoun** is an object pronoun such as *myself*, *yourself*, *himself*, *herself* and *ourselves* that forms part of German reflexive verbs like **sich waschen** (meaning *to wash*) or **sich setzen** (meaning *to sit down*). A reflexive verb is a verb whose subject and object are the same and whose action is "reflected back" to its subject.

➤ German reflexive pronouns have two forms: accusative (for the direct object pronoun) and dative (for the indirect object pronoun), as follows:

Accusative Form	Dative Form	Meaning
mich	**mir**	myself
dich	**dir**	yourself (*familiar*)
sich	**sich**	himself/herself/itself
uns	**uns**	ourselves
euch	**euch**	yourselves (*plural*)
sich	**sich**	themselves
sich	**sich**	yourself/yourselves (*polite*)

Er hat sich rasiert. — He had a shave.
Du hast dich gebadet. — You had a bath.
Ich will es mir zuerst überlegen. — I'll have to think about it first.

ℹ Note that unlike personal pronouns and possessives, the polite forms have no capital letter.

Setzen Sie sich bitte. — Please take a seat.
Nehmen Sie sich ruhig etwas Zeit. — Take your time.

➤ The reflexive pronoun usually follows the first verb in the sentence, with certain exceptions:

Sie wird sich darüber freuen. — She'll be pleased about that.

- If the subject and verb are swapped round in the sentence, and the subject is a personal pronoun, then the reflexive pronoun must come AFTER the personal pronoun.

Darüber wird sie sich freuen. — She'll be pleased about that.

- If the sentence is made of up two parts or clauses, then the reflexive pronoun comes AFTER the subject in the second clause.

Ich frage mich, ob sie sich darüber freuen wird. — I wonder if she'll be pleased about that.

➪ *For more information on **Word order**, see page 175.*
➪ *For more information on **Reflexive verbs**, see page 102.*

➤ Unlike English, reflexive pronouns are also used after prepositions when the pronoun "reflects back" to the subject of the sentence.

Er hatte nicht genug Geld bei sich.	He didn't have enough money on him.
Hatten Sie nicht genug Geld bei sich?	Didn't you have enough money on you?

➤ Another use of reflexive pronouns in German is with transitive verbs where the action is performed for the benefit of the subject, as in the English phrase: I bought *myself* a new hat. The pronoun is not always translated in English.

Ich hole mir einen Kaffee.	I'm going to get (myself) a coffee.
Sie hat sich eine neue Jacke gekauft.	She bought (herself) a new jacket.

➤ Reflexive pronouns are usually used in German where *each other* and *one another* would be used in English.

Wir sind uns letzte Woche begegnet.	We met (each other) last week.

[i] Note that **einander**, (meaning *one another, each other*), which does not change in form, may be used instead of a reflexive pronoun in such cases.

Wir kennen uns schon OR **Wir kennen einander schon.**	We already know each other.

➤ After prepositions, **einander** is always used instead of a reflexive pronoun. The preposition and **einander** are then joined to form one word.

Sie redeten miteinander.	They were talking to each other.

➤ In English, pronouns used for emphasis are the same as normal reflexive pronouns, for example, *I did it myself*. In German **selbst** or, in informal spoken language, **selber** are used instead of reflexive pronouns for emphasis. They never change their form and are always stressed, regardless of their position in the sentence:

Ich selbst habe es nicht gelesen, aber ...	I haven't read it *myself*, but ...

Key points

✔ German reflexive pronouns have two forms: accusative for the direct object pronoun and dative for the indirect object pronoun.

✔ Reflexive pronouns are also used after prepositions when the pronoun "reflects back" to the subject of the sentence.

✔ Reflexive pronouns are usually used in German where *each other* or *one another* would be used in English, but **einander** can be used as an alternative and is always used after prepositions.

✔ **Selbst** or, in informal spoken German, **selber** are used instead of reflexive pronouns for emphasis.

Relative pronouns

What is a relative pronoun?
In English a **relative pronoun** is one of the words *who*, *which* and *that* (and the more formal *whom*). These pronouns are used to introduce information that makes it clear which person or thing is being talked about, for example, *The man who has just come in is Ann's boyfriend; The vase that you broke was quite valuable.*

Relative pronouns can also introduce further information about someone or something, for example, *Peter, who is a brilliant painter, wants to study art; Jane's house, which was built in 1890, needs a lot of repairs.*

➤ In German the most common relative pronouns **der**, **den**, **dessen**, **dem** etc have the same forms as the definite article, except in the dative plural and genitive singular and plural. They are declined as follows:

Case	Masculine Singular	Feminine Singular	Neuter Singular	All Genders Plural
Nominative	der	die	das	die
Accusative	den	die	das	die
Genitive	dessen	deren	dessen	deren
Dative	dem	der	dem	denen

➤ Relative pronouns must agree in gender and number with the noun to which they refer, but the case they have depends on their function in the relative clause. The relative clause is simply the part of the sentence in which the relative pronoun appears. Relative clauses are ALWAYS separated by commas from the rest of the sentence.

- In the following example, the relative pronoun **den** is in the accusative because it is the direct object in the relative clause.

  Der Mann, den ich gestern gesehen habe, kommt aus Zürich. — The man that I saw yesterday comes from Zürich.

- In this second example, the relative pronoun **dessen** is in the genitive because it is used to show that something belongs to someone.

  Der Student, dessen Smartphone gestohlen wurde, ging zur Polizei. — The student whose smartphone was stolen went to the police.

For further explanation of grammatical terms, please see pages viii–xii.

> ***Tip***
>
> In English we often miss out the object pronouns *who*, *which* and *that*. For example, we can say both *the friends that I see most*, or *the friends I see most*, and *the house which we want to buy*, or *the house we want to buy*. In German you can NEVER miss out the relative pronoun in this way.
>
> | | |
> |---|---|
> | **Die Frau, mit der ich gestern gesprochen habe, kennt deine Mutter.** | The woman I spoke to yesterday knows your mother. |

ℹ Note that the genitive forms are used in relative clauses in much the same way as in English, but to translate *one of whom*, *some of whom* use the following constructions.

Das Kind, dessen Fahrrad gestohlen worden war, fing an zu weinen.	The child whose bicycle had been stolen started to cry.
Die Kinder, von denen einige schon lesen konnten, ...	The children, some of whom could already read, ...
Meine Freunde, von denen einer ...	My friends, one of whom ...

Grammar Extra!

When a relative clause is introduced by a preposition, the relative pronoun can be replaced by **wo-** or **wor-** if the noun or pronoun it stands for refers to an object or something abstract. The full form of the pronoun plus preposition is much more common.

Das Buch, woraus ich vorgelesen habe, gehört dir.

OR:

Das Buch, aus dem ich vorgelesen habe, gehört dir.	The book I read aloud from belongs to you.

➤ In German **wer** and **was** are normally used as interrogative pronouns (meaning *who?* and *what?*) to ask questions. They can also be the subject of a sentence or a relative pronoun. For example, *he who*, *a woman who*, *anyone who*, *those who* etc.

Wer das glaubt, ist verrückt.	Anyone who believes that is mad.
Was du gestern gekauft hast, steht dir ganz gut.	The things you bought yesterday really suit you.

Note that **was** is the relative pronoun used in set expressions with certain neuter forms. For example:

alles, was ...	everything which
das, was ...	that which
nichts, was ...	nothing that
vieles, was ...	a lot that
wenig, was ...	little that
Nichts, was er sagte, hat gestimmt.	Nothing that he said was right.
Das, was du jetzt machst, ist unpraktisch.	What you are doing now is impractical.
Mit allem, was du gesagt hast, sind wir einverstanden.	We agree with everything you said.

Key points

- ✔ The most common relative pronouns **der**, **den**, **dessen**, **dem** etc have the same forms as the definite article, except in the dative plural and genitive singular and plural.
- ✔ Relative pronouns must agree in gender and number with the noun to which they refer, but take their case from their function in the relative clause.
- ✔ In German you can NEVER miss out the relative pronoun, unlike in English.
- ✔ Relative clauses are always separated by commas from the rest of the sentence.
- ✔ **Wer** and **was** are normally used as interrogative pronouns but can also be the subject of a sentence or a relative pronoun.

Interrogative pronouns

What is an interrogative pronoun?
This is one of the words *who*, *whose*, *whom*, *what* and *which* when they are used instead of a noun to ask questions, for example, *What's happening?*; *Who's coming?*

1 Wer? and was?

➤ **Wer** and **was** only have a singular form.

Case	Persons	Things
Nominative	wer?	was?
Accusative	wen?	was?
Genitive	wessen?	–
Dative	wem?	–

- They can be used in direct questions.

Wer hat es gemacht?	Who did it?
Mit wem bist du gekommen?	Who did you come with?
Wo ist der Kugelschreiber, mit dem du es geschrieben hast?	Where is the pen you wrote it with?

- They can also be used in indirect questions.

Ich weiß nicht, wer es gemacht hat.	I don't know who did it.
Sie wollte wissen, mit wem sie fahren sollte.	She wanted to know who she was to travel with.

2 Interrogative pronouns with prepositions

➤ When used with prepositions, **was** usually becomes **wo-** and is combined with the preposition to form one word. Where the preposition begins with a vowel, **wor-** is used instead.

Wodurch ist es zerstört worden?	How was it destroyed?
Worauf sollen wir sitzen? Es gibt keine Stühle.	What should we sit on? There aren't any chairs.

3 Was für ein?, welcher?

➤ These are used to mean *what kind of ...?* and *which one?* and are declined like the definite article.

„Er hat jetzt ein Auto" –	"He has a car now." -
„Was für eins hat er gekauft?"	"What kind (of one) did he buy?"
Welches hast du gewollt?	Which one did you want?

⇨ *For more information on* ***Words declined like the definite article****, see page 31.*

➤ They can refer to people or things and require the appropriate endings.

Für welchen (e.g. **welchen Job, welchen Whisky** etc**) hat sie sich entschieden?** OR:

Für welches (e.g. **welches Haus, welches Buch** etc**) hat sie sich entschieden?** OR:

Für welche (e.g. **welche Person, welche Jacke** etc**) hat sie sich entschieden?**

Which one did she choose?

Key points

✔ The interrogative pronouns **wer** and **was** can be used for direct and indirect questions and only have a singular form.

✔ When used with prepositions, **was** becomes **wo-**, or **wor-** when the preposition begins with a vowel.

✔ **Was für ein?** and **welcher?** are used to mean *what kind of ...?* and *which one?*

Verbs

What is a verb?
A **verb** is a 'doing' word which describes what someone or something does, what someone or something is, or what happens to them, for example, *be, sing, live*.

Weak, strong and mixed verbs

➤ Verbs are usually used with a noun, with a pronoun such as *I*, *you* or *she*, or with somebody's name. They can relate to the present, the past and the future; this is called their tense.

➪ *For more information on* ***Nouns*** *and* ***Pronouns****, see pages 1 and 69.*

➤ Verbs are either:

- weak; their forms follow a set pattern. These verbs may also be called regular.
- strong and irregular; their forms change according to different patterns.

OR

- mixed; their forms follow a mixture of the patterns for weak and strong verbs.

➤ Regular English verbs have a base form (the form of the verb without any endings added to it, for example, *walk*). This is the form you look up in a dictionary. The base form can have *to* in front of it, for example, *to walk*. This is called the infinitive.

➤ German verbs also have an infinitive, which is the form shown in a dictionary; most weak, strong and mixed verbs end in **-en**. For example, **holen** (meaning *to fetch*) is weak, **helfen** (meaning *to help*) is strong and **denken** (meaning *to think*) is mixed. All German verbs belong to one of these groups. We will look at each of these three groups in turn on the next few pages.

➤ English verbs have other forms apart from the base form and infinitive: a form ending in -*s* (*walks*), a form ending in -*ing* (*walking*), and a form ending in -*ed* (*walked*).

➤ German verbs have many more forms than this, which are made up of endings added to a stem. The stem of a verb can usually be worked out from the infinitive and can change, depending on the tense of the verb and who or what you are talking about.

➤ German verb endings also change, depending on who or what you are talking about: **ich** (*I*), **du** (*you* (informal)), **er/sie/es** (*he/she/it*), **Sie** (*you* (formal)) in the singular, or **wir** (*we*), **ihr** (*you* (informal)), **Sie** (*you* (formal)) and **sie** (*they*) in the plural. German verbs also have different forms depending on whether you are referring to the present, future or past.

➪ *For* ***Verb Tables****, see supplement.*

Key points

✔ German verbs have different forms depending on what noun or pronoun they are used with, and on their tense.

✔ They are made up of a stem and an ending. The stem is based on the infinitive and can change in form.

✔ All German verbs fit into one of three patterns or conjugations: weak (and regular), strong (and irregular) or mixed (a mixture of the two).

For further explanation of grammatical terms, please see pages viii–xii.

The present tense

What is the present tense?
The **present tense** is used to talk about what is true at the moment, what happens regularly and what is happening now, for example, *I'm a student, I travel to college by train, I'm studying languages.*

1 Using the present tense

➤ In English there are two forms of the present tense. One is used to talk about things happening now and the other is used for things that happen all the time. In German, you use the same form for both of these.

- things that are happening now

Es regnet.	It's raining.
Sie spielen Fußball.	They're playing football.

- things that happen all the time, or things that you do as a habit

Hier regnet es viel.	It rains a lot here.
Samstags spielen sie Fußball.	They play football on Saturdays.

➤ In German there are three alternative ways of emphasizing that something is happening now:

- present tense + an adverb

Er kocht gerade das Abendessen.	He's cooking dinner.

- **beim** + an infinitive being used as a noun

Ich bin beim Bügeln.	I am ironing

- **eben/gerade dabei sein zu** (meaning *to be in the process of*) + an infinitive

Sie ist gerade dabei, eine E-Mail zu schreiben.	She is just writing an email.

➤ In English you can also use the present tense to talk about something that is going to happen in the near future. You can do the same in German.

Morgen spiele ich Tennis.	I'm going to play tennis tomorrow.
Wir nehmen den Zug um zehn Uhr.	We're getting the ten o'clock train.

Tip

Although English sometimes uses parts of the verb *to be* to form the present tense of other verbs (for example, *I am listening, she's talking*), German NEVER uses the verb **sein** in this way.

When using **seit** or **seitdem** to describe an action which began in the past and is continuing in the present, the present tense is used in German, where in English a verb form with *have* or *has* is used.

Ich wohne seit drei Jahren hier.	I have been living here for three years.
Seit er krank ist, hat er uns nicht besucht.	He hasn't visited us since he's been ill.
Seitdem sie am Gymnasium ist, hat sie kaum mehr Zeit.	Since she's been going to grammar school, she's hardly had any time.

ℹ Note that if the action is finished, the perfect tense is used in German.

Seit seinem Unfall habe ich ihn nur ein einziges Mal gesehen.	I have only seen him once since his accident.

2 Forming the present tense of weak verbs

- ➤ Nearly all weak verbs in German end in **-en** in their infinitive form. This is the form of the verb you find in the dictionary, for example, **spielen**, **machen**, **holen**. Weak verbs are regular and their changes follow a set pattern or conjugation.
- ➤ To know which form of the verb to use in German, you need to work out what the stem of the verb is and then add the correct ending. The stem of most verbs in the present tense is formed by chopping the **-en** off the infinitive.

Infinitive	**Stem** (without **-en**)
spielen (*to play*)	**spiel-**
machen (*to make*)	**mach-**
holen (*to fetch*)	**hol-**

- ➤ Where the infinitive of a weak verb ends in **-eln** or **-ern**, only the **-n** is chopped off to form the stem.

Infinitive	**Stem** (without **-n**)
wandern (*to hillwalk*)	**wander-**
segeln (*to sail*)	**segel-**

For further explanation of grammatical terms, please see pages viii–xii.

➤ Now you know how to find the stem of a verb, you can add the correct ending. Which one you choose will depend on whether you are referring to **ich**, **du**, **er**, **sie**, **es**, **wir**, **ihr**, **Sie** or **sie**.

➪ *For more information on **Pronouns**, see page 69.*

➤ Here are the present tense endings for weak verbs ending in **-en**:

Pronoun	Ending	Add to Stem, e.g. spiel-	Meanings
ich	-e	ich spiele	I play I am playing
du	-st	du spielst	you play you are playing
er sie es	-t	er spielt sie spielt es spielt	he/she/it plays he/she/it is playing
wir	-en	wir spielen	we play we are playing
ihr	-t	ihr spielt	you (*plural*) play you are playing
sie Sie	-en	sie spielen Sie spielen	they play they are playing you (*polite*) play you are playing

Sie macht ihre Hausaufgaben. She's doing her homework.
Er holt die Kinder. He's fetching the children.

ⓘ Note that you add **-n**, not **-en** to the stem of weak verbs ending in **-ern** and **-eln** to get the **wir**, **sie** and **Sie** forms of the present tense.

Pronoun	Ending	Add to Stem, e.g. wander-	Meanings
wir	-n	wir wandern	we hillwalk we are hillwalking
sie Sie	-n	sie wandern Sie wandern	they hillwalk they are hillwalking you (*polite*) hillwalk you are hillwalking

Sie wandern gern, oder? You like hillwalking, don't you?
Im Sommer wandern wir fast jedes Wochenende. In the summer we go hillwalking most weekends.

➤ If the stem of a weak verb ends in **-d** or **-t**, an extra **-e** is added before the usual endings in the **du**, **er**, **sie** and **es** and **ihr** parts of the verb to make pronunciation easier.

Pronoun	Ending	Add to Stem, e.g. red-	Meanings
du	-est	**du red<u>est</u>**	you talk you are talking
er sie es	-et	**er red<u>et</u>** **sie red<u>et</u>** **es red<u>et</u>**	he/she/it talks he/she/it is talking
ihr	-et	**ihr red<u>et</u>**	you (*plural*) talk you are talking

Du red<u>est</u> doch die ganze Zeit über deine Arbeit! You talk about your work all the time!

Pronoun	Ending	Add to Stem, e.g. arbeit-	Meanings
du	-est	**du arbeit<u>est</u>**	you work you are working
er sie es	-et	**er arbeit<u>et</u>** **sie arbeit<u>et</u>** **es arbeit<u>et</u>**	he/she/it works he/she/it is working
ihr	-et	**ihr arbeit<u>et</u>**	you (*plural*) work you are working

Sie arbeit<u>et</u> übers Wochenende. She's working over the weekend.
Ihr arbeit<u>et</u> ganz schön viel. You work a lot.

➤ If the stem of a weak verb ends in **-m** or **-n**, this extra **-e** is added to make pronunciation easier. If the **-m** or **-n** has a consonant in front of it, the **-e** is added, except if the consonant is *l*, *r* or *h*, for example **le<u>r</u>nen**.

Pronoun	Ending	Add to Stem, e.g. atm-	Meanings
du	-est	**du atm<u>est</u>**	you breathe you are breathing
er sie es	-et	**er atm<u>et</u>** **sie atm<u>et</u>** **es atm<u>et</u>**	he/she/it breathes he/she/it is breathing
ihr	-et	**ihr atm<u>et</u>**	you (*plural*) breathe you are breathing

Du atm<u>est</u> ganz tief. You're breathing very deeply.

For further explanation of grammatical terms, please see pages viii–xii.

Pronoun	Ending	Add to Stem, e.g. lern-	Meanings
du	**-est**	**du lernst**	you learn you are learning
er **sie** **es**	**-t**	**er lernt** **sie lernt** **es lernt**	he/she/it learns he/she/it is learning
ihr	**-t**	**ihr lernt**	you (*plural*) learn you are learning

Sie lernt alles ganz schnell. She learns everything very quickly.

Key points

✔ Weak verbs are regular and most of them form their present tense stem by losing the **-en** from the infinitive.

✔ The present tense endings for weak verbs ending in **-en** are: **-e**, **-st**, **-t**, **-en**, **-t**, **-en**, **-en**.

✔ If the stem of a weak verb ends in **-d**, **-t**, **-m** or **-n**, an extra **-e** is added before the endings to make pronunciation easier.

3 Forming the present tense of strong verbs

➤ The present tense of most strong verbs is formed with the same endings that are used for weak verbs.

Pronoun	Ending	Add to Stem, e.g. sing-	Meanings
ich	**-e**	**ich singe**	I sing I am singing
du	**-st**	**du singst**	you sing you are singing
er **sie** **es**	**-t**	**er singt** **sie singt** **es singt**	he/she/it sings he/she/it is singing
wir	**-en**	**wir singen**	we sing we are singing
ihr	**-t**	**ihr singt**	you (*plural*) sing you are singing
sie **Sie**	**-en**	**sie singen** **Sie singen**	they sing they are singing you (*polite*) sing you are singing

Sie singen in einer Gruppe. They sing in a band.

➤ However, the vowels in stems of most strong verbs change for the **du** and **er/sie/es** forms. The vowels listed below change as shown in nearly all cases:

long **e** → **ie** (*see* **sehen**)
short **e** → **i** (*see* **helfen**)
a → **ä** (*see* **fahren**)
au → **äu** (*see* **laufen**)
o → **ö** (*see* **stoßen**)

- long **e** → **ie**

Pronoun	Ending	Add to Stem, e.g. seh-	Meanings
ich	**-e**	**ich sehe**	I see I am seeing
du	**-st**	**du siehst**	you see you are seeing
er **sie** **es**	**-t**	**er sieht** **sie sieht** **es sieht**	he/she/it sees he/she/it is seeing
wir	**-en**	**wir sehen**	we see we are seeing
ihr	**-t**	**ihr seht**	you (*plural*) see you are seeing
sie **Sie**	**-en**	**sie sehen** **Sie sehen**	they see they are seeing you (*polite*) see you are seeing

Siehst du fern? Are you watching TV?

- short **e** → **i**

Pronoun	Ending	Add to Stem, e.g. helf-	Meanings
ich	**-e**	**ich helfe**	I help I am helping
du	**-st**	**du hilfst**	you help you are helping
er **sie** **es**	**-t**	**er hilft** **sie hilft** **es hilft**	he/she/it helps he/she/it is helping
wir	**-en**	**wir helfen**	we help we are helping
ihr	**-t**	**ihr helft**	you (*plural*) help you are helping
sie **Sie**	**-en**	**sie helfen** **Sie helfen**	they help they are helping you (*polite*) help you are helping

Heute hilft er beim Kochen. He's helping with the cooking today.

For further explanation of grammatical terms, please see pages viii–xii.

- a → ä

Pronoun	Ending	Add to Stem, e.g. fahr-	Meanings
ich	-e	**ich fahre**	I drive I am driving
du	-st	**du fährst**	you drive you are driving
er sie es	-t	**er fährt** **sie fährt** **es fährt**	he/she/it drives he/she/it is driving
wir	-en	**wir fahren**	we drive we are driving
ihr	-t	**ihr fahrt**	you (*plural*) drive you are driving
sie Sie	-en	**sie fahren** **Sie fahren**	they drive they are driving you (*polite*) drive you are driving

Am Samstag fährt sie nach Italien. She's driving to Italy on Saturday.

- au → äu

Pronoun	Ending	Add to Stem, e.g. lauf-	Meanings
ich	-e	**ich laufe**	I run I am running
du	-st	**du läufst**	you run you are running
er sie es	-t	**er läuft** **sie läuft** **es läuft**	he/she/it runs he/she/it is running
wir	-en	**wir laufen**	we run we are running
ihr	-t	**ihr lauft**	you (*plural*) run you are running
sie Sie	-en	**sie laufen** **Sie laufen**	they run they are running you (*polite*) run you are running

Er läuft die 100 Meter in Rekordzeit. He runs the 100 metres in record time.

- o → ö

Pronoun	Ending	Add to Stem, e.g. stoß-	Meanings
ich	-e	ich stoße	I push I am pushing
du	-st	du stößt	you push you are pushing
er sie es	-t	er stößt sie stößt es stößt	he/she/it pushes he/she/it is pushing
wir	-en	wir stoßen	we push we are pushing
ihr	-t	ihr stoßt	you (*plural*) push you are pushing
sie Sie	-en	sie stoßen Sie stoßen	they push they are pushing you (*polite*) push you are pushing

Pass auf, dass du nicht an den Tisch stößt. — Watch out that you don't bump into the table.

i Note that strong AND weak verbs whose stem ends in **-s**, **-z**, **-ss** or **-ß** (such as **stoßen**) add **-t** rather than **-st** to get the **du** form in the present tense. However, if the stem ends in **-sch**, the normal **-st** is added.

Verb	Stem	Du Form
wachsen	wachs-	wächst
waschen	wasch-	wäschst

Key points

✔ Strong verbs have the same endings in the present tense as weak verbs.

✔ The vowel or vowels of the stem of strong verbs change(s) in the present for the **du** and **er/sie/es** forms.

4 Forming the present tense of mixed verbs

➤ There are nine mixed verbs in German. They are very common and are formed according to a mixture of the rules already explained for weak and strong verbs.

➤ The nine mixed verbs are:

Mixed Verb	Meaning	Mixed Verb	Meaning	Mixed Verb	Meaning
brennen	to burn	**kennen**	to know	**senden**	to send
bringen	to bring	**nennen**	to name	**wenden**	to turn
denken	to think	**rennen**	to run	**wissen**	to know

➤ The present tense of mixed verbs has the same endings as weak verbs and has no vowel or consonant changes in the stem: **ich bringe**, **du bringst**, **er/sie/es bringt**, **wir bringen**, **ihr bringt**, **sie bringen**, **Sie bringen**.

Sie bringt mich nach Hause. — She's bringing me home.
Bringst du mir etwas mit? — Will you bring something for me?

i Note that the present tense of the most important strong, weak and mixed verbs is shown in the Verb Tables.

⇨ *For **Verb Tables**, see supplement.*

Key points

✔ There are nine mixed verbs in German.

✔ The present tense of mixed verbs has the same endings as weak verbs and has no vowel or consonant changes in the stem.

Reflexive verbs

What is a reflexive verb?
A **reflexive verb** is one where the subject and object are the same, and where the action 'reflects back' on the subject. Reflexive verbs are used with a reflexive pronoun such as *myself*, *yourself* and *herself* in English, for example, *I washed myself*; *He shaved himself*.

1 Using reflexive verbs

➤ In German, reflexive verbs are much more common than in English, and many are used in everyday German. Reflexive verbs consist of two parts: the reflexive pronoun **sich** (meaning *himself, herself, itself, themselves* or *oneself*) and the infinitive of the verb.

For more information on ***Reflexive pronouns****, see page 84.*

2 Forming the present tense of reflexive verbs

➤ Reflexive verbs are often used to describe things you do (to yourself) every day or that involve a change of some sort (getting dressed, sitting down, getting excited, being in a hurry).

➤ The reflexive pronoun is either the direct object in the sentence, which means it is in the accusative case, or the indirect object in the sentence, which means it is in the dative case. Only the reflexive pronouns used with the **ich** and **du** forms of the verb have separate accusative and dative forms:

Accusative Form	Dative Form	Meaning
mich	**mir**	myself
dich	**dir**	yourself (*familiar*)
sich	**sich**	himself/herself/itself
uns	**uns**	ourselves
euch	**euch**	yourselves (*plural*)
sich	**sich**	themselves
sich	**sich**	yourself/yourselves (*polite*)

➤ The present tense forms of a reflexive verb work in just the same way as an ordinary verb, except that the reflexive pronoun is used as well.

➤ Below you will find the present tense of the common reflexive verbs **sich setzen** (meaning *to sit down*) which has its reflexive pronoun in the accusative and **sich erlauben** (meaning *to allow oneself*) which has its reflexive pronoun in the dative.

Reflexive Forms	Meaning
ich setze mich	I sit down
du setzt dich	you sit down
er/sie/es setzt sich	he/she/it sits down
wir setzen uns	we sit down
ihr setzt euch	you (*plural*) sit down
sie setzen sich	they sit down
Sie setzen sich	you (*polite form*) sit down

Ich setze mich neben dich. — I'll sit beside you.
Sie setzen sich aufs Sofa. — They sit down on the sofa.

Reflexive Forms	Meaning
ich erlaube mir	I allow myself
du erlaubst dir	you allow yourself
er/sie/es erlaubt sich	he/she/it allows himself/herself/itself
wir erlauben uns	we allow ourselves
ihr erlaubt euch	you (*plural*) allow yourselves
sie erlauben sich	they allow themselves
Sie erlauben sich	you (*polite form*) allow yourself

Ich erlaube mir jetzt ein Bier. — Now I'm going to allow myself a beer.
Er erlaubt sich ein Stück Kuchen. — He's allowing himself a piece of cake.

➤ Some of the most common German reflexive verbs are listed here:

Reflexive Verb with Reflexive Pronoun in Accusative	Meaning
sich anziehen	to get dressed
sich aufregen	to get excited
sich beeilen	to hurry
sich beschäftigen mit	to be occupied with
sich bewerben um	to apply for
sich erinnern an	to remember
sich freuen auf	to look forward to
sich interessieren für	to be interested in
sich irren	to be wrong
sich melden	to report (for duty etc) *or* to volunteer
sich rasieren	to shave
sich setzen *or* **hinsetzen**	to sit down
sich trauen	to dare
sich umsehen	to look around

Ich ziehe mich schnell an und dann gehen wir. — I'll get dressed quickly and then we can go.
Wir müssen uns beeilen. — We must hurry.

Reflexive Verb with Reflexive Pronoun in Dative	Meaning
sich abgewöhnen	to give up (something)
sich ansehen	to have a look at
sich einbilden	to imagine (wrongly)
sich erlauben	to allow oneself
sich leisten	to afford
sich nähern	to get close to
sich vornehmen	to plan to do
sich vorstellen	to imagine
sich wünschen	to want

Ich muss mir das Rauchen abgewöhnen. I must give up smoking.

Sie kann sich ein neues Auto nicht leisten. She can't afford a new car.

Was wünscht ihr euch zu Weihnachten? What do you want for Christmas?

Note that a direct object reflexive pronoun changes to an indirect object pronoun if another direct object is present.

Ich wasche mich. I'm having a wash.
mich = direct object reflexive pronoun

Ich wasche mir die Hände. I am washing my hands.
mir = indirect object reflexive pronoun
die Hände = direct object

For more information on ***Pronouns****, see page 69.*

➤ Some German verbs which are not usually reflexive can be made reflexive by adding a reflexive pronoun.

Soll ich es melden? Should I report it?

Ich habe mich gemeldet. I volunteered.

For more information on word order with ***Reflexive pronouns****, see page 84.*

Key points

- ✔ A reflexive verb is made up of a reflexive pronoun and a verb.
- ✔ The direct object pronouns in the accusative are **mich**, **dich**, **sich**, **uns**, **euch**, **sich**, **sich**.
- ✔ The indirect object pronouns in the dative are **mir**, **dir**, **sich**, **uns**, **euch**, **sich**, **sich**.
- ✔ In the present tense the reflexive pronoun usually comes after the verb.

The imperative

What is the imperative?
An **imperative** is a form of the verb used when giving orders and instructions, for example, *Shut the door!; Sit down!; Don't go!*

1 Using the imperative

➤ In German, there are three main forms of the imperative that are used to give instructions or orders to someone. These correspond to the three different ways of saying *you*: **du**, **ihr** and **Sie**. However, it is only in the **Sie** form of the imperative that the pronoun usually appears – in the **du** and **ihr** forms, the pronoun is generally dropped, leaving only the verb.

Hör zu! Listen!
Hören Sie zu! Listen!

2 Forming the present tense imperative

➤ Most weak, strong and mixed verbs form the present tense imperative in the following way:

Pronoun	Form of Imperative	Verb Example	Meaning
du (singular)	verb stem (+ **e**)	**hol(e)!**	fetch!
ihr (plural)	verb stem + **t**	**holt!**	fetch!
Sie (polite singular and plural)	verb stem + **en** + **Sie**	**holen Sie!**	fetch!

ℹ Note that the **-e** of the **du** form is often dropped, but NOT where the verb stem ends, for example, in **chn-**, **fn-**, or **tm-**. In such cases, the **-e** is kept to make the imperative easier to pronounce.

Hör zu! Listen!
Hol es! Fetch it!

BUT: **Öffne die Tür!** Open the door!
Atme richtig durch! Take a deep breath!
Rechne nochmal nach! Do your sums again!

Grammar Extra!

Weak verbs ending in **-eln** or **-ern** also retain this **-e**, but the other **-e** in the stem itself is often dropped in spoken German.

Verb	Meaning	Imperative	Meaning
wandern	to walk	**wand(e)re!**	walk!
handeln	to act	**hand(e)le!**	act!

➤ Any vowel change in the present tense of a strong verb also occurs in the **du** form of its imperative and the **-e** mentioned above is generally not added. However, if this vowel change in the present tense involves adding an umlaut, this umlaut is NOT added to the **du** form of the imperative.

Verb	Meaning	2nd Person Singular	Meaning	2nd Person Singular Imperative	Meaning
nehmen	to take	**du nimmst**	you take	**nimm!**	take!
helfen	to help	**du hilfst**	you help	**hilf!**	help!
laufen	to run	**du läufst**	you run	**lauf(e)!**	run!
stoßen	to push	**du stößt**	you push	**stoß(e)!**	push!

3 Word order with the imperative

➤ An object pronoun is a word like **es** (meaning *it*), **mir** (meaning *me*) or **ihnen** (meaning *them/to them*) that is used instead of a noun as the object of a sentence. In the imperative, the object pronoun comes straight after the verb. However, you can have orders and instructions containing both direct object and indirect object pronouns. In these cases, the direct object pronoun always comes before the indirect object pronoun.

Hol mir das Buch! Fetch me that book!
Hol es mir! Fetch me it!

Holt mir das Buch! Fetch me that book!
Holt es mir! Fetch me it!

Holen Sie mir das Buch! Fetch me that book!
Holen Sie es mir! Fetch me it!

⇨ *For more information on* ***Word order with indirect object pronouns****, see page 77.*

➤ In the imperative form of a reflexive verb such as **sich waschen** (meaning *to wash oneself*) or **sich setzen** (meaning *to sit down*), the reflexive pronoun comes immediately after the verb.

For further explanation of grammatical terms, please see pages viii–xii.

Reflexive verb	Meaning	Imperative Forms	Meaning
sich setzen	to sit down	**setz dich!**	sit down!
		setzt euch!	sit down!
		setzen Sie sich!	do sit down!

➪ *For more information on* ***Reflexive pronouns****, see page 84.*

➤ In verbs which have separable prefixes, the prefix comes at the end of the imperative.

Verb with Separable Prefix	Meaning	Imperative Example	Meaning
zumachen	to close	**Mach die Tür zu!**	Close the door!
aufhören	to stop	**Hör aber endlich auf!**	Do stop it!

➪ *For more information on* ***Separable prefixes****, see page 109.*

4 Other points about the imperative

➤ In German, imperatives are usually followed by an exclamation mark, unless they are not being used to give an order or instruction. For example, they can also be used where we might say *Can you*... or *Could you* ... in English.

Lass ihn in Ruhe! — Leave him alone!
Sagen Sie mir bitte, wie spät es ist. — Can you tell me what time it is please?

➤ The verb **sein** (meaning *to be*) is a strong, irregular verb. Its imperative forms are also irregular and the **du**, **Sie** and less common **wir** forms are not the same as the present tense forms of the verb.

Sei ruhig! — be quiet!
Seid ruhig! — be quiet!
Seien Sie ruhig! — be quiet!

Tip

The words **auch**, **nur**, **mal** and **doch** are frequently used with imperatives to change their meanings in different ways, but are often not translated since they have no direct equivalent in English.

Geh doch! — Go on!/Get going!
Sag mal, wo warst du? — Tell me, where were you?
Versuchen Sie es mal! — Give it a try!
Komm schon! — Do come/Please come.
Mach es auch richtig! — Be sure to do it properly.

Grammar Extra!

There are some alternatives to using the imperative in German:

- Infinitives (the *to* form of a verb) are often used instead of the imperative in written instructions or public announcements

Einsteigen!	All aboard!
Zwiebeln abziehen und in Ringe schneiden.	Peel the onions and slice them.

- Nouns, adjectives or adverbs can also be used as imperatives

Ruhe!	Be quiet!/Silence!
Vorsicht!	Careful!/Look out!

Some of these have become set expressions

Achtung!	Listen!/Attention!
Rauchen verboten!	No smoking.

Key points

✔ The imperative has four forms: **du**, **ihr**, **Sie** and **wir**.

✔ The forms are the same as the **ihr**, **Sie** and **wir** forms of the present tense for most strong, weak and mixed verbs, but the **du** form drops the **-st** present tense ending and sometimes adds an **-e** on the end.

✔ Any vowel change in the stem of a strong verb also occurs in the imperative, except if it involves adding an umlaut.

✔ Object pronouns always go after the verb, with the direct object pronoun coming before the indirect object pronoun.

✔ Reflexive pronouns also come after the verb, while separable verb prefixes come at the end of the imperative sentence.

✔ **Sein** has irregular imperative forms.

Verb prefixes in the present tense

What is a phrasal verb?
In English, words such as *up* or *down* can be used with verbs to create new verbs with an entirely different meaning. These are called **phrasal verbs**.

get → get up → get down
put → put up → put down
shut → shut up → shut down

➤ In German there is a similar system, but the words are put before the infinitive and joined to it:

zu (meaning *to*) + **geben** (meaning *to give*) = **zugeben** (meaning *to admit*)
an (meaning *on, to, by*) + **ziehen** (meaning *to pull*) = **anziehen** (meaning *to put on* or *to attract*)

➤ Prefixes can be found in strong, weak and mixed verbs. Some prefixes are always joined to the verb and never separated from it – these are called inseparable prefixes. However, the majority are separated from the verb in certain tenses and forms, and come at the end of the sentence. They are called separable prefixes.

1 Inseparable prefixes

➤ There are eight inseparable prefixes in German, highlighted in the table of common inseparable verbs below:

Inseparable Verb	Meaning	Inseparable Verb	Meaning	Inseparable Verb	Meaning	Inseparable Verb	Meaning
beschreiben	to describe	**enttäuschen**	**to disappoint**	**gehören**	to belong	**verlieren**	to lose
empfangen	to receive	**erhalten**	**to preserve**	**misstrauen**	to mistrust	**zerlegen**	to dismantle

i Note that when you pronounce an inseparable verb, the stress is NEVER on the inseparable prefix:

er*hal*ten
ver*lie*ren
emp*fan*gen
ver*ges*sen

Das darf ich wirklich nicht ver*ges*sen. I really mustn't forget that.

2 Separable prefixes

➤ There are many separable prefixes in German and some of them are highlighted in the table below which shows a selection of the most common separable verbs:

Separable Verb	Meaning	Separable Verb	Meaning
abfahren	to leave	**mitmachen**	to join in
ankommen	to arrive	**nachgeben**	to give way/in
aufstehen	to get up	**vorziehen**	to prefer
ausgehen	to go out	**weglaufen**	to run away
einsteigen	to get on	**zuschauen**	to watch
feststellen	to establish/see	**zurechtkommen**	to manage
freihalten	to keep free	**zurückkehren**	to return
herkommen	to come (here)	**zusammenpassen**	to be well-suited; to go well together
hinlegen	to put down		

Der Zug fährt in zehn Minuten ab.	The train is leaving in ten minutes.
Ich stehe jeden Morgen früh auf.	I get up early every morning.
Sie gibt niemals nach.	She'll never give in.

3 Word order with separable prefixes

➤ In tenses consisting of one verb part only, for example the present and the imperfect, the separable prefix is placed at the end of the main clause.

Der Bus kam immer spät an.	The bus was always late.

➪ *For more information on* ***Separable prefixes in the perfect tense****, see page 115.*

➤ In subordinate clauses, the prefix is attached to the verb, which is then placed at the end of the subordinate clause.

Weil der Bus spät ankam, verpasste sie den Zug.	Because the bus arrived late, she missed the train.

➪ *For more information on* ***Subordinate clauses****, see page 177.*

➤ In infinitive phrases using **zu**, the **zu** is inserted between the verb and its prefix to form one word.

Um rechtzeitig aufzustehen, muss ich den Wecker stellen.	In order to get up on time I'll have to set the alarm.

➪ *For more information on the* ***Infinitive****, see page 134.*

4 Verb combinations

➤ Below you will see some other types of word which can be combined with verbs. These combinations are mostly written as two separate words and behave like separable verbs:

- Noun + verb combinations

Ski fahren	to ski
Ich fahre gern Ski.	I like skiing
Schlittschuh laufen	to ice-skate
Im Winter kann man Schlittschuh laufen.	You can ice-skate in winter.

- Infinitive + verb combinations

kennenlernen	to meet or to get to know
Meine Mutter möchte dich kennenlernen.	My mother wants to meet you.
Er lernt sie nie richtig kennen.	He'll never get to know her properly.
sitzen bleiben	to remain seated
Bleiben Sie bitte sitzen.	Please remain seated.
spazieren gehen	to go for a walk
Er geht jeden Tag spazieren.	He goes for a walk every day.

- Other adjective + verb combinations

bekannt machen	to announce
Die Regierung will das morgen bekannt machen.	The government plans to announce it tomorrow.

- Some adverb + verb combinations

kaputt machen	to break
Mach mir bloß mein Fahrrad nicht kaputt!	Don't you dare break my bike!

- Verb combinations with **-seits**

abseitsstehen	to stand apart
Sie steht immer abseits von den anderen.	She always stands apart from the others.

- Prefix combinations with **sein**

auf sein	to be open or to be up
Das Fenster ist auf.	The window is open.
Die Geschäfte sind am Sonntag nicht auf.	The shops are closed on Sundays.
Sie ist noch nicht auf.	She isn't up yet.

zu sein	to be shut
Das Fenster <u>ist</u> <u>zu</u>.	The window is shut.

i Note that **auf** (meaning *open*) is another word for **geöffnet** and **zu** (meaning *shut* or *closed*) is another word for **geschlossen**.

Key points

- ✔ Prefixes can be found in strong, weak and mixed verbs.
- ✔ Eight prefixes are inseparable and are never separated from the verb.
- ✔ Most prefixes are separable and are separated from the verb in certain tenses and forms and come at the end of the sentence.

The perfect tense

What is the perfect tense?
The **perfect** is one of the verb tenses used to talk about the past, especially about a single, rather than a repeated action.

Den Nachtisch habe ich schon gegessen.	I've already eaten dessert.

1 Using the perfect tense

➤ The German perfect tense is the one generally used to translate an English form such as *I have finished*.

I have finished the book.	**Ich habe das Buch zu Ende gelesen.**

➤ The perfect tense is also sometimes used to translate an English form such as *I gave*.

I gave him my phone number.	**Ich habe ihm meine Nummer gegeben.**

Tip

When a specific time in the past is referred to, you use the perfect tense in German. In English you use the *-ed* form instead.

Gestern Abend habe ich einen Krimi im Fernsehen gesehen.	Last night I watched a thriller on TV.

➤ The perfect tense is used with **seit** or **seitdem** to describe a completed action in the past, whereas the present tense is used to describe an action which started in the past and is still continuing in the present.

Seit dem Unfall habe ich sie nur einmal gesehen.	I've only seen her once since the accident.

⇨ *For more information on this use of the **Present tense**, see page 94.*

2 Forming the perfect tense

➤ Unlike the present and imperfect tenses, the perfect tense has TWO parts to it:

- the present tense of the irregular weak verb **haben** (meaning *to have*) or the irregular strong verb **sein** (meaning *to be*). They are also known as auxiliary verbs.
- a part of the main verb called the *past participle*, like *given*, *finished* and *done* in English.

➤ In other words, the perfect tense in German is like the form *I have done* in English.

Pronoun	Ending	Present Tense	Meanings
ich	**-e**	**ich habe**	I have
du	**-st**	**du hast**	you have
er **sie** **es**	**-t**	**er hat** **sie hat** **es hat**	he/she/it has
wir	**-en**	**wir haben**	we have
ihr	**-t**	**ihr habt**	you (*plural*) have
sie **Sie**	**-en**	**sie haben** **Sie haben**	they have you (*polite*) have

Pronoun	Ending	Present Tense	Meanings
ich	–	**ich bin**	I am
du	–	**du bist**	you are
er **sie** **es**	–	**er ist** **sie ist** **es ist**	he/she/it is
wir	–	**wir sind**	we are
ihr	–	**ihr seid**	you (*plural*) are
sie	–	**sie sind**	they are
Sie	–	**Sie sind**	you (*polite*) are

3 Forming the past participle

➤ To form the past participle of weak verbs, you add **ge-** to the beginning of the verb stem and **-t** to the end.

Infinitive	Take off -en	Add ge- and -t
holen (*to fetch*)	**hol-**	**geholt**
machen (*to do*)	**mach-**	**gemacht**

ℹ Note that one exception to this rule is weak verbs ending in **-ieren**, which omit the **ge**.

studieren (*to study*) **studiert** (*studied*)

➤ To form the past participle of strong verbs, you add **ge-** to the beginning of the verb stem and **-en** to the end. The vowel in the stem may also change.

Infinitive	Take off -en	Add ge- and -en
laufen (*to run*)	**lauf-**	**gelaufen**
singen (*to sing*)	**sing-**	**gesungen**

For further explanation of grammatical terms, please see pages viii–xii.

- To form the past participle of mixed verbs, you add **ge-** to the beginning of the verb stem and, like weak verbs, **-t** to the end. As with many strong verbs, the stem vowel may also change.

Infinitive	Take off -en	Add ge- and -t
bringen (*to run*)	**bring-**	**gebracht**
denken (*to think*)	**denk-**	**gedacht**

- The perfect tense of separable verbs is also formed in the above way, except that the separable prefix is joined on to the front of the **ge-: ich habe die Flasche aufgemacht, du hast die Flasche aufgemacht** and so on.

- With inseparable verbs, the only difference is that past participles are formed without the **ge-: ich habe Kaffee bestellt, du hast Kaffee bestellt** and so on.

*For more information on **Separable** and **Inseparable verbs**, see page 109.*

4 Verbs that form their perfect tense with haben

- Most weak, strong and mixed verbs form their perfect tense with **haben**, for example **machen**:

Pronoun	haben	Past Participle	Meaning
ich	**habe**	**gemacht**	I did, I have done
du	**hast**	**gemacht**	you did, you have done
er **sie** **es**	**hat**	**gemacht**	he/she/it did, he/she/it has done
wir	**haben**	**gemacht**	we did, we have done
ihr	**habt**	**gemacht**	you (*plural*) did, you have done
sie	**haben**	**gemacht**	they did, they have done
Sie	**haben**	**gemacht**	you (*singular/plural formal*) did, you have done

Sie hat ihre Hausaufgaben schon gemacht.	She has already done her homework.
Haben Sie gut geschlafen?	Did you sleep well?
Er hat fleißig gearbeitet.	He has worked hard.

5 haben or sein?

➤ MOST verbs form their perfect tense with **haben**.

Ich habe das schon gemacht.	I've already done that.
Wo haben Sie früher gearbeitet?	Where did you work before?

➤ With reflexive verbs the reflexive pronoun comes immediately after **haben**.

Ich habe mich heute Morgen geduscht.	I had a shower this morning.
Sie hat sich nicht daran erinnert.	She didn't remember.

⇨ *For more information on **Reflexive verbs**, see page 102.*

➤ There are two main groups of verbs which form their perfect tense with **sein** instead of **haben**, and most of them are strong verbs:

- verbs which take no direct object and are used mainly to talk about movement or a change of some kind, such as:

gehen	to go
kommen	to come
ankommen	to arrive
abfahren	to leave
aussteigen	to get off
einsteigen	to get on
sterben	to die
sein	to be
werden	to become
bleiben	to remain
begegnen	to meet
gelingen	to succeed
aufstehen	to get up
fallen	to fall
Gestern bin ich ins Kino gegangen.	I went to the cinema yesterday.
Sie ist heute Morgen ganz früh abgefahren.	She left really early this morning.
An welcher Haltestelle sind Sie ausgestiegen?	Which stop did you get off at?

- two verbs which mean *to happen*.

Was ist geschehen/passiert?	What happened?

➩ Here are the perfect tense forms of a very common strong verb, **gehen**, in full:

Pronoun	sein	Past Participle	Meanings
ich	bin	gegangen	I went, I have gone
du	bist	gegangen	you went, you have gone
er sie es	ist	gegangen	he/she/it went, he/she/it has gone
wir	sind	gegangen	we went, we have gone
ihr	seid	gegangen	you (*plural*) went, you have gone
sie	sind	gegangen	they went, they have gone
Sie	sind	gegangen	you (*singular/plural formal*) went, you have gone

ℹ Note that the perfect tense of the most important strong, weak and mixed verbs is shown in the Verb Tables.

➩ *For **Verb Tables**, see supplement.*

Key points

✔ The perfect tense describes things that happened and were completed in the past.

✔ The perfect tense is formed with the present tense of **haben** or **sein** and a past participle.

✔ The past participle begins in **ge-** and ends in **-t** for weak verbs, in **ge-** and **-en** for strong verbs often with a stem vowel change, and in **ge-** and **-t** for mixed verbs, with a stem vowel change.

✔ Most verbs take **haben** in the perfect tense. Many strong verbs, especially those referring to movement or change, take **sein**.

The imperfect tense

What is the imperfect tense?
The **imperfect tense** is one of the verb tenses used to talk about the past, especially in descriptions, and to say what used to happen, for example, *It was sunny at the weekend; I used to walk to school.*

1 Using the imperfect tense

➤ The German imperfect tense is used:

- to describe actions in the past which the speaker feels have no link with the present

Er kam zu spät, um teilnehmen zu können.	He arrived too late to take part.

- to describe what things were like and how people felt in the past

Ich war ganz traurig, als sie wegging.	I was very sad when she left.
Damals gab es ein großes Problem mit Drogen.	There was a big problem with drugs at that time.

- to say what used to happen or what you used to do regularly in the past

Wir machten jeden Tag einen Spaziergang.	We used to go for a walk every day.
Samstags spielte ich Tennis.	I used to play tennis on Saturdays.

ℹ Note that if you want to talk about an event or action that took place and was completed in the past, you normally use the perfect tense in German conversation. The imperfect tense is normally used in written German.

Was hast du heute gemacht?	What have you done today?

⇨ *For more information on the **Perfect tense**, see page 113.*

➤ When using **seit** or **seitdem** to describe something that had happened or had been true at a point in the past, the imperfect is used in German, where in English a verb form with *had* is used.

Sie war seit ihrer Heirat als Lehrerin beschäftigt.	She had been working as a teacher since her marriage.

⇨ *For more information on the **Pluperfect tense**, see page 127.*

> ### *Tip*
> Remember that you NEVER use the verb **sein** to translate *was* or *were* in forms like *was raining* or *were looking* and so on. You change the German verb ending instead.

2 Forming the imperfect tense of weak verbs

➤ To form the imperfect tense of weak verbs, you use the same stem of the verb as for the present tense. Then you add the correct ending, depending on whether you are referring to **ich**, **du**, **er**, **sie**, **es**, **wir**, **ihr**, **sie** or **Sie**.

Pronoun	Ending	Add to Stem, e.g. spiel-	Meanings
ich	**-te**	**ich spielte**	I played I was playing
du	**-test**	**du spieltest**	you played you were playing
er **sie** **es**	**-te**	**er spielte** **sie spielte** **es spielte**	he/she/it played he/she/it was playing
wir	**-ten**	**wir spielten**	we played we were playing
ihr	**-tet**	**ihr spieltet**	you (*plural*) played you were playing
sie **Sie**	**-ten**	**sie spielten** **Sie spielten**	they played they were playing you (*polite*) played you were playing

Sie holte ihn jeden Tag von der Arbeit ab. — She picked him up from work every day.

Normalerweise machte ich nach dem Abendessen meine Hausaufgaben. — I usually did my homework after dinner.

➤ As with the present tense, some weak verbs change their spellings slightly when they are used in the imperfect tense.

- If the stem ends in **-d**, **-t**, **-m** or **-n** an extra **-e** is added before the usual imperfect endings to make pronunciation easier.

Pronoun	Ending	Add to Stem, e.g. arbeit-	Meanings
ich	-ete	ich arbeitete	I worked I was working
du	-etest	du arbeitetest	you worked you were working
er sie es	-ete	er arbeitete sie arbeitete es arbeitete	he/she/it worked he/she/it was working
wir	-eten	wir arbeiteten	we worked we were working
ihr	-etet	ihr arbeitetet	you (*plural*) worked you were working
sie	-eten	sie arbeiteten	they worked they were working
Sie	-eten	Sie arbeiteten	you (*polite*) worked you (*polite*) were working

Sie arbeitete übers Wochenende. She was working over the weekend.

Ihr arbeitetet ganz schön viel. You worked a lot.

- If the **-m** or **-n** has one of the consonants *l*, *r* or *h* in front of it, the **-e** is not added as shown in the **du**, **er**, **sie** and **es**, and **ihr** forms below.

Pronoun	Ending	Add to Stem, e.g. lern-	Meanings
du	-test	du lerntest	you learned you were learning
er sie es	-te	er lernte sie lernte es lernte	he/she/it learned he/she/it was learning
ihr	-tet	ihr lerntet	you (*plural*) learned you were learning

Sie lernte alles ganz schnell. She learned everything very quickly.

3 Forming the imperfect tense of strong verbs

➤ The main difference between strong verbs and weak verbs in the imperfect is that strong verbs have a vowel change and take a different set of endings. For example, let's compare **sagen** and **rufen**:

	Infinitive	Meaning	Present	Imperfect
Weak	**sagen**	to say	**er sagt**	**er sagte**
Strong	**rufen**	to shout	**er ruft**	**er rief**

➤ To form the imperfect tense of strong verbs you add the following endings to the stem, which undergoes a vowel change.

Pronoun	Ending	Add to Stem, e.g. rief-	Meanings
ich	–	ich rief	I shouted I was shouting
du	-st	du riefst	you shouted you were shouting
er sie es	–	er rief sie rief es rief	he/she/it shouted he/she/it was shouting
wir	-en	wir riefen	we shouted we were shouting
ihr	-t	ihr rieft	you (*plural*) shouted you were shouting
sie	-en	sie riefen	they shouted they were shouting
Sie		Sie riefen	you (*polite*) shouted you were shouting

Sie rief mich immer freitags an. She always called me on Friday.
Sie liefen die Straße entlang. They ran along the street.
Als Kind sangst du viel. You used to sing a lot as a child.

➤ As in other tenses, the verb **sein** is a very irregular strong verb since the imperfect forms seem to have no relation to the infinitive form of the verb: **ich war, du warst, er/sie/es war, wir waren, ihr wart, sie/Sie waren**.

4 Forming the imperfect tense of mixed verbs

➤ The imperfect tense of mixed verbs is formed by adding the weak verb endings to a stem whose vowel has been changed as for a strong verb.

Pronoun	Ending	Add to Stem, e.g. kann-	Meanings
ich	-te	ich kannte	I knew
du	-test	du kanntest	you knew
er sie es	-te	er kannte sie kannte es kannte	he/she/it knew
wir	-ten	wir kannten	we knew
ihr	-tet	ihr kanntet	you (*plural*) knew
sie Sie	-ten	sie kannten Sie kannten	they knew you (*polite*) knew

Er kannte die Stadt nicht. He didn't know the town.

➤ **Bringen** (meaning *to bring*) and **denken** (meaning *to think*) have a vowel AND a consonant change in their imperfect forms

bringen (*to bring*)	**denken** (*to think*)
ich brachte	**ich dachte**
du brachtest	**du dachtest**
er/sie/es brachte	**er/sie/es dachte**
wir brachten	**wir dachten**
ihr brachtet	**ihr dachtet**
sie/Sie brachten	**sie/Sie dachten**

[i] Note that the imperfect tense of the most important strong, weak and mixed verbs is shown in the Verb Tables.

⇨ *For* ***Verb Tables****, see supplement.*

Key points

✔ The imperfect tense is generally used for things that happened regularly or for descriptions in the past, especially in written German.

✔ The imperfect of weak verbs is formed using the same stem of the verb as for the present tense + these endings: **-te**, **-test**, **-te**, **-ten**, **-tet**, **-ten**.

✔ If the stem of a weak verb ends in **-d**, **-t**, **-m** or **-n** an extra **-e** is added before the usual imperfect endings to make pronunciation easier. If the **-m** or **-n** has one of the consonants *l*, *r* or *h* in front of it, the **-e** is not added.

✔ The imperfect tense of strong verbs is formed by adding the following endings to the stem, which undergoes a vowel change: **-**, **-st**, **-**, **-en**, **-t**, **-en**.

✔ The imperfect tense of mixed verbs is formed by adding the weak verb endings to a stem whose vowel has been changed as for a strong verb. The verbs **bringen** and **denken** also have a consonant change.

The future tense

What is the future tense?
The **future tense** is a verb tense used to talk about something that will happen or will be true.

1 Using the future tense

➤ In English the future tense is often shown by *will* or its shortened form *'ll*.

What will you do?
The weather will be warm and dry tomorrow.
He'll be here soon.
I'll give you a call.

➤ Just as in English, you can use the present tense in German to refer to something that is going to happen in the future.

Wir fahren nächstes Jahr nach Griechenland.	We're going to Greece next year.
Ich nehme den letzten Zug heute Abend.	I'm taking the last train tonight.

➤ The future tense IS used however to:

- emphasize the future

Das werde ich erst nächstes Jahr machen können.	I won't be able to do that until next year.

- express doubt or suppose something about the future

Wenn sie zurückkommt, wird sie mir bestimmt helfen.	I'm sure she'll help me when she returns.

➤ In English we often use *going to* followed by an infinitive to talk about something that will happen in the immediate future. You CANNOT use the German verb **gehen** (meaning *to go*) followed by an infinitive in the same way. Instead, you use either the present or the future tense.

Das wirst du bereuen.	You're going to regret that.
Wenn er sich nicht beeilt, verpasst er den Zug.	He's going to miss the train if he doesn't hurry up.

2 Forming the future tense

➤ The future tense has TWO parts to it and is formed in the same way for all verbs, be they weak, strong or mixed:

- the present tense of the strong verb **werden** (meaning *to become*), which acts as an auxiliary verb like **haben** and **sein** in the perfect tense

Pronoun	Ending	Present Tense	Meanings
ich	-e	**ich werde**	I become
du	-st	**du wirst**	you become
er sie es	–	**er wird** **sie wird** **es wird**	he/she/it becomes
wir	-en	**wir werden**	we become
ihr	-t	**ihr werdet**	you (*plural*) become
sie Sie	-en -en	**sie werden** **Sie werden**	they become you (*polite*) become

- the infinitive of the main verb, which normally goes at the end of the clause or sentence.

Pronoun	Present Tense of werden	Infinitive of Main Verb	Meanings
ich	**werde**	**holen**	I will fetch
du	**wirst**	**holen**	you will fetch
er sie es	**wird**	**holen**	he/she/it will fetch
wir	**werden**	**holen**	we will fetch
ihr	**werdet**	**holen**	you (*plural*) will fetch
sie Sie	**werden**	**holen**	they will fetch you (*polite*) will fetch

Morgen werde ich mein Fahrrad holen. I'll fetch my bike tomorrow.
Sie wird dir meine Adresse geben. She'll give you my address.
Wir werden draußen warten. We'll wait outside.

i Note that in reflexive verbs, the reflexive pronoun comes after the present tense of **werden**.

Ich werde mich nächste Woche vorbereiten. I'll prepare next week.

Key points

- ✔ You can use a present tense in German to talk about something that will happen or be true in the future, just as in English.
- ✔ The future tense is formed from the present tense of **werden** and the infinitive of the main verb.
- ✔ You CANNOT use **gehen** with an infinitive to refer to things that will happen in the immediate future.
- ✔ The future tense is used to emphasize the future and express doubt or suppose something about the future.

The conditional

> **What is the conditional?**
> The **conditional** is a verb form used to talk about things that would happen or that would true under certain conditions, for example, *I would help you if I could*. It is also used to say what you would like or need, for example, *Could you give me the bill?*

1 Using the conditional

➤ You can often recognize a conditional in English by the word *would* or its shortened form *'d*.

I would be sad if you left.
If you asked him, he'd help you.

➤ In German, the conditional is also used to express *would*.

Ich würde dir schon helfen, ich habe aber keine Zeit.	I would help you, but I don't have the time.
Was würden Sie an meiner Stelle tun?	What would you do in my position?

2 Forming the conditional

➤ The conditional has TWO parts to it and is formed in the same way for all verbs, be they weak, strong or mixed:

- the **würde** form or subjunctive of the verb **werden** (meaning *to become*)
- the infinitive of the main verb, which normally goes at the end of the clause.

Pronoun	Subjunctive of werden	Infinitive of Main Verb	Meanings
ich	**würde**	**holen**	I would fetch
du	**würdest**	**holen**	you would fetch
er **sie** **es**	**würde**	**holen**	he/she/it would fetch
wir	**würden**	**holen**	we would fetch
ihr	**würdet**	**holen**	you (*plural*) would fetch
sie **Sie**	**würden**	**holen**	they would fetch you (*polite*) would fetch

Das würde ich nie machen.	I would never do that.
Würdest du mir etwas Geld leihen?	Would you lend me some money?
Würden Sie jemals mit dem Rauchen aufhören?	Would you ever stop smoking?

i Note that you have to be careful not to mix up the present tense of **werden**, used to form the future tense, and the subjunctive of **werden**, used to form the conditional. They look similar.

FUTURE USE	CONDITIONAL USE
ich werde	**ich würde**
du wirst	**du würdest**
er/sie/es wird	**er/sie/es würde**
wir werden	**wir würden**
ihr werdet	**ihr würdet**
sie/Sie werden	**sie/Sie würden**

Key points

✔ The conditional tense is formed from the subjunctive or **würde** part of **werden** and the infinitive of the main verb.

✔ The conditional tense is often used with the subjunctive.

The pluperfect tense

What is the pluperfect tense?
The **pluperfect** is a verb tense which describes something that had happened or had been true at a point in the past, for example, *I'd forgotten to finish my homework*.

1 Using the pluperfect tense

➤ You can often recognize a pluperfect tense in English by a form like *I had arrived*, *you'd fallen*.

Sie waren schon weggefahren.	They had already left.
Diese Bücher hatten sie schon gelesen.	They had already read these books.
Ich hatte mir das neueste iPad-Modell zum Geburtstag gewünscht.	I had asked for the latest iPad for my birthday.

Note that when translating *had done/had been doing* in conjunction with **seit**/**seitdem**, you use the imperfect tense in German.

Sie machte es seit Jahren.	She had been doing it for years.

*For more information on the **Imperfect tense**, see page 118.*

2 Forming the pluperfect tense

➤ Like the perfect tense, the pluperfect tense in German has two parts to it:

- the imperfect tense of the verb **haben** (meaning *to have*) or **sein** (meaning *to be*)
- the past participle.

➤ If a verb takes **haben** in the perfect tense, then it will take **haben** in the pluperfect too. If a verb takes **sein** in the perfect, then it will take **sein** in the pluperfect.

*For more information on the **Imperfect tense** and the **Perfect tense**, see pages 118 and 113.*

3 Verbs taking haben

➤ Here are the pluperfect tense forms of **holen** (meaning *to fetch*) in full.

Pronoun	haben	Past Participle	Meanings
ich	hatte	geholt	I had fetched
du	hattest	geholt	you had fetched
er sie es	hatte	geholt	he/she/it had fetched
wir	hatten	geholt	we had fetched
ihr	hattet	geholt	you (*plural*) had fetched
sie	hatten	geholt	they had fetched
Sie			you (*polite*) had fetched

Ich <u>hatte</u> schon mit ihm <u>gesprochen</u>. I had already spoken to him.

4 Verbs taking sein

➤ Here are the pluperfect tense forms of **reisen** (meaning *to travel*) in full.

Pronoun	sein	Past Participle	Meanings
ich	war	gereist	I had travelled
du	warst	gereist	you had travelled
er sie es	war	gereist	he/she/it had travelled
wir	waren	gereist	we had travelled
ihr	wart	gereist	you (*plural*) had travelled
sie	waren	gereist	they had travelled
Sie			you (*polite*) had travelled

Sie war sehr spät angekommen. She had arrived very late.

Key points

✔ The pluperfect tense describes things that had happened or were true at a point in the past before something else happened.

✔ It is formed with the imperfect tense of **haben** or **sein** and the past participle.

✔ Verbs which take **haben** in the perfect tense will take **haben** in the pluperfect tense and those which take **sein** in the perfect tense will take **sein** in the pluperfect tense.

The subjunctive

What is the subjunctive?
The **subjunctive** is a verb form that is used in certain circumstances to express some sort of feeling, or to show there is doubt about whether something will happen or whether something is true. It is only used occasionally in modern English, for example, *If I were you, I wouldn't bother; So be it.*

1 Using the subjunctive

➤ In German, subjunctive forms are used much more frequently than in English, to express uncertainty, speculation or doubt.

Es könnte doch wahr sein.	It could be true.

➤ Subjunctives are also commonly used in indirect speech, also known as reported speech. What a person asks or thinks can be reported directly:

Sie sagte: „Er kennt deine Schwester"	She said, "He knows your sister"

OR indirectly:

Sie sagte, er kenne meine Schwester.	She said he knew my sister.

ℹ Note that the change from direct to indirect speech is indicated by a change of tense in English, but is shown by a change to the subjunctive form in German.

Grammar Extra!

➤ There are two ways of introducing indirect speech in German, as in English.

- The conjunction **dass** (meaning *that*) begins the clause containing the indirect speech and the verb goes to the end of the clause.

Sie hat uns gesagt, dass sie Italienisch spreche.	She told us that she spoke Italian.

- **dass** is dropped and normal word order applies in the second clause – the verb comes directly after the subject.

Sie hat uns gesagt, sie spreche Italienisch.	She told us she spoke Italian.

➤ If you want to express a possible situation in English, for example, *I would be happy if you came*, you use '*if*' followed by the appropriate tense of the verb. In German you use the conjunction **wenn** followed by a subjunctive form of the verb.

ℹ Note that the verb ALWAYS goes to the end of a clause beginning with **wenn**.

- **wenn** (meaning *if, whenever*)

  Wenn du kä̲m̲(̲e̲)̲s̲t̲ *(subjunctive)*, **w̲ä̲r̲e̲** *(subjunctive)* **ich froh.**
  OR
  Wenn du käm(e)st, würde ich froh sein. — I would be happy if you came.

[i] Note that the main clause can either have a subjunctive form or the conditional tense.

Wenn es mir nicht gefiele, würde ich es nicht bezahlen.
OR
Wenn es mir nicht gefiele, bezahlte *(subjunctive)* **ich es nicht.** — If I wasn't happy with it, I wouldn't pay for it.

> **Tip**
> The imperfect forms of **bezahlen**, and of all weak verbs, are exactly the same as the imperfect subjunctive forms, so it's better to use a conditional tense to avoid confusion.

➤ **wenn ... nur** (meaning *if only*), **selbst wenn** (meaning *even if* or *even though*) and **wie** (meaning *how*) work in the same way as **wenn**. This means that the normal word order is changed and the verb comes at the end of the clause.

- **wenn ... nur**

  Wenn wir nur erfolgreich wären! — If only we were successful!

- **selbst wenn**

  Selbst wenn er etwas wüsste, würde er nichts sagen. — Even if he knew about it, he wouldn't say anything.

- **wie**, expressing uncertainty

  Er wunderte sich, wie es ihr wohl ginge. — He wondered how she was.

➤ Unlike **wenn** and **wie** etc, the word order does not change after **als** (meaning *as if* or *as though*) when it is used in conditional clauses: it is immediately followed by the verb.

Sie sah aus, als sei sie krank. — She looked as if she were ill.

> **Tip**
> It is quite common to hear the subjunctive used when someone is asking you something politely, for example, the person serving you in a shop might ask:
> **Wäre da sonst noch etwas?** — Will there be anything else?

2 Forming the present subjunctive

➤ The three main forms of the subjunctive are the present subjunctive, the imperfect subjunctive and the pluperfect subjunctive.

➤ The present subjunctive of weak, strong and mixed verbs has the same endings:

Pronoun	Present Subjunctive: Weak and Strong Verb Endings
ich	-e
du	-est
er/sie/es	-e
wir	-en
ihr	-et
sie/Sie	-en

- **holen** (weak verb, meaning *to fetch*)

  ich hole — I fetch
  du holest — you fetch

- **fahren** (strong verb, meaning *to drive, to go*)

  ich fahre — I drive, I go
  du fahrest — you drive, you go

- **denken** (mixed verb, meaning *to think*)

  ich denke — I think
  du denkest — you think

> **Tip**
> The present and the present subjunctive endings are exactly the same for the **ich**, **wir** and **sie/Sie** forms.

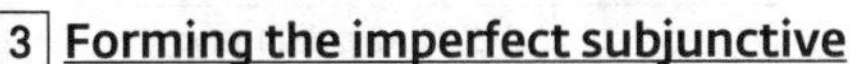

3 Forming the imperfect subjunctive

➤ The imperfect subjunctive is very common and is not always used to describe actions in the past. It can, for example, express the future.

Wenn ich nur früher kommen könnte! — If only I could come earlier!

➤ The imperfect tense and the imperfect subjunctive of weak verbs are identical.

Pronoun	Imperfect/Imperfect Subjunctive	Meaning
ich	**holte**	I fetched
du	**holtest**	you fetched
er/sie/es	**holte**	he/she/it fetched
wir	**holten**	we fetched
ihr	**holtet**	you (*plural*) fetched
sie/Sie	**holten**	they/you (*polite*) fetched

➤ The imperfect subjunctive of strong verbs is formed by adding the following endings to the stem of the imperfect. If there is an **a**, **o** or **u** in this stem, an umlaut is also added to it.

Pronoun	Imperfect Subjunctive: Strong Verb Endings
ich	-e
du	-(e)st
er/sie/es	-e
wir	-en
ihr	-(e)t
sie/Sie	-en

ℹ Note that you add the **-e** to the **du** and **ihr** parts of the verb if it makes pronunciation easier, for example:

du stießest you pushed
ihr stießet you pushed

Pronoun	Imperfect Subjunctive	Meaning
ich	**gäbe**	I gave
du	**gäb(e)st**	you gave
er/sie/es	**gäbe**	he/she/it gave
wir	**gäben**	we gave
ihr	**gäb(e)t**	you (*plural*) gave
sie/Sie	**gäben**	they/you (*polite*) gave

➤ The imperfect subjunctive forms of the mixed verbs **brennen**, **kennen**, **senden**, **nennen**, **rennen** and **wenden** add weak verb imperfect endings to the stem of the verb, which DOES NOT change the vowel. The imperfect subjunctive forms of the remaining mixed verbs **bringen**, **denken** and **wissen** are also the same as the imperfect with one major difference: not only does the stem vowel change, but an umlaut is also added to the **a** or **u**. However, all of these forms are rare, with the conditional tense being used much more frequently instead.

Wenn ich du wäre, <u>würde</u> ich <u>rennen</u>.

INSTEAD OF

Wenn ich du wäre, <u>rennte</u> ich.	If I were you, I would run.

Ich <u>würde</u> so etwas nie <u>denken</u>!

INSTEAD OF

Ich <u>dächte</u> so etwas nie!	I would never think such a thing!

➪ *For more information on the **Conditional**, see page 125.*

Grammar Extra!

The pluperfect subjunctive is formed from the imperfect subjunctive of **haben** or **sein** + the past participle. This subjunctive form is frequently used to translate the English structure 'If I had done something, ...'

Wenn ich Geld <u>gehabt hätte</u>, <u>wäre</u> ich <u>gereist</u>.	If I had had money, I would have travelled.

Key points

- ✔ In German, subjunctive forms are used much more frequently than in English, to express uncertainty, speculation or doubt.
- ✔ Subjunctive forms are commonly used in indirect speech and in conditional sentences.
- ✔ The present subjunctive of weak, strong and mixed verbs have the same endings.
- ✔ The imperfect tense and the imperfect subjunctive of weak verbs are identical.
- ✔ The imperfect subjunctive of strong verbs is formed by adding the endings **-e**, **-(e)st**, **-e**, **-en**, **-(e)t**, **-en** to the stem of the imperfect and often has an umlaut change.
- ✔ The imperfect subjunctive of mixed verbs is rare and the conditonal form of **würde** + infinitive is normally used instead.

The infinitive

What is the infinitive?
The **infinitive** is the 'to' form of the verb, for example, *to go*, and is the form you look up in a dictionary. It is the **-en** form of the verb in German.

Using the infinitive

➤ **zu** is used with the infinitive:

- after other verbs

Ich versuchte zu kommen.	I tried to come.

- after adjectives

Es war leicht zu sehen.	It was easy to see.
Es ist schwierig zu verstehen.	It's hard to understand.

- after nouns

Ich habe keine Zeit, Sport zu treiben.	I don't have the time to do any sport.
Ich habe keine Lust, meine Hausaufgaben zu machen.	I don't want to do my homework.

➤ The infinitive is used without **zu** after the following:

- modal verbs, such as **können** (meaning *to be able, can*)

Sie kann gut schwimmen.	She can swim very well.

➪ *For more information on **Modal verbs**, see page 136.*

Tip

The English *–ing* form is often translated by the German infinitive, as shown in some of the examples below.

- the verbs **lassen** (meaning *to stop, to leave*), **bleiben** (meaning *to stay*) and **gehen** (meaning *to go*)

Sie ließen uns warten.	They kept us waiting.
Sie blieb sitzen.	She remained seated.
Er ging einkaufen.	He went shopping.

- verbs of perception such as **hören** (meaning *to hear, to listen (to)*) and **sehen** (meaning *to see, to watch*)

Ich sah ihn kommen.	I saw him coming.
Er hörte sie singen.	He heard her singing.

For further explanation of grammatical terms, please see pages viii–xii.

➤ The infinitive can be used to give an order or instruction.

Bitte nicht in diesen Zug <u>einsteigen</u>! Please don't board this train!

➤ It can also be used as a noun with a capital letter. It is always neuter.

rauchen = to smoke

Sie hat <u>das Rauchen</u> aufgegeben. She's given up smoking.

Key points

✔ The infinitive is the 'to' form of the verb, the one you look up in a dictionary.

✔ **zu** is used with the infinitive after other verbs, adjectives and nouns.

✔ The infinitive is used WITHOUT **zu** after certain verbs, mostly modal verbs.

✔ The infinitive can be used to give an order or instruction.

✔ It can be used as a noun with a capital letter and is always neuter.

Modal verbs

What are modal verbs?
Modal verbs are used to modify or change other verbs to show such things as *ability, permission* or *necessity*. For example, *he can swim; may I come?; we ought to go*.

1 Using modal verbs

➤ In German, the modal verbs are **dürfen**, **können**, **mögen**, **müssen**, **sollen** and **wollen**.

➤ Modal verbs are different from other verbs in their conjugation, which is shown in the Verb Tables.

⇨ *For **Verb Tables**, see supplement.*

➤ Here are the main uses of **dürfen**:

- Meaning *to be allowed to* or *may*
  Darfst du mit ins Kino kommen? — Are you allowed to/Can you come to the cinema with us?
- Meaning *must not* or *may not*
  Ich darf keine Schokolade essen. — I mustn't eat any chocolate.
- Expressing politeness
  Darf ich? — May I?

➤ Here are the main uses of **können**:

- Meaning *to be able to* or *can*
  Wir können es nicht schaffen. — We can't make it.
- Meaning *would be able to* or *could*
  Könntest du morgen hinfahren? — Could you go there tomorrow?
- As a more common, informal alternative to **dürfen**, with the meaning *to be allowed to* or *can*
  Kann ich/darf ich einen Kaffee haben? — Can I/may I have a coffee?
- Expressing possibility
  Das kann sein. — That may be so.
  Das kann nicht sein. — That can't be true.

➤ Here are the main uses of **mögen**:

- Meaning *to like*, when expressing likes and dislikes
  Magst du Schokolade? — Do you like chocolate?
  Sie mögen es nicht. — They don't like it.
- Meaning *would like to*, when expressing wishes and polite requests
  Möchtest du sie besuchen? — Would you like to visit her?
  Möchten Sie etwas trinken? — Would you like something to drink?

- Expressing possibility or probability

Es mag sein, dass es falsch war.	It may well be that it was wrong.

➤ Here are the main uses of **müssen**:

- Meaning *to have to* or *must* or *need to*

Sie musste jeden Tag um sechs aufstehen.	She had to get up at six o'clock every day.

- Certain common, informal uses

Muss das sein?	Is that really necessary?
Den Film muss man gesehen haben.	That film is worth seeing.

ℹ Note that you can use a negative form of **brauchen** (meaning *to need*) instead of **müssen** for *don't have to* or *need not*

Das brauchst du nicht zu sagen.	You don't have to say that.

➤ Here are the main uses of **sollen**:

- Meaning *ought to* or *should*

Das sollten Sie sofort machen.	You ought to do that straight away.
Sie wusste nicht, was sie tun sollte.	She didn't know what to do. (*what she should do*)

- Meaning *to be supposed to* where someone else has asked you to do something

Du sollst deine Freundin anrufen.	You are supposed to/should phone your girlfriend. (*she has left a message asking you to ring*)

- Meaning *to be said to be*

Sie soll sehr reich sein.	I've heard she's very rich/ She is said to be very rich.

➤ Here are the main uses of **wollen**:

- Meaning *to want* or *to want to*

Sie will Lkw-Fahrerin werden.	She wants to be a lorry driver.

- As a common, informal alternative to **mögen**, meaning *to want* or *to wish*

Willst du eins?	Do you want one?
Willst du/möchtest du etwas trinken?	Do you want/would you like something to drink?

- Meaning *to be willing to*

Er will nichts sagen.	He refuses to say anything.

- Expressing something you previously intended to do

Ich wollte gerade anrufen.	I was just about to phone.

2 Modal verb forms

➤ Modal verbs have unusual present tenses:

dürfen	*können*	*mögen*
ich darf	ich kann	ich mag
du darfst	du kannst	du magst
er/sie/es/man darf	er/sie/es/man kann	er/sie/es/man mag
wir dürfen	wir können	wir mögen
ihr dürft	ihr könnt	ihr mögt
sie/Sie dürfen	sie/Sie können	sie/Sie mögen

müssen	*sollen*	*wollen*
ich muss	ich soll	ich will
du musst	du sollst	du willst
er/sie/es/man muss	er/sie/es/man soll	er/sie/es/man will
wir müssen	wir sollen	wir wollen
ihr müsst	ihr sollt	ihr wollt
sie/Sie müssen	sie/Sie sollen	sie/Sie wollen

➤ In tenses consisting of one verb part, the infinitive of the verb used with the modal comes at the end of the sentence or clause.

Sie kann sehr gut schwimmen. She is a very good swimmer.

Grammar Extra!

In sentences with modal verbs where the other verb expresses movement, it can be dropped if there is an adverb or adverbial phrase to show movement instead.

Ich muss nach Hause. I must go home.
Die Kinder sollen jetzt ins Bett. The children have to go to bed now.

➪ *For more information on **Adverbs**, see page 57.*

Key points

✔ Modal verbs are used to modify the meaning of other verbs.

✔ In German, the modal verbs are **dürfen**, **können**, **mögen**, **müssen**, **sollen** and **wollen**.

✔ Modal verbs are different from other verbs in their conjugation.

mpersonal verbs

What is an impersonal verb?
An **impersonal verb** is one that does not relate to a real person or thing and where the subject is represented by *it*, for example, *It's going to rain*; *It's ten o'clock*.

- In German, impersonal verbs are used with **es** (meaning *it*) and the third person singular form of the verb.

Es regnet.	It's raining.
Es gibt ein Problem.	There's a problem.

- Here are the most common impersonal verbs. In some of these expressions it is possible to drop the **es**, in which case a personal pronoun such as **mich** or **mir** begins the clause. For example:

Es ist mir egal, ob er mitkommt.	
OR	
Mir ist egal, ob er mitkommt.	I don't care if he comes with us.

*For more information on **Personal pronouns**, see page 70.*

- These expressions are marked with a * in the list below:

• **es freut mich, dass/zu**	I am glad that/to
Es freut mich, dass du gekommen bist.	I'm pleased that you have come.
Es freut mich, Sie in unserer Stadt begrüßen zu dürfen.	I'm pleased to welcome you to our town.
• **es gefällt mir**	I like it
Es gefällt mir gar nicht.	I don't like it at all.
• **Es geht mir gut/schlecht.**	I'm fine/not too good.
• **Es geht nicht.**	It's not possible
• **es geht um**	it's about
Es geht um die Liebe.	It's about love.
• **es gelingt mir (zu)**	I succeed (in)
Es ist mir gelungen, ihn zu überzeugen.	I managed to convince him.
• **es handelt sich um**	it's a question of
Es handelt sich um Zeit und Geld.	It's a question of time and money.
• **es hängt davon ab**	it depends
Es hängt davon ab, ob ich arbeiten muss.	It depends whether I have to work or not.

• **Es hat keinen Zweck.**	There's no point.
• **es ist mir egal (ob)***	it's all the same to me (if)
Es ist mir egal, ob du kommst oder nicht.	I don't care if you come or not.
• **es ist möglich(, dass)**	it's possible (that)
Es is doch möglich, dass sie ihr Handy nicht dabei hat.	It's always possible she doesn't have her mobile with her.
• **es ist nötig**	it's necessary
Es wird nicht nötig sein, mir Bescheid zu sagen.	It won't be necessary to let me know.
• **es ist schade(, dass)**	it's a pity (that)
Es ist schade, dass sie nicht kommt.	It's a pity (that) she isn't coming.
• **es ist mir warm** OR **es ist mir kalt***	I'm warm OR I'm cold
• **es klingelt**	someone's ringing the bell OR the phone is ringing
Es hat gerade geklingelt.	The bell just went OR the phone just rang.
• **es klopft**	someone's knocking (at the door)
• **es kommt darauf an(, ob)**	it all depends (whether)
Es kommt darauf an, ob ich arbeiten muss.	It all depends whether I have to work.
• **es lohnt sich (nicht)**	it's (not) worth it
Ich weiß nicht, ob es sich lohnt oder nicht.	I don't know if it's worth it or not.
• **es macht nichts**	it doesn't matter
• **es macht nichts aus**	it makes no difference
Macht es dir etwas aus, wenn wir morgen gehen?	Would you mind if we went tomorrow?
• **es stimmt, dass ...**	it's true that ...
Es stimmt, dass sie keine Zeit hat.	It's true that she doesn't have any time.
• **es tut mir leid(, dass) ...**	I'm sorry(that) ...
• **Wie geht es (dir)?**	How are you?
• **Mir wird schlecht.***	I feel sick.

For further explanation of grammatical terms, please see pages viii–xii.

➤ All weather verbs are impersonal.

Infinitive	Expression	Meaning
donnern und blitzen	**es donnert und blitzt**	there's thunder and lightning
frieren	**es friert**	it's freezing
gießen	**es gießt**	it's pouring
regnen	**es regnet**	it's raining
schneien	**es schneit**	it's snowing
sein	**es ist warm/kalt**	it's cold/warm

Key points

✔ Impersonal verbs are used with **es** (meaning it) and the third person singular form of the verb.

✔ All weather verbs are impersonal.

There is/There are

➤ There are two main ways of expressing this in German.

1 Es gibt

- This is always used in the singular form and is followed by a singular or plural object in the accusative case.

Es gibt zu viele Probleme dabei.	There are too many problems involved.
Es gibt keinen besseren Wein.	There is no better wine.

- **Es gibt** is used to refer to things of a general nature.

Es gibt bestimmt Regen.	It's definitely going to rain.
Wenn wir zu spät kommen, gibt es Ärger.	If we arrive late, there'll be trouble.

- It is often used informally.

Was gibts (=gibt es) zu essen?	What is there to eat?
Was gibts?	What's wrong?, What's up?
Das gibts doch nicht!	That's impossible!

2 Es ist/es sind

- Here, the **es** simply introduces the real subject of the sentence, so if the subject is plural, **es sind** is used. The subject is in the nominative case.

Es sind kaum Leute da.	There are hardly any people there.

- Where the subject and verb swap places in the clause or sentence, the **es** is dropped.

Da sind kaum Leute.	There are hardly any people there.

i Note that **es gibt** is frequently used instead of **es ist/es sind** in the above two examples.

- **Es ist** or **es sind** are used to refer to a temporary situation.

Es war niemand da.	There was no-one there.

- They are also used to begin a story.

Es war einmal eine Königin.	Once upon a time there was a Queen ...

Key point

✔ In German there are two main ways of translating *there is/there are*: **es gibt** and **es ist/es sind**.

Use of "es" as an anticipatory object

➤ The object of many verbs can be a clause beginning with **dass** (meaning *that*) or an infinitive with **zu**.

Er wusste, dass wir pünktlich kommen würden.	He knew that we would come on time.
Sie fing an zu lachen.	She began to laugh.

➤ With some verbs, **es** is often used as the object to anticipate this clause or infinitive phrase.

Er hatte es abgelehnt, mitzukommen.	He refused to come.

➤ When the **dass** clause or infinitive phrase begins the sentence, **es** is not used in the main clause. Instead, it can be replaced by the pronoun **das** (meaning *that*).

Dass es Karla war, das haben wir ihr verschwiegen.	We hid from her the fact that it was Karla.

[i] Note that **dass** is a subordinating conjunction and **das** is a demonstrative pronoun.

⇨ *For more information on **Subordinating conjunctions**, see page 172.*

➤ The following common verbs usually have the **es** object:

- **es ablehnen, zu ...** — to refuse to
- **es aushalten, zu tun/dass ...** — to stand doing/that
  Ich halte es nicht mehr aus, bei ihnen zu arbeiten. — I can't stand working for them any longer.
- **es ertragen, zu tun/dass ...** — to bear doing/that
  Ich ertrage es nicht, dass sie mir widerspricht. — I can't bear her contradicting me.
- **es leicht haben, zu ...** — to find it easy to
  Sie hatte es nicht leicht, sie zu überreden. — She didn't have an easy job persuading them.
- **es nötig haben, zu ...** — to need to
  Ich habe es nicht nötig, mit dir darüber zu reden. — I don't have to talk to you about it.
- **es satt haben, zu ...** — to have had enough of (doing)
  Ich habe es satt, englische Verben zu lernen. — I've had enough of learning English verbs.
- **es verstehen, zu ...** — to know how to
  Sie versteht es, Autos zu reparieren. — She knows about repairing cars.

➤ The following common verbs <u>often</u> have the **es** object.

- **es jemandem anhören/ansehen, dass ...** — to tell by listening to/looking at someone that

  Man hörte <u>es</u> ihm an, dass er kein Deutscher war. — You could tell by listening to him that he wasn't German.

- **es bereuen, zu tun/dass ...** — to regret having done/that

  Ich bereue <u>es</u> nicht, dass ich gekommen bin. — I don't regret coming.

- **es jemandem verbieten, zu ...** — to forbid someone to

  Ihre Mutter hat <u>es</u> ihr verboten, dort hinzugehen. — Her mother forbade her to go there.

  es wagen zu ... — to dare to

  Er wagte <u>es</u> nicht, ein neues Auto zu kaufen. — He didn't dare buy a new car.

Key points

✔ The object of many verbs can be a clause beginning with **dass** (meaning *that*) or an infinitive with **zu**.

✔ With some verbs, **es** is used as the object to anticipate this clause or infinitive phrase.

✔ When the **dass** clause or infinitive phrase begins the sentence, **es** is not used in the main clause. Instead, it can be replaced by the pronoun **das** (meaning *that*).

Verbs followed by prepositions

➤ Some English verbs must be followed by prepositions for certain meanings, for example, *to wait for*, *to ask for*. This also happens in German:

sich sehnen nach	to long for
warten auf	to wait for
bitten um	to ask for

Tip

As you can see from the examples above, the preposition that is used in German is not always the same as the one that is used in English. Whenever you learn a new verb, try to learn which preposition is used after it too.

➤ As in English, using different prepositions with a verb creates completely different meanings.

bestehen	to pass (a test etc)
bestehen aus	to consist of
bestehen auf	to insist on
sich freuen auf	to look forward to
sich freuen über	to be pleased about

ℹ Note that you occasionally need to use a preposition with a German verb whose English equivalent does not have one.

diskutieren über	to discuss

➤ Prepositions used with these verbs behave like normal prepositions and affect the case of the following noun in the normal way. For instance, with verbs followed by **für** the accusative case is always used.

sich interessieren für	to be interested in
Sie interessiert sich nicht für den neuen Wagen.	She isn't interested in the new car.

➤ A verb plus preposition is not always followed by a noun or pronoun. It can also be followed by a clause containing another verb. This is often used to translate an *-ing* form in English and is dealt with in one of two ways:

- If the verbs in both parts of the sentence have the same subject, **da-** or **dar-** is added to the beginning of the preposition and the following verb becomes an infinitive used with **zu**.

Ich freue mich sehr darauf, mal wieder mit ihr zu arbeiten.	I am looking forward to working with her again.

- If the subject is not the same for both verbs, a **dass** (meaning *that*) clause is used.

Ich freue mich sehr darauf, dass du morgen kommst.	I am looking forward to you coming tomorrow.

1 Verbs followed by a preposition + the accusative case

➤ The following list contains the most common verbs followed by a preposition plus the accusative case:

• **sich amüsieren über**	to laugh at, to smile about
Sie haben sich über ihn amüsiert.	They laughed at him.
• **sich ärgern über**	to get annoyed about/with
• **sich bewerben um**	to apply for
Sie hat sich um die Stelle als Direktorin beworben.	She applied for the position of director.
• **bitten um**	to ask for
• **denken an**	to be thinking of
Daran habe ich gar nicht mehr gedacht.	I'd forgotten about that.
• **denken über**	to think about, to hold an opinion of
Wie denkt ihr darüber?	What do you think about it?
• **sich erinnern an**	to remember
• **sich freuen auf**	to look forward to
• **sich freuen über**	to be pleased about
Ich freue mich sehr darüber, dass du gekommen bist.	I'm very glad you came.
• **sich gewöhnen an**	to get used to
• **sich interessieren für**	to be interested in
Sie interessiert sich sehr für Politik.	She's very interested in politics.
• **kämpfen um**	to fight for
• **sich kümmern um**	to take care of, to see to
Kannst du dich um meine Pflanzen kümmern?	Can you see to my plants?
• **nachdenken über**	to think about
Er hatte schon lange darüber nachgedacht.	He had been thinking about it for a long time.
• **sich unterhalten über**	to talk about
• **sich verlassen auf**	to rely on, to depend on
Kann sie sich auf ihn verlassen?	Can she rely on him?
• **warten auf**	to wait for

2 Verbs followed by a preposition + the dative case

➤ The following list contains the most common verbs followed by a preposition plus the dative case:

- **abhängen von** — to depend on
  Das hängt von der Zeit ab, die uns noch bleibt. — That depends how much time we have left.
- **sich beschäftigen mit** — to occupy oneself with
  Sie beschäftigen sich im Moment mit dem neuen Haus. — They're busy with their new house at the moment.
- **bestehen aus** — to consist of
- **leiden an/unter** — to suffer from
  Sie hat lange an dieser Krankheit gelitten. — She suffered from this illness for a long time.
- **riechen nach** — to smell of
- **schmecken nach** — to taste of
  Es schmeckt nach Zimt. — It tastes of cinnamon.
- **sich sehnen nach** — to long for
- **sterben an** — to die of
  Sie ist an Krebs gestorben. — She died of cancer.
- **teilnehmen an** — to take part in
  Du solltest am Wettbewerb teilnehmen. — You should take part in the competition.
- **träumen von** — to dream of
- **sich verabschieden von** — to say goodbye to
  Ich habe mich noch nicht von ihm verabschiedet. — I haven't said goodbye to him yet.
- **sich verstehen mit** — to get along with, get on with
  Sie versteht sich ganz gut mit ihr. — She gets on really well with her.

Key points

✔ German prepositions after verbs are often not the same as the ones used in English.

✔ Using different prepositions with a verb creates completely different meanings.

✔ German verbs occasionally use prepositions where their English equivalents don't.

✔ Prepositions used with verbs behave like normal prepositions and affect the case of the following noun.

Verbs followed by the dative case

1 Verbs with a direct and indirect object

➤ Some verbs are generally used with a direct object and an indirect object. For example, in the English sentence, *She gave me a book*, the direct object of *gave* is *a book* and would be in the accusative case in German, and *me* (= *to me*) is the indirect object and would be in the dative case in German.

Sie gab mir ein Buch. She gave me a book.
direct object = **ein Buch**
indirect object = **mir**

➤ In German, as in English, this type of verb is usually concerned with giving or telling someone something, or with doing something for someone else.

Sie erzählte ihm eine Geschichte. She told him a story.
direct object = **eine Geschichte**
indirect object = **ihm**

i Note that the normal word order after such verbs is for the direct object to follow the indirect, EXCEPT where the direct object is a personal pronoun.

Kaufst du mir das Buch? Will you buy me the book?
BUT
Kaufst du es mir? Will you buy it for me?

⇨ *For more information on* ***Direct*** *and* ***Indirect object pronouns****, see pages 74-77.*

➤ Here are some of the most common examples of verbs which are used with both a direct and an indirect object:

- **anbieten** to offer
  Sie bot ihr die Arbeitsstelle an. She offered her the job.
- **bringen** to bring
  Bringst du mir eins? Will you bring me one?
- **beweisen** to prove
  Können Sie es mir beweisen? Can you prove it to me?
- **fehlen** to be absent or missing
  Mir fehlt das nötige Geld. I don't have enough money.
- **geben** to give
  Gib mir das sofort! Give me that now!

- **schenken** to give (as a present)
  Ich schenke ihr einen Computer zum Geburtstag. I'm giving her a computer for her birthday.
- **schreiben** to write
  Schreib ihm mal einen Brief. Write him a letter sometime.
- **zeigen** to show
  Zeig es mir! Show me it!

2 Verbs with their object in the dative

➤ Certain verbs in German, such as **helfen** (meaning *to help*) can ONLY be followed by an object in the dative case. In many cases, their English equivalents have a direct object, and you need to learn the most common verbs which are different in this way.

➤ Here are some of the most common ones.

- **begegnen** to bump into, meet
  Er ist seinem Freund in der Stadt begegnet. He bumped into his friend in town.
- **gehören** to belong to
  Wem gehört dieses Buch? Whose book is this?
- **helfen** to help
  Er wollte ihr nicht helfen. He refused to help her.
- **danken** to thank
  Ich danke dir! Thank you!
- **schaden** to damage
  Rauchen schadet der Gesundheit Smoking is bad for your health.
- **schmecken** to taste
  Das Essen hat ihnen gut geschmeckt. They enjoyed the meal.
- **trauen** to trust
  Ich traue dir nicht. I don't trust you.

Key points

✔ Some German verbs are usually used with a direct AND an indirect object.

✔ The indirect object is ALWAYS in the dative case.

✔ The normal word order after such verbs is for the direct object to follow the indirect, EXCEPT where the direct object is a personal pronoun.

✔ Certain German verbs can only be followed by an object in the dative case.

The passive

What is the passive?
The **passive** is the form of the verb that is used when the subject of the verb is the person or thing that is affected by the action, for example, *I was given*, *we were told*, *it had been made*.

1 Using the passive

➤ In a normal, or *active* sentence, the 'subject' of the verb is the person or thing that carries out the action described by the verb. The 'object' of the verb is the person or thing that the verb 'happens' to.

Ryan (*subject*) hit (*active verb*) me (*object*).

➤ In English, as in German, you can turn an active sentence round to make a passive sentence.

I (*subject*) was hit (*passive verb*) by Ryan (*agent*).

➤ Very often, however, you cannot identify who is carrying out the action indicated by the verb.

I was hit in the face.
The trees will be chopped down.
I've been chosen to represent the school.

2 Forming the passive

➤ In English we use the verb *to be* with the past participle (*was hit, was given*) to form the passive and the word 'by' usually introduces the agent. In German the passive is formed using **werden** and the past participle, while the agent is introduced by

- **von**, for a person or organisation,
- or **durch**, for a thing.

Das Kind wurde von einem Hund gebissen.	The child was bitten by a dog.
Die Tür wurde durch den Wind geöffnet.	The door was opened by the wind.

➪ *For more information on the **Past participle**, see page 114.*

➤ Here is the present tense of the verb **sehen** (meaning *to see*) in its passive form.

ich werde gesehen	I am seen
du wirst gesehen	you are seen
er/sie/es wird gesehen	he/she/it is seen
wir werden gesehen	we are seen
ihr werdet gesehen	you (*plural*) are seen
sie/Sie werden gesehen	they/you (*formal*) are seen

Tip

There is/there are can be translated by a verb in the passive tense in German.

Es wird immer viel getrunken auf seiner Party.	There is always a lot of drinking at his party.

➤ You can form other tenses of the passive by changing the tense of the verb **werden**, for example, the imperfect passive.

ich wurde gesehen	I was seen

⇨ *For more information on the* ***Imperfect tense****, see page 118.*

Tip

There is a very important difference between German and English in sentences containing an indirect object. In English we can quite easily turn a normal (active) sentence with an indirect object into a passive sentence.

Active
Someone (*subject*) gave (*active verb*) me (*indirect object*) a book (*direct object*).

Passive
I (*subject*) was given (*passive verb*) a book (*direct object*).

In German, an indirect object can NEVER become the subject of a passive verb. Instead, the indirect object must remain in the dative case, with either the direct object becoming the subject of the passive sentence OR use of an impersonal passive construction.
Ein Buch (*subject*) **wurde mir geschenkt**.

3 Avoiding the passive

➤ Passives are not as common in German as in English. There are <u>three</u> main ways that German speakers express the same idea.

- by using the pronoun **man** (meaning *they* or *one*) with a normal, active verb.

<u>Man</u> hatte es mir schon gesagt.	I had already been told.

i Note that **man** is not always translated as *they* or *one*.

<u>Man</u> hatte es schon verkauft.	It had already been sold.

- by using **sich lassen** plus a verb in the infinitive.

Das lässt sich machen.	That can be done.

- by using an active tense where the agent of the action is known.

Susi schenkte ihr ein Auto.	Susi gave her a car.

INSTEAD OF

Ihr wurde von Susi ein Auto geschenkt.	She was given a car by Susi.

Key points

✔ The present tense of the passive is formed by using the present tense of **werden** with the past participle.

✔ In German, an indirect object can <u>NEVER</u> become the subject of a passive verb.

✔ You can often avoid a passive construction by using the pronoun **man** or **sich lassen** plus an infinitive or an active tense where the agent is known.

Prepositions

What is a preposition?
A **preposition** is a word such as *at*, *for*, *with*, *into* or *from*, which is usually followed by a noun, pronoun or, in English, a word ending in *-ing*. Prepositions show how people and things relate to the rest of the sentence, for example, *She's at home; a tool for cutting grass; it's from David.*

Using prepositions

➤ Prepositions are used in front of nouns and pronouns (such as *me*, *him*, *the man* and so on), and show the relationship between the noun or pronoun and the rest of the sentence. Some prepositions can be used before verb forms ending in *-ing* in English.

I showed my ticket to the inspector.
Come with me.
This brush is really good for cleaning shoes.

⇨ *For more information on **Nouns** and **Pronouns**, see pages 1 and 69.*

➤ In English, a preposition does not affect the word or phrase it introduces, for example:

the inspector	to the inspector
me	with me
cleaning shoes	for cleaning shoes

➤ In German, however, the noun following a preposition must be put into the accusative, genitive or dative case.

Tip
It is important to learn each preposition with the case or cases it governs.

1 Prepositions followed by the dative case

➤ Some of the most common prepositions taking the dative case are:
aus, **außer**, **bei**, **gegenüber**, **mit**, **nach**, **seit**, **von**, **zu**

- **aus** *out of, from*

Er trinkt aus der Flasche.	He is drinking out of the bottle.
Sie kommt aus Essen.	She comes from Essen.

- **außer** *out of; except*

Der Fahrstuhl war außer Betrieb.	The lift was out of order.
Der Patient ist jetzt außer Gefahr.	The patient is out of danger now.
Alle außer mir kamen zu spät.	All except me came too late.

- **bei** *at the home/shop/work etc of; near*

Feiern wir bei uns?	Shall we celebrate at our house?
Bei uns in Schottland ist das kein Problem.	At home in Scotland that isn't a problem.
Sie ist beim Bäcker.	She is at the baker's.
Er ist noch beim Friseur.	He is still at the hairdresser's.
Er wohnt immer noch bei seinen Eltern.	He still lives with his parents.

Note that **bei** plus the definite article can be shortened to **beim**.

*For more information on **Shortened forms of prepositions**, see page 165.*

- **gegenüber** *opposite; towards*

Er wohnt uns gegenüber.	He lives opposite us.
Sie ist mir gegenüber immer sehr freundlich gewesen.	She has always been very friendly towards me.

Note that when used as a preposition, **gegenüber** is placed AFTER a pronoun, but can be placed BEFORE or AFTER a noun.

- **mit** *with*

Er ging mit seinen Freunden spazieren.	He went for a walk with his friends.

- **nach** *after; to*

Nach zwei Stunden kam er wieder.	He returned two hours later.
Sie ist nach London gereist.	She went to London.
Ihrem Dialekt nach ist sie Süddeutsche.	From the way she talks I would say she is from southern Germany.

Note that when **nach** means *according to*, as in the last example, it can be placed AFTER the noun.

- **seit** *since; for (of time)*

Seit er krank ist, spielt er nicht mehr Fußball.	He's stopped playing football since he became ill.

Note that after **seit**, meaning *for*, we use the present tense in German, but the perfect tense in English.

Ich wohne seit zwei Jahren in Frankfurt.	I've been living in Frankfurt for two years.
Sie arbeitet seit acht Jahren bei uns.	She's been working for us for eight years.

*For more information on **Tenses**, see page 94.*

- **von** *from; about; by (when used in the passive tense)*

Von Berlin sind wir weiter nach Krakau gefahren.	From Berlin we went on to Krakow.
Ich weiß nichts von ihm.	I know nothing about him.
Sie ist von unseren Argumenten überzeugt worden.	She was convinced by our arguments.

*For more information on the **Passive**, see page 150.*

Note that **von** can be used as a common alternative to the genitive case.

Die Mutter von diesen Mädchen ist Künstlerin.	The mother of these girls is an artist.
Sie ist eine Freundin von Alexander.	She is a friend of Alexander's.

*For more information on the **Genitive case**, see page 11.*

- **zu** *to; for*

Er ging zum Arzt.	He went to the doctor's.
Wir sind zum Essen eingeladen.	We're invited for dinner.

Note that **zu** plus the definite article can be shortened to **zum** or **zur**.

*For more information on **Shortened forms of prepositions**, see page 165.*

Grammar Extra!

Some of the above prepositions are also used as separable verb prefixes, that is the part at the beginning of a separable German verb.

aushalten	to endure
Ich halte es nicht mehr aus.	I can't stand it any longer.
(jemandem) beistehen	to stand by (somebody)
Er stand seinem Freund bei.	He stood by his friend.
gegenüberstehen	to have an attitude towards
Er steht ihnen kritisch gegenüber.	He has a critical attitude towards them.
jemanden mitnehmen	to give somebody a lift
Nimmst du mich bitte mit?	Will you give me a lift please?
nachmachen	to copy
Sie macht mir alles nach.	She copies everything I do.
zumachen	to shut
Mach die Tür zu!	Shut the door!

*For more information on **Separable verbs**, see page 109.*

Key points

- ✔ **gegenüber**, **aus**, **bei**, **mit**, **nach**, **seit**, **von**, **zu**, **außer** are the most common prepositions used with the dative case.
- ✔ Each of them has several different possible meanings, depending on the context they are used in.
- ✔ **aus**, **nach**, **mit**, **bei** and **zu** can also be used as separable verb prefixes.

2 Prepositions followed by the accusative case

➤ The most common prepositions taking the accusative case are:
durch, **entlang**, **für**, **gegen**, **ohne**, **um**, **wider**

Tip

If you want an easy way to remember which prepositions take the accusative case, you could think of the word DOGWUF, which can stand for the prepositions **durch ohne gegen wider um für**.

- **durch** *through*

Sie guckte durch das Loch.	She looked through the hole.
Durch Zufall trafen sie sich wieder.	They met again, by chance.

- **entlang** *along*

Die Kinder kommen die Straße entlang.	The children are coming along the street.

Note that **entlang** comes AFTER the noun in this meaning.

- **für** *for; to*

Ich habe es für dich getan.	I did it for you.
Das ist für ihn sehr wichtig.	That is very important to him.
Was für eins hat er?	What kind (of one) does he have?
Was für einen Wagen hat sie?	What kind of car does she have?
Was für Äpfel sind das?	What kind of apples are they?

- **gegen** *against; around*

Stelle es gegen die Wand.	Put it against the wall.
Haben Sie etwas gegen Heuschnupfen?	Have you got something for hayfever?
Wir sind gegen vier angekommen.	We arrived at around four o'clock.

- **ohne** *without*

Ohne sie gehts nicht.	It won't work without her.

- **um** *(a)round, round about; at (with time); by (with quantity)*

Der Bahnhof liegt um die Ecke.	The station is round the corner.
Es fängt um neun Uhr an.	It begins at nine.
Es ist um zehn Euro billiger.	It is cheaper by ten euros.

Note that **um** is used after certain verbs.

Sie baten um ein bisschen mehr Zeit.	They asked for a bit more time.
Es handelt sich um dein Benehmen.	It's a question of your behaviour.

*For more information on **Verbs followed by prepositions**, see page 145.*

- **wider** *contrary to, against*

Das geht mir wider die Natur.	That's against my nature.

Grammar Extra!

Some of the above prepositions are also used as separable verb prefixes, that is the part at the beginning of a separable German verb.

durchmachen
Sie hat viel durchgemacht in ihrem Leben. — She's been through a lot in her life.

entlanggehen
Wir gingen die Straße entlang. — We went along the street.

um and **wider** are also used as separable or inseparable verb prefixes (variable verb prefixes), depending on the verb and meaning.

umarmen	*inseparable*	to embrace
Er hat sie umarmt.		He gave her a hug.
umfallen	*separable*	to fall over
Sie ist umgefallen.		She fell over.
widersprechen	*inseparable*	to go against
Das hat meinen Wünschen widersprochen.		That went against my wishes.
(sich) widerspiegeln	*separable*	to reflect
Der Baum spiegelt sich im Wasser wider.		The tree is reflected in the water.

➪ *For more information on **Separable verbs** and **Inseparable verbs**, see pages 109 and 110.*

Key points

- ✔ **durch**, **entlang**, **für**, **gegen**, **ohne**, **um**, and **wider** are the most common prepositions used with the accusative case.
- ✔ Most of them have several different possible meanings, depending on the context they are used in.
- ✔ **durch**, **entlang** and **gegen** can also be used as separable verb prefixes.
- ✔ **um** and **wider** can also be used as variable verbal prefixes.

3 Prepositions followed by the accusative or the dative case

➤ There are a number of prepositions which can be followed by the accusative or the dative case. You use:

- the accusative case when there is some movement towards a different place
- the dative case when a location is described rather than movement, or when there is movement within the same place

- The most common prepositions in this category are:

an, **auf**, **hinter**, **in**, **neben**, **über**, **unter**, **vor**, **zwischen**

- You use **an**:
  - with the accusative case

Die Lehrerin schrieb das Wort an die Tafel.	The teacher wrote the word on the board.
Ich habe einen Brief an meine Mutter geschrieben.	I wrote a letter to my mother.
Ich ziehe im Sommer an die Küste.	In the summer I move to the coast.

  - with the dative case

Das Wort stand an der Tafel.	The word was written on the blackboard.
Wir treffen uns am Bahnhof.	We're meeting at the station.

Note that **an** plus the definite article can be shortened to **am**.

For more information on ***Shortened forms of prepositions****, see page* 165.

- You use **auf**:
  - with the accusative case

Stell die Suppe bitte auf den Tisch.	Put the soup on the table please.
Wir fahren morgen aufs Land.	We're going to the country tomorrow.
Er warf einen Blick auf das Buch.	He glanced at the book.

Note that **auf** plus the definite article can be shortened to **aufs**.

For more information on ***Shortened forms of prepositions****, see page* 165.

  - with the dative case

Die Suppe steht auf dem Tisch.	The soup's on the table.
Auf dem Land ist die Luft besser.	The air is better in the country.

- You use **hinter**:
  - with the accusative case

Stell dich hinter deinen Bruder.	Stand behind your brother.

  - with the dative case

Sie saß hinter mir.	She was sitting behind me.

➤ You use **in**:

- with the accusative case

Sie ging ins Zimmer.	She entered the room.
Er wollte nicht in die Schule gehen.	He didn't want to go to school.

- with the dative case

Was hast du heute in der Schule gemacht?	What did you do at school today?
Im Zimmer warteten viele Leute auf ihn.	A lot of people were waiting for him in the room.

ⓘ Note that **in** plus the definite article can be shortened to **im** or **ins**.

⇨ *For more information on **Shortened forms of prepositions**, see page 165.*

➤ You use **neben**:

- with the accusative case

Stell dein Rad neben meines.	Put your bike next to mine.

- with the dative case

Dein Rad steht neben meinem.	Your bike's next to mine.

➤ You use **über**:

- with the accusative case

Zieh den Pullover über deinen Kopf!	Pull the jumper over your head!
Sie ging quer über das Feld.	She went across the field.
Flugzeuge dürfen nicht über dieses Gebiet fliegen.	Planes are not allowed to fly over this area.

- with the dative case

Die Lampe soll über dem Tisch hängen.	The lamp should hang over the table.

ⓘ Note that when **über** means *about*, it is always followed by the accusative case, NOT the dative.

Wir haben viel über sie gesprochen.	We talked about her a lot.

➤ You use **unter**:

- with the accusative case

Sie stellte sich unter den Baum.	She (came and) stood under the tree.

- with the dative case

Sie lebte dort unter Freunden.	She lived there among friends.

➤ You use **vor**:

- with the accusative case

Stell den Stuhl vor das Fenster.	Put the chair in front of the window.

- with the dative case

Auf dem Foto stand sie vor dem Haus.	In the photo she was standing in front of the house.
Ich war vor ihm da.	I was there before him.
Vor dem Krankenhaus links abbiegen.	Turn left at the hospital.

➤ You use **zwischen**:

- with the accusative case

Er legte es zwischen die beiden Teller.	He put it between the two plates.

- with the dative case

Das Dorf liegt zwischen den Bergen.	The village lies between the mountains.

➤ Each of these prepositions can also be used with verbs and are then called prepositional objects.

abhängen von + *dative*	to depend on
Das hängt von dir ab.	That depends on you.
schmecken nach + *dative*	to taste of
Der Nachtisch schmeckt nach Zimt.	The dessert tastes of cinnamon.

➤ When **auf** or **an** is used in this way, the case used depends on the verb – it's much easier to learn such examples together with the case which follows them.

sich verlassen auf + *accusative*	to depend on
Ich verlasse mich auf dich.	I'm depending on you.
bestehen auf + *dative*	to insist on
Wir bestehen auf sofortiger Bezahlung.	We insist on immediate payment.
glauben an + *accusative*	to believe in
Sie glaubt an ihre Schwester.	She believes in her sister.
leiden an + *dative*	to suffer from
Er leidet an einer tödlichen Krankheit.	He is suffering from a terminal illness.

sich freuen auf + *accusative*	to look forward to
Ich freue mich auf die Sommerferien.	I'm looking forward to the summer holidays.
warten auf + *accusative*	to wait for
Er wartet jeden morgen auf den Bus.	Every morning he waits for the bus.

➪ *For more information on* ***Verbs with prepositional objects****, see page 145.*

Grammar Extra!

Some of the above prepositions are also used as separable or inseparable verb prefixes.

anrechnen	*separable*	to charge for
Das wird Ihnen später angerechnet.		You'll be charged for that later.
aufsetzen	*separable*	to put on
Er setzte sich die Mütze auf.		He put his cap on.
überqueren	*inseparable*	to cross
Sie hat die Straße überquert.		She crossed the street.

➪ *For more information on* ***Separable verbs*** *and* ***Inseparable verbs****, see pages 109 and 110.*

Key points

- ✔ **an**, **auf**, **hinter**, **in**, **neben**, **über**, **unter**, **vor** and **zwischen** are the most common prepositions which can be followed by the accusative or dative case.
- ✔ Most of them have several different possible meanings, depending on the context they are used in.
- ✔ Each of them can also be prepositional objects of certain verbs.
- ✔ Many of them can also be used as verb prefixes.

4 Prepositions followed by the genitive case

➤ The following are some of the more common prepositions which take the genitive case:

außerhalb, **infolge**, **innerhalb**, **statt**, **trotz**, **um ... willen**, **während**, **wegen**

- **außerhalb** *outside*

Es liegt außerhalb der Stadt.	It's outside the town.

- **infolge** *as a result of*

Infolge des starken Regens kam es zu Überschwemmungen.	As a result of the heavy rain, there were floods.

- **innerhalb** *within, inside*

Ich schaffe das nicht innerhalb der gesetzten Frist.	I won't manage that within the deadline.

- **statt** *instead of*

Statt nach Hause zu gehen, sind wir noch in die Stadt gegangen.	Instead of going home, we went into town.
Sie kam statt ihres Bruders.	She came instead of her brother.

- **trotz** *in spite of*

Trotz ihrer Krankheit ging sie jeden Tag spazieren.	In spite of her illness, she went for a walk every day.

- **um ... willen** *for ... sake, because of ...*

Ich komme um deinetwillen.	I'm coming for your sake.
Tun Sie das bitte um meiner Mutter willen.	Please do it, for my mother's sake.

- **während** *during*

Was hast du während der Ferien gemacht?	What did you do during the holidays?

- **wegen** *because of, on account of*

Wegen des schlechten Wetters wurde die Veranstaltung abgesagt.	The event was cancelled because of bad weather.

[i] Note that **statt**, **trotz**, **während** and **wegen** can also be followed by the dative case.

Statt dem Abendessen musste ich arbeiten.	Instead of having dinner, I had to work.
Trotz allem will ich weiterstudieren.	In spite of everything, I want to continue studying.
Während dem Vortrag schlief er ein.	He fell asleep during the lecture.
Wegen mir musste sie früh nach Hause.	She had to go home early because of me.

Grammar Extra!

There are some other prepositions which take the genitive case:

- **beiderseits** *on both sides of*

Beiderseits des Flusses gibt es ein Ufer.	On both sides of the river there is a river bank.

- **diesseits** *on this side of*

Diesseits der Grenze spricht man Polnisch und Deutsch.	On this side of the border Polish and German are spoken.

- **... halber**

Vorsichtshalber nehme ich heute meinen Regenschirm mit.	To be on the safe side I'm taking an umbrella today.
Sicherheitshalber verschließt er die Tür.	For safety's sake he locks the door.

- **hinsichtlich** *with regard to*

Hinsichtlich Ihrer Beschwerde habe ich Ihren Brief an die zuständigen Behörden geschickt.	With regards to your complaint, I have passed on your letter to the relevant authorities.

- **jenseits** *on the other side of*

Das Dorf liegt 2 km jenseits der Grenze.	The village is 2km on the other side of the border.

Grammar Extra!

Special forms of the possessive and relative pronouns are used with **wegen**:

- **meinetwegen**

Hat er sich meinetwegen so aufgeregt?	Did he get so upset on my account?

- **deinetwegen**

Ich ging nicht deinetwegen nach Hause.	I didn't go home because of you.

- **seinetwegen**

Ihr müsst seinetwegen nicht auf euren Urlaub verzichten.	You don't have to do without your holiday for his sake.

- **ihretwegen**

Wir sind ihretwegen früher gegangen.	We went earlier because of them.

- **unsertwegen**

Sie musste unsertwegen Strafe zahlen.	She had to pay a fine because of us.

- **euretwegen**

Euretwegen durfte er nicht mitspielen.	Because of you he wasn't allowed to play.

- **Ihretwegen**

Sollte es Ihretwegen Probleme geben, dann gehen wir alle nach Hause.	Should you cause any problems, then we'll all go home.

➪ *For more information on* ***Possessive pronouns*** *and* ***Relative pronouns****, see pages 80 and 86.*

Key points

- ✔ **außerhalb**, **beiderseits**, **diesseits**, **... halber**, **hinsichtlich**, **infolge**, **innerhalb**, **jenseits**, **statt**, **trotz**, **um ... willen**, **während** and **wegen** are the most common prepositions which take the genitive case.
- ✔ **statt**, **trotz**, **während** and **wegen** can also take the dative case.
- ✔ Special forms of possessive and relative pronouns are used with **wegen**.

5 Shortened forms of prepositions

➤ After many German prepositions, a shortened or contracted form of the definite article can be merged with the preposition to make one word.

auf + das → **aufs**
bei + dem → **beim**
zu + der → **zur**

➪ *For more information on the **Definite article**, see page 25.*

➤ This can be done with all of the following prepositions:

Preposition	+ das	+ den	+ dem	+ der
an	ans		am	
auf	aufs			
bei			beim	
durch	durchs			
für	fürs			
hinter	hinters	hintern	hinterm	
in	ins		im	
über	übers	übern	überm	
um	ums			
unter	unters	untern	unterm	
vor	vors		vorm	
von			vom	
zu			zum	zur

Er ging ans Fenster. He went to the window.

Wir waren gestern am Meer. We were at the seaside yesterday.

Er ist beim Friseur. He's at the hairdresser's.

Wir gehen heute Abend ins Kino. We're going to the cinema tonight.

Im Sommer lese ich gern im Garten. In the summer I like reading in the garden.

Es ging immer ums Thema Geld. It was always about the subject of money.

Der Hund lief unters Auto. The dog ran under the car.

Der Ball rollte untern Tisch. The ball rolled under the table.

Die Katze lag unterm Schreibtisch. The cat lay under the desk.

Er erzählte vom Urlaub. He talked about his holiday.

Sie fährt zum Bahnhof. She drives to the station.

Er geht zur Schule. He goes to school.

➤ The following shortened forms are normally only used in informal, spoken German:

- **aufs**

  Wir fahren morgen aufs Land. We're going to the country tomorrow.

- **durchs**

  Sie fiel durchs Abitur. She failed her 'A' Levels.

- **fürs**

  Das ist fürs neue Haus. That's for the new house.

- **hinters, hintern, hinterm**

  Er lief hinters Auto. He ran behind the car.

  Stell es hintern Tisch. Put it behind the table.

  Es liegt hinterm Sofa. It's behind the couch.

- **übers, übern, überm**

  Sie legten ein Brett übers Loch. They put a board over the hole.

  Man muss das übern Kopf ziehen. You have to pull it over your head.

  Überm Tisch hängt eine Lampe. There's a lamp hanging over the table.

- **unters, untern, unterm**

  Die Katze ging unters Bett. The cat went under the bed.

  Der Ball rollte untern Tisch. The ball rolled under the table.

  Der Hund liegt unterm Tisch. The dog is lying under the table.

- **vors, vorm**

Stell den Stuhl <u>vors</u> Fenster.	Put the chair in front of the window.
Er stand <u>vorm</u> Spiegel.	He stood in front of the mirror.

ℹ Note that if you want to stress the article in a sentence, shortened forms are <u>NOT</u> used.

<u>In</u> <u>dem</u> Anzug kann ich mich nicht sehen lassen!	I can't go out in that suit!

➤ Shortened forms of prepositions can also be used:

- with personal pronouns representing inanimate objects, that is objects which are not living things

Sie war <u>damit</u> zufrieden.	She was satisfied with that.
Er hat es <u>darauf</u> angelegt, dass er die beste Note kriegen würde.	He was determined to get the best grade.

➪ *For more information on **Personal pronouns**, see page 70.*

Key points

✔ It is often possible to combine the definite article and a preposition to create a shortened form.

✔ Some of these shortened forms should only be used in spoken German.

Conjunctions

What is a conjunction?
A **conjunction** is a linking word such as *and*, *but*, *if* and *because*, that links two words or phrases of a similar type, for example, *Diane and I have been friends for years*. Conjunctions also link two clauses, for example, *I left because I was bored*. In German there are two types of conjunctions, called **co-ordinating conjunctions** and **subordinating conjunctions**.

Co-ordinating conjunctions

➤ **aber**, **denn**, **oder**, **sondern** and **und** are the most important co-ordinating conjunctions.

- **aber** but

Wir wollten ins Kino, aber wir hatten kein Geld.	We wanted to go to the cinema, but we had no money.

ℹ Note that you can't use **aber** after a negative to mean *not ... but ...*: you must use **sondern**.

- **aber** however

Ich wollte nach Hause, er aber wollte nicht mit.	I wanted to go home; however, he wouldn't come.

ℹ Note that when **aber** means 'however', it comes between the subject and verb in the clause.

- **denn** because, since

Wir wollten heute fahren, denn montags ist weniger Verkehr.	We wanted to travel today because there is less traffic on Mondays.

- **oder** or

Sie hatte noch nie Whisky oder Schnaps getrunken.	She had never drunk whisky or schnapps.
Willst du eins oder hast du vielleicht keinen Hunger?	Do you want one or aren't you hungry?

- **sondern** but

Es kostet nicht zwanzig, sondern fünfzig Euro.	It doesn't cost twenty euros, but fifty.

- **und** and

Susi und Oliver	Susi and Oliver
Er ging in die Stadt und kaufte sich ein neues Hemd.	He went into town and bought himself a new shirt.

For further explanation of grammatical terms, please see pages viii–xii.

➤ If you use a co-ordinating conjunction, you do not put the verb at the end of the clause beginning with the conjunction.

Wir wollten ins Theater, <u>aber</u> <u>wir</u> <u>hatten</u> kein Geld.	We wanted to go to the theatre but we had no money.

wir = subject
hatten = verb

Co-ordinating conjunctions with two parts

➤ German, like English, also has conjunctions which have more than one part. Here are the most common ones:

- **sowohl ... als (auch)** both ... and

  The verb is plural, whether the individual subjects are singular or plural.

Sowohl sein Vater als auch seine Mutter haben sich darüber gefreut.	Both his father and mother were pleased about it.
Sowohl unser Lehrkörper als auch unsere Schüler haben teilgenommen.	Both our staff and pupils took part.

- **weder ... noch** neither ... nor

  With this conjunction, the verb is plural unless both subjects are singular, as shown below.

Weder die Lehrer noch die Schüler haben recht.	Neither the teachers nor the pupils are right.
Weder du noch ich würde es schaffen.	Neither you nor I would be able to do it.

  When **weder ... noch** is used to link clauses, the subject and verb are swapped round in BOTH clauses.

Weder mag ich ihn noch respektiere ich ihn.	I neither like nor respect him.

- **nicht nur ... sondern auch** not only ... but also

  The verb agrees in number with the subject nearest to it.

Nicht nur sie, sondern auch ich habe es gehört.	They weren't the only ones to hear it – I heard it too.

  When **nicht nur ... sondern auch** is used to link clauses, the subject and verb are only swapped round in the first clause, not the second, BUT if **nicht nur** does not begin the clause, word order is normal.

  Nicht nur ist sie geschickt, sondern auch intelligent.

  OR

Sie ist nicht nur geschickt, sondern auch intelligent.	She is not only skilful but also intelligent.

- **entweder ... oder** either ... or

  The verb agrees in number with the subject nearest to it. When **entweder ... oder** is used to link clauses, the subject and verb are only swapped round in the first clause, not the second.

Entweder du oder Karla muss es getan haben.	It must have been either you or Karla.
Entweder komme ich vorbei, oder ich rufe dich an.	I'll either drop in or I'll give you a ring.

For further explanation of grammatical terms, please see pages viii–xii.

Key points

- ✔ A conjunction is a word that links two words or clauses of a similar type, or two parts of a sentence.
- ✔ **Aber**, **denn**, **oder**, **sondern** and **und** are the most important co-ordinating conjunctions.
- ✔ Single-word co-ordinating conjunctions do not change the order of the subject and the verb in the clause.

Subordinating conjunctions

➤ The subordinate clause is always separated from the main clause by a comma. It is called a subordinate clause because it cannot stand on its own without the other clause in the sentence and is linked to this by a subordinating conjunction.

Sie ist zu Fuß gekommen, <u>weil</u> der Bus zu teuer <u>ist</u>.	She came on foot because the bus is too dear.
MAIN CLAUSE	= **Sie ist zu Fuß gekommen**
SUBORDINATE CLAUSE	= **weil der Bus zu teuer ist**

[i] Note that the verb comes at the end of the subordinate clause.

➤ **als**, **da**, **damit**, **dass**, **ob**, **obwohl**, **während**, **wenn**, **weil**, **um ... zu**, and **ohne ... zu** are some of the most important subordinating conjunctions.

- **als** (when)

Es regnete, <u>als</u> ich in Glasgow ankam.	It was raining when I arrived in Glasgow.

- **da** (as, since)

<u>Da</u> du nicht kommen willst, gehe ich allein.	Since you don't want to come, I'll go on my own.

- **damit** so (that)

Ich sage dir das, <u>damit</u> du es weißt.	I'm telling you so that you know.

- **dass** that

Ich weiß, <u>dass</u> du besser in Mathe bist als ich.	I know (that) you're better at maths than me.

- **ob** if, whether

Sie fragt, <u>ob</u> du auch kommst.	She wants to know if you're coming too.

- **obwohl** although

Sie blieb lange auf, <u>obwohl</u> sie müde war.	She stayed up late although she was tired.

- **während** while

Sie sah fern, <u>während</u> sie ihre Hausaufgaben machte.	She was watching TV while she was doing her homework.

- **wenn** when, whenever/if

<u>Wenn</u> ich nach Hause komme, dusche ich erst mal.	When I get home, the first thing I'm going to do is have a shower.
<u>Wenn</u> er anruft, sag mir Bescheid.	If he calls, tell me.

For further explanation of grammatical terms, please see pages viii–xii.

Tip

If translating *when* in a sentence which describes a single, completed action in the past, you use **als**, NOT **wenn**. You use **wenn** for single, momentary actions in the present or future.

- **weil** because

Morgen komme ich nicht, weil ich keine Zeit habe.	I'm not coming tomorrow because I don't have the time.

- **um ... zu** in order to ...

Um früh aufzustehen, musste sie den Wecker stellen.	In order to get up early, she had to set the alarm.

Note that **zu** is inserted between a separable verb and its prefix.

*For more information on **Separable verbs**, see page 109.*

- **ohne ... zu** without ...

Er verließ das Haus, ohne ein Wort zu sagen.	He left the house without saying a word.

Note that **um ... zu** and **ohne ... zu** are always used with infinitive constructions.

Note that with the subordinating conjunctions **als**, **da**, **damit**, **dass**, **ob**, **obwohl**, **während**, **wenn**, **weil**, **um ... zu**, and **ohne ... zu**, the subordinate clause can come BEFORE the main clause, as seen in the example with **da**. When this happens, the verb and subject of the main clause swap places.

*For more information on the **Infinitive**, see page 134.*

➤ In tenses which only have one verb part, such as the present and imperfect, the verb comes last in the subordinate clause.

Wenn er mich sah, lief er davon.	Whenever he saw me, he ran away.

➤ In tenses which have two verb parts, such as the perfect tense, it is the form of **haben**, **sein** or **werden** which comes last in the subordinate clause, after the past participle.

Sie will nicht ausgehen, weil sie noch nichts gegessen hat.	She doesn't want to go out because she hasn't eaten anything yet.

*For more information on the **Perfect** and **Imperfect tenses**, see pages 113 and 118.*

➤ Any modal verb, for example **mögen** (meaning *to like*) and **können** (meaning *can*, *to be able to*), used in a subordinate clause is placed last in the clause.

Sie wusste nicht, ob sie kommen konnte.	She didn't know if she could come.

*For more information on **Modal verbs**, see page 136.*

Key points

- ✔ Subordinating conjunctions link the main clause and subordinating clause in a sentence.
- ✔ After subordinating conjunctions, verbs go to the end of the clause.
- ✔ **Als**, **da**, **damit**, **dass**, **ob**, **obwohl**, **während**, **wenn**, **weil**, **um ... zu**, and **ohne ... zu** are some of the most important subordinating conjunctions.
- ✔ The subordinate clause can come before the main clause. When this happens, the verb and subject of the main clause swap places.
- ✔ In tenses which only have one verb part, the verb comes last in the subordinate clause. In tenses which have two verb parts, **haben**, **sein** or **werden** comes last in the subordinate clause, after the past participle.

For further explanation of grammatical terms, please see pages viii–xii.

Word order

➤ Here is a ready-reference guide to the key points of German word order.

1 Main clauses

➤ In a main clause the subject comes first and is followed by the verb, as in English.

Seine Mutter *(subject)* **trinkt** *(verb)* **Whisky.**	His mother *(subject)* drinks *(verb)* whisky.

➤ In tenses with more than one verb element, such as the perfect tense and the passive, the part of **haben**, **sein** or **werden** comes after the subject, and the past participle or infinitive goes to the end of the clause.

Sie hat mir nichts gesagt.	She told me nothing.
Er ist spät angekommen.	He arrived late.
Es wurde für ihn gekauft.	It was bought for him.

➤ A direct object usually follows an indirect object, except where the direct object is a personal pronoun.

Ich gab dem Mann *(indirect object)* **das Geld** *(direct object)*.	I gave the man the money.
Ich gab ihm *(indirect object)* **das Geld** *(direct object)*.	I gave him the money.
BUT	
Ich gab es *(direct object)* **ihm** *(indirect object)*.	I gave it to him.

i Note that the indirect object can also be placed last for emphasis, providing it is NOT a pronoun.

Er gab das Geld seiner Schwester.	He gave the money to his sister. *(not his brother)*

⇨ *For more information on **Direct** and **Indirect objects**, see pages 9 and 13.*

⇨ *For more information on **Using direct** and **Indirect object pronouns**, see pages 74 and 76.*

➤ As a general rule, adverbs are placed next to the words to which they refer.

- Adverbs of time often come first in the clause, but this is not fixed.

  Gestern gingen wir ins Theater
  OR
  Wir gingen gestern ins Theater — We went to the theatre yesterday.

- Adverbs of place can also come first in the clause when you want to emphasize something.

  Dort haben sie Fußball gespielt. — That's where they played football.

- Adverbs of manner comment on verbs and so are likely to come immediately after the verb they refer to.

Sie spielen gut Fußball.	They play football well.

- Where there is more than one adverb, a useful rule of thumb is: "TIME, MANNER, PLACE"

Wir haben gestern gut hierhin gefunden.	We found our way here all right yesterday.

gestern = adverb of time
gut = adverb of manner
hierhin = adverb of place

- If there is a pronoun object (a word like *her*, *it*, *me* or *them*) in the clause, it comes before all adverbs.

Sie haben es gestern sehr billig gekauft.	They bought it very cheaply yesterday.

➤ The normal word order in a main clause is subject followed by verb. The subject can be replaced as the first element by any of the words and phrases below. In such cases, the verb is the second element in the clause.

- an adverb

Gestern sind wir ins Theater gegangen.	We went to the theatre yesterday.

- a direct or indirect object

Seinen Freunden wollte er es nicht zeigen.	He wouldn't show it to his friends.

- an infinitive phrase

Ihren Freunden zu helfen, hat sie nicht versucht.	She didn't try to help her friends.

- another noun or pronoun

Deine Schwester war es.	It was your sister.
Sie war es.	It was her.

- a past participle

Geraucht hatte er nie.	He had never, ever smoked.

- a phrase with a preposition

In diesem Haus bin ich auf die Welt gekommen.	I was born in this house.

- a clause which acts as the object of the verb

Was mit ihm los war, haben wir nie herausgefunden.	We never found out what was wrong with him.

For further explanation of grammatical terms, please see pages viii–xii.

- a subordinate clause

<u>Nachdem ich ihn gesehen hatte,</u> ging ich nach Hause.	I went home after seeing him.

2 Subordinate clauses

➤ A subordinate clause may be introduced by a relative pronoun (a word such as **der**, **die** or **dessen**) or a subordinating conjunction (a word such as **da**, **als** or **ob**).

Die Kinder, <u>die</u> wir gesehen haben ...	The children whom we saw ...
<u>Da</u> sie nicht schwimmen wollte, ist sie nicht mitgekommen.	As she didn't want to swim, she didn't come.

➤ The subject follows the conjunction or relative pronoun.

Ich weiß nicht, <u>ob</u> <u>er</u> kommt.	I don't know if he's coming.

➤ The main verb ALMOST ALWAYS goes to the end of a subordinate clause.

<u>Als</u> ich nach Hause <u>kam</u>, war ich ganz müde.	When I came home I was really tired.

Grammar Extra!

The exceptions to this are:

- A clause which normally begins with **wenn**, but from which it can be left out.

Findest du mein Handy, so ruf mich bitte an.	
INSTEAD OF	
<u>Wenn</u> du mein Handy findest, ruf mich bitte an.	If you find my mobile, please give me a call.

- Indirect speech without the conjunction **dass** (meaning that).

Sie meint, sie werde es innerhalb einer Stunde schaffen.	
INSTEAD OF	
Sie meint, <u>dass</u> sie es innerhalb einer Stunde schaffen wird.	She thinks (that) she will manage it inside an hour.

➤ The rules applying to the order of articles, nouns, adjectives, adverbs, direct and indirect objects are the same in subordinate clauses as in main clauses, EXCEPT that all these words are placed between the subject of the clause and the relevant verb part.

MAIN CLAUSE:

Sie ist <u>gestern mit ihrer Mutter in die Stadt</u> gefahren. She went into town with her mother yesterday.

SUBORDINATE CLAUSE:

<u>Da</u> sie <u>gestern mit ihrer Mutter in die Stadt</u> gefahren ist. Since she went into town with her mother yesterday.

Tip

The rule "time, manner, place" applies equally to subordinate clauses, EXCEPT that the verb goes to the end.

➪ *For more information on **Subordinate clauses**, see page 193.*

➤ Word order in the imperative, in direct and indirect speech and in verbs with separable prefixes is covered in the relevant chapters:

➪ *For more information on the **Imperative**, see page 105.*

➪ *For more information on **Direct** and **Indirect speech**, see page 129.*

➪ *For more information on **Verbs with separable prefixes**, see page 109.*

Negatives

What is a negative?
A **negative** question or statement is one which contains a word such as *not*, *never* or *nothing* and is used to say that something is not happening, is not true or is absent.

1 Using negatives

- In English we use words like *not*, *no*, *nothing* and *never* to show a negative.

  I'm not very pleased.
  Dan never rang me.
  Nothing ever happens here!
  There's no milk left.

- In German, if you want to make something negative, you generally add **nicht** (meaning *not*) or **nie** (meaning *never*) next to the phrase or word referred to.

Ich will nicht mitgehen.	I don't want to come.
Sie fährt nie mit ans Meer.	She never comes with us to the seaside.

- Here is a list of the other common German negatives:
  - **nein** (meaning *no*)

    Nein, ich habe keine Zeit. — No, I don't have any time.
  - **nichts** (meaning *nothing*)

    Sie hat nichts damit zu tun. — She has nothing to do with it.
  - **nicht mehr** (meaning *not ... any more, no longer*)

    Ich rauche nicht mehr. — I don't smoke any more/ I no longer smoke.

    Sie geht nicht mehr hin. — She doesn't go any more.

i Note that **nicht** and **mehr** always appear next to each other.

kein (meaning *none*)

Keiner meiner Freunde wollte kommen.	None of my friends wanted to come.
Wo ist die Milch? – Es ist keine mehr da.	Where is the milk? – There is none left.

> ***Tip***
>
> **Nicht** applies to verbs. Remember that when you want to make a negative statement about a noun, you must use **kein**. If you want to say *I don't drink milk any more*, you would say **Ich trinke keine Milch mehr**.

➪ *For more information on the **Indefinite article in negative sentences** and on **Indefinite pronouns**, see pages 36 and 82.*

- **niemand** (meaning *nobody* or *no one*)

Es war niemand im Büro.	There was nobody in the office.

➪ *For more information on **Indefinite pronouns**, see page 82.*

- **nirgendwo** or **nirgends** (meaning *nowhere, not ... anywhere*)

Nirgends sonst gibt es so schöne Blumen.	Nowhere else will you find such beautiful flowers.
Hier gibts nirgendwo ein Schwimmbad.	There isn't a swimming pool anywhere here.

- **weder noch** (meaning *neither of two things*)

Karotten oder Erbsen? – Weder noch, danke.	Carrots or peas? – Neither, thanks.

- **weder ... noch** (meaning *neither ... nor*)

Weder Sabina noch Oliver kommen zur Party.	Neither Sabina nor Oliver is coming to the party.

➪ *For more information on **Co-ordinating conjunctions with two parts**, see page 170.*

- **... auch nicht** (meaning *neither have I, nor does he, nor are we* etc)

Ich mag ihn nicht. – Ich auch nicht!	I don't like him. – Neither do I!
Er war noch nie im Spanien. – Sie auch nicht!	He's never been to Spain. – Neither has she!

2 Word order with negatives

➤ In a sentence with only one verb part, such as the present tense, **nicht** and **nie** usually come directly after the verb. However, in direct questions, the negative word comes after the subject.

Du arbeitest nicht.	You're not working.
BUT	
Arbeitest du nicht?	Aren't you working?

➤ In a sentence with two verb parts, such as the perfect tense and the passive, the part of **haben**, **sein** or **werden** comes after the subject and the negative word usually comes directly before the past participle or infinitive. The position of the negative doesn't change in direct questions.

Sie haben es nicht gemacht.	You haven't done it.
Haben Sie es nicht gemacht?	Haven't you done it?

- You can change the emphasis in a sentence by moving the position of the negative. For example, **nie** can be placed at the start of the sentence. The subject and verb then swap positions.

Nie waren sie glücklicher gewesen.	They had never been happier.
Nie im Leben hatte er so etwas gesehen.	Never in his life had he seen such a thing.

- **nicht** comes at the end of a negative imperative, except if the verb is separable, in which case it comes before the separable prefix.

Iss das nicht!	Don't eat that!
Setzen Sie sich nicht!	Don't sit down!
BUT	
Geh nicht weg!	Don't go away!

- **nicht** + the indefinite article **ein** is usually replaced by forms of **kein**.

Gibt es keine Plätzchen?	Aren't there any biscuits?
Kein einziger Student hatte die done **Arbeit gemacht.**	Not a single student had the work.

⇨ *For more information on the **Indefinite article**, see page 35.*

- To contradict a negative statement, **doch** is used instead of **ja**, to mean *yes*.

Du kommst nicht mit. – Doch, ich komme mit.	You're not coming. – Yes I am.
Das ist nicht wahr. – Doch!	That isn't true! – Yes it is!

- **nicht ... sondern** (meaning *not ... but*) is used to correct a wrong idea or false impression.

Nicht Susi, sondern ihr Bruder war es.	It wasn't Susi, it was her brother.

Key points

- ✔ A statement is usually made negative by adding **nicht** (meaning *not*) or **nie** (meaning *never*).
- ✔ The most common German negatives are: **nicht**, **nein**, **nie**, **nichts**, **nicht mehr**, **kein**, **niemand**, **nirgends** or **nirgendwo**, **weder noch**, **weder ... noch** and ... **auch nicht**.
- ✔ **Nicht** comes at the end of a negative imperative, except if the verb is separable, in which case it comes before the separable prefix.
- ✔ **Nicht** + the indefinite article **ein** is usually replaced by forms of **kein**.
- ✔ To contradict a negative statement, **doch** is used instead of **ja**, to mean *yes*.
- ✔ **Nicht ... sondern** (meaning *not ... but*) is used to correct a wrong idea or false impression.

Questions

What is a question?
A **question** is a sentence which is used to ask someone about something and which in English normally has the verb in front of the subject. Question words such as *why*, *where*, *who*, *which* or *how* are also used to ask a question.

How to ask a question in German

1 The basic rules

➤ There are three ways of asking direct questions in German:

- by changing round the order of words in a sentence
- by adding **nicht**, **nicht wahr**, **oder** or **doch** (meaning *isn't it*) to a sentence
- by using a question word

2 Asking a question by changing word order

➤ Many questions are formed in German by simply changing the normal word order of a sentence. You swap round the subject and verb, and add a question mark.

Magst *(verb)* **du** *(subject)* **ihn?**	Do you like him?
Gehst *(verb)* **du** *(subject)* **ins Kino?**	Do you go to the cinema? OR Are you going to the cinema?

➤ In tenses with more than one verb, such as the perfect tense and the passive, the part of **haben**, **sein** or **werden** comes BEFORE the subject, and the past participle or infinitive goes to the end of the clause.

Haben Sie es gesehen?	Did you see it?

3 Asking a question by adding nicht, nicht wahr, oder or doch

➤ A statement can be made into a question by adding **nicht**, **nicht wahr**, **oder** or **doch**, in the same way as *isn't it*, *won't you* etc is added in English. You'd normally expect the answer to such questions to be a simple *yes* or *no*.

Das stimmt, nicht wahr?	That's true, isn't it?
Das Essen ist fertig, nicht?	The food's ready, isn't it?
Sie machen das, oder?	They'll do it, won't they?
Das schaffst du doch?	You'll manage, won't you?

➤ When a question is put in the negative, **doch** can be used to answer it more positively than **ja**.

Glaubst du mir nicht? – Doch!	Don't you believe me? – Yes, I do!

For further explanation of grammatical terms, please see pages viii–xii.

4 Asking a question by using a question word

➤ A question word is a word like *when* or *how* that is used to ask for information. In German, these words are a mixture of interrogative adverbs, pronouns and adjectives. Listed below are the most common question words:

wie? (*how?*)	**wo?** (*where?*)	**wem?** (*whom?*)
was? (*what?*)	**welcher?** (*which?*)	**wessen?** (*whose?*)
wann? (*when?*)	**wer?** (*who?*)	**warum?** (*why?*)

ⓘ Note that **wer** means *who*, NOT *where*.

➤ When questions are formed with interrogative adverbs like **wann**, **wo**, **wie** and **warum**, normal word order changes and the subject and verb swap places.

Wann ist er gekommen?	When did he come?
Wo willst du hin?	Where are you off to?
Wie haben Sie das gemacht?	How did you do that?
Warum ist sie so spät aufgestanden?	Why did she get up so late?

Tip

Remember to use **woher** and **wohin** when direction is involved.

Woher kommst du?	Where do you come from?
Wohin fahren Sie?	Where are you going?

➤ When questions are formed with interrogative pronouns and adjectives, word order is normal if the interrogative pronoun or adjective is the subject of the verb at the beginning of the clause.

Wer (*subject*) **hat** (*verb*) **das gemacht?**	Who did that?

➤ If the interrogative pronoun or adjective is NOT the subject of the verb at the beginning of the clause, the subject and verb swap places.

Wem hast (*verb*) **du** (*subject*) **es geschenkt?**	Who did you give it to?

➪ *For more information on* ***Interrogative pronouns****, see page 89.*

ⓘ Note that in indirect questions, that is questions following verbs of *asking* and *wondering*, the verb comes at the end of the question.

Sie fragte, ob du mitkommen wolltest.	She asked if you wanted to come.

Key points

- ✔ There are three basic ways of asking direct questions in German: changing the word order; adding **nicht**, **nicht wahr**, **oder** or **doch**; and using a question word.
- ✔ When a question is put in the negative, **doch** can be used to answer it more positively than **ja**.
- ✔ The most common question words are the interrogative adverbs **wann**, **wo**, **wie** and **warum**, the interrogative pronouns **was**, **wer**, **wem** and **wessen**, and the interrogative adjective **welcher**.

For further explanation of grammatical terms, please see pages viii–xii.

Numbers

0	**null**
1	**eins**
2	**zwei**
3	**drei**
4	**vier**
5	**fünf**
6	**sechs**
7	**sieben**
8	**acht**
9	**neun**
10	**zehn**
11	**elf**
12	**zwölf**
13	**dreizehn**
14	**vierzehn**
15	**fünfzehn**
16	**sechzehn**
17	**siebzehn**
18	**achtzehn**
19	**neunzehn**
20	**zwanzig**
21	**einundzwanzig**
22	**zweiundzwanzig**
30	**dreißig**
40	**vierzig**
50	**fünfzig**
60	**sechzig**
70	**siebzig**
80	**achtzig**
90	**neunzig**
a hundred	**hundert**
one hundred	**einhundert**
101	**hunderteins**
102	**hundertzwei**
121	**hunderteinundzwanzig**
200	**zweihundert**
a thousand	**tausend**
one thousand	**eintausend**
1001	**tausendeins**
2000	**zweitausend**
100,000	**hunderttausend**
1,000,000	**eine Million**

Note that **zwo** often replaces **zwei** in speech, to distinguish it clearly from **drei**.

> **Tip**
>
> In German, spaces or full stops are used with large numbers where English uses a comma. Decimals are written with a comma instead of a full stop.

1,000,000	**1.000.000** *or* **1 000 000**
7.5 (*seven point five*)	7,5 (**sieben Komma fünf**)
1st	1. **der erste**
2nd	2. **der zweite**
3rd	3. **der dritte**
4th	4. **der vierte**
5th	5. **der fünfte**
6th	6. **der sechste**
7th	7. **der siebte**
8th	8. **der achte**
9th	9. **der neunte**
10th	10. **der zehnte**
11th	11. **der elfte**
12th	12. **der zwölfte**
13th	13. **der dreizehnte**
14th	14. **der vierzehnte**
15th	15. **der fünfzehnte**
16th	16. **der sechzehnte**
17th	17. **der siebzehnte**
18th	18. **der achtzehnte**
19th	19. **der neunzehnte**
20th	20. **der zwanzigste**
21st	21. **der einundzwanzigste**
22nd	22. **der zweiundzwanzigste**
30th	30. **der dreißigste**
40th	40. **der vierzigste**
50th	50. **der fünfzigste**
60th	60. **der sechzigste**
70th	70. **der siebzigste**
80th	80. **der achtzigste**
90th	90. **der neunzigste**
100th	100. **der hunderste**
101st	101. **der hunderterste**
102nd	102. **der hundertzweite**
121st	121. **der hunderteinundzwanzigste**
200th	200. **der zweihundertste**

For further explanation of grammatical terms, please see pages viii–xii.

1000th	1000.	**der tausendste**
1001st	1001.	**der tausenderste**
2000th	2000.	**der zweitausendste**
100,000th	100 000.	**der hunderttausendste**
1,000,000th	1 000 000.	**der millionste**

Tip

When these numbers are used as nouns, they are written with a capital letter.

Sie ist die Zehnte. She's the tenth.

half	½	**halb**
third	⅓	**das Drittel**
two thirds	⅔	**zwei Drittel**
quarter	¼	**das Viertel**
three quarters	¾	**drei Viertel**
one and a half	1½	**anderthalb, eineinhalb**
two and a half	2½	**zweieinhalb**

BEISPIELE	EXAMPLES
Sie hat zwei Autos.	She has two cars.
Er ist zwanzig Jahre alt.	He is twenty years old.
Sie wohnt im dritten Stock.	She lives on the third floor.
Er hat am 31. August Geburtstag.	His birthday is on the 31st of August.
Ich brauche anderthalb Stunden, um nach Hause zu kommen.	I need an hour and a half *or* one and a half hours to get home.
Sie aß zwei Drittel von dem Kuchen.	She ate two thirds of the cake.

Note that ordinal numbers (**erste**, **zweite**, and so on) are declined according to the number, case and gender of the noun.

Ich habe gerade mein erstes Auto gekauft.	I've just bought my first car.
Sie kam zum zweiten Mal mit Verspätung an.	She arrived late for the second time.

*For more information on **Nouns**, see page 1.*

DIE ZEIT	THE TIME
Wie spät ist es? *or* **Wie viel Uhr ist es?**	What time is it?
Es ist ...	It's ...
Mitternacht *or* **null Uhr** *or* **vierundzwanzig Uhr** *or* **zwölf Uhr**	midnight *or* twelve o'clock
zehn (Minuten) nach zwölf *or* **null Uhr zehn**	ten (minutes) past twelve
Viertel nach zwölf *or* **null Uhr fünfzehn**	quarter past twelve
halb eins *or* **null Uhr dreißig**	half past twelve
zwanzig (Minuten) vor eins *or* **null Uhr vierzig**	twenty (minutes) to one
Viertel vor eins *or* **drei viertel eins** *or* **null Uhr fünfundvierzig**	quarter to one
ein Uhr	one o'clock
zehn (Minuten) nach eins *or* **ein Uhr zehn**	ten (minutes) past one
Viertel nach eins *or* **ein Uhr fünfzehn**	quarter past one
halb zwei *or* **ein Uhr dreißig**	half past one
zwanzig (Minuten) vor zwei *or* **ein Uhr vierzig**	twenty (minutes) to two
Viertel vor zwei *or* **drei viertel zwei** *or* **ein Uhr fünfundvierzig**	quarter to two
zehn (Minuten) vor zwei *or* **ein Uhr fünfzig**	ten (minutes) to two
zwölf Uhr	twelve o'clock (midday)
halb eins *or* **zwölf Uhr dreißig**	half past twelve
ein Uhr *or* **dreizehn Uhr**	one o'clock
halb fünf *or* **sechzehn Uhr dreißig**	half past four
zehn Uhr *or* **zweiundzwanzig Uhr** *or* **zwoundzwanzig Uhr**	ten o'clock
Um wie viel Uhr?	At what time?
Wann?	**When?**
morgen um halb drei	tomorrow at half past two
um drei Uhr (nachmittags)	at three (pm)
kurz vor zehn Uhr	just before ten o'clock
gegen vier Uhr (nachmittags)	around four o'clock (in the afternoon)
erst um halb neun	not until half past-eight
ab neun Uhr	from nine o'clock onwards
morgen früh	tomorrow morning
morgen Abend	tomorrow evening

DAS DATUM	THE DATE
WOCHENTAGE	**DAYS OF THE WEEK**
Montag	Monday
Dienstag	Tuesday
Mittwoch	Wednesday
Donnerstag	Thursday
Freitag	Friday
Samstag	Saturday
Sonntag	Sunday
Wann?	**When?**
Montag	(on) Monday
montags	(on) Mondays
jeden Montag	every Monday
letzten Dienstag	last Tuesday
nächsten Freitag	next Friday
Samstag in einer Woche *or* **in acht Tagen**	a week on Saturday
Samstag in zwei Wochen	two weeks on Saturday
MONATE	**MONTHS**
Januar	January
Februar	February
März	March
April	April
Mai	May
Juni	June
Juli	July
August	August
September	September
Oktober	October
November	November
Dezember	December
Wann?	**When?**
im Dezember	in December
im April	in April
nächsten Januar	next January
letzten August	last August
Anfang/Ende September	at the beginning/ end of September

Der Wievielte is heute?	What's the date today?
Welches Datum haben wir heute?	
Heute ist ...	It's ...
der zwanzigste März	the twentieth of March
der Zwanzigste	the twentieth
Heute haben wir ...	It's ...
den zwanzigsten März	the twentieth of March
den Zwanzigsten	the twentieth
Am Wievielten findet es statt?	When does it take place?
am ersten April ...	... on the first of April
am Ersten ...	... on the first
(am) Montag, den ersten April *or*	on Monday, the first of April *or*
Montag, den 1. April	April 1st

JAHRESZEITEN	**SEASONS**
im Winter	in winter
im Sommer	in summer
im Herbst	in autumn
im Frühling	in spring

NÜTZLICHE VOKABELN	**USEFUL VOCABULARY**
Wann?	**When?**
heute	today
heute Morgen	this morning
heute Nachmittag	this afternoon
heute Abend	this evening
(im Jahr(e)) 2015	in 2015
Wie oft?	**How often?**
jeden Tag	every day
alle zwei Tage	every other day
einmal in der Woche/pro Woche	once a week
zweimal pro Woche	twice a week
einmal im Monat/pro Monat	once a month

For further explanation of grammatical terms, please see pages viii–xii.

Wann ist das passiert?	**When did it happen?**
am Morgen/Vormittag	in the morning
morgens/vormittags	in the mornings
am Abend	in the evening
abends	in the evenings
gestern	yesterday
gestern Abend	yesterday evening
vorgestern	the day before yesterday
vor einer Woche	a week ago
vor zwei Wochen	two weeks ago
letztes Jahr	last year
Wann passiert das?	**When is it going to happen?**
morgen	tomorrow
morgen früh	tomorrow morning
übermorgen	the day after tomorrow
in zwei Tagen	in two days
in einer Woche	in a week
in vierzehn Tagen/zwei Wochen	in two weeks
nächsten Monat	next month
nächstes Jahr	next year

[i] Note that to talk about the year in which something happens, you don't use **in** in German.

Das findet 2016 statt.	That's taking place in 2016.
Sie wurde 2002 geboren.	She was born in 2002.
Ich ging 2011 für ein Jahr nach Deutschland.	I went to Germany for a year in 2011.

Some common difficulties

General problems

➤ You can't always translate German into English and English into German word for word. While occasionally it is possible to do this, often it is not. For example:

- Sentences which contain a verb and preposition in English might NOT contain a preposition in German.

Jemanden/etwas ansehen	to look at somebody/something
Jemandem/etwas zuhören	to listen to somebody/something

- However, many sentences which contain a verb and preposition in German DO contain a preposition in English.

sich interessiern für	to be interested in
denken über	to think about

➤ Remember that German prepositions are of two types:

- Some are only ever used with one case, such as **gegen** (accusative), **bei** (dative) and **außerhalb** (genitive). For all of these it is useful to learn the preposition and its case by heart.
- The second type are used either with the accusative or the dative, according to whether movement from one place to another is involved or not. The translation of the same preposition from the last group can change according to the case being used.

Sie schrieb einen Brief an ihren Bruder.	She wrote a letter to her brother.
Wir treffen uns am Bahnhof.	We're meeting at the station.

➪ *For more information on* ***Prepositions****, see page* 153.

➤ A word which is plural in English may not be in German.

eine Brille	glasses, spectacles
eine Schere	scissors
eine Hose	trousers

ⓘ Note that they are only used in the plural in German to mean more than one pair, for example, **zwei Hosen** = two pairs of trousers.

➪ *For more information on* ***Nouns****, see page* 1.

➤ In English, you use *'s* to show who or what something belongs to; in German you generally either use the genitive case or **von** + the dative case.

Das Auto meiner Schwester	
OR	
Das Auto von meiner Schwester	My sister's car

➪ *For more information on the **Genitive case**, see page 11.*

➤ German punctuation differs from English in several ways.

- Decimal places are always shown by a comma, NOT a full stop.

3,4 (drei Komma vier)	3.4 (three point four)

- Large numbers are separated by means of a space or a full stop, NOT a comma.

20 000	
OR: **20.000 (zwanzigtausend)**	20,000 (twenty thousand)

- Subordinate clauses are always separated from the rest of the sentence by a comma.

Er bleibt gesund, obwohl er zu viel trinkt.	He stays healthy, even though he drinks too much.

➪ *For more information on **Subordinate clauses**, see page 177.*

- When two main clauses are linked by **und** (meaning *and*) or **oder** (meaning *or*), no comma is required.

Wir gehen ins Kino oder wir bleiben zu Hause.	We'll go to the cinema or stay at home.

Specific problems

1 Nouns with capital letters

➤ Unlike English, ALL German nouns start with a capital letter, not just proper names.

der Tisch	the table
die Politikerin	the politician
die Königin	the Queen

ℹ Note that this also applies to verbs being used as nouns.

Sie hat ihr Können bewiesen.	She has proved her ability.

2 Three forms of you

➤ In English we have only one way of saying *you*. In German, there are three words: **du**, **ihr** and **Sie**. You use:

- the familiar **du** if talking to one person you know well, such as a friend, someone younger than you or a relative.

Kommst du mit ins Kino?	Are you coming to the cinema?

- the familiar **ihr** if talking to more than one person you know well.

Also, was wollt ihr heute Abend machen?	So, what do you want to do tonight?

- the formal or polite **Sie** if talking to one or more people you do not know so well, such as your teacher, your boss or a stranger.

Was haben Sie gemacht?	What did you do?

3 -ing

➤ Although English sometimes uses parts of the verb *to be* to form the present tense of other verbs (for example, *I am listening*, *she's talking*), German NEVER uses the verb **sein** in this way. Instead, it uses the normal present tense of the verb.

Ich spiele Tennis.	I play tennis OR: I am playing tennis

4 To be

➤ The verb *to be* is generally translated by **sein**.

Es ist spät.	It's late.
Das ist nicht möglich.	That's not possible.

➤ When you are talking about the physical position of something you can use **liegen**. You may also come across **sich befinden** in more formal contexts.

Wo liegt/befindet sich der Bahnhof?	Where's the station?

➤ In certain set phrases which describe how you are feeling or a state you are in, the verb **haben** is used.

Hunger haben	to be hungry
Durst haben	to be thirsty
Angst haben	to be afraid
unrecht haben	to be wrong
recht haben	to be right

[i] Note that to say *I* etc *am hot* or *I* etc *am cold*, you use a personal pronoun in the dative case followed by **sein**.

Mir ist heiß NOT **Ich bin heiß**	I am hot
Ihr ist kalt NOT **Sie ist kalt**	She is cold

➤ When talking about your health, use the following forms of the verb **gehen**.

Wie geht es dir/Ihnen?	How are you?
Es geht mir gut OR **Mir geht es gut.**	I'm fine.

5 It

➤ There are three ways of saying *it* in German: **er**, **sie** and **es**. These correspond to the three different genders, masculine, feminine and neuter.

Wo ist der Wagen? – Er steht da drüben.	Where is the car? – It's over There.
Ich finde meine Uhr nicht. Hast du sie gesehen?	I can't find my watch. Have you seen it?
Was hältst du von meinem Haus? – Es ist ganz schön.	What do you think of my house? – It's really nice.

➪ *For more information on **Gender**, see page 3.*

6 Date and time

➤ When talking about a particular day or date, use the preposition **an** + the dative case in the following constructions:

Ich fahre am Montag nach Hause.	I'm going home on Monday.
Sie wurde am Dienstag, den 1. April aus dem Krankenhaus entlassen.	She was discharged from hospital on Tuesday, the 1st of April.
Meine Nichte hat am 6. September Geburtstag.	My niece's birthday is on the 6th of September.

➤ When stating the time of a particular event, use the preposition **um** + the accusative case in the following construction.

Ich bin um 9 Uhr aufgestanden.	I got up at 9 o'clock.
Der Zug ist um 22.30 Uhr abgefahren.	The train left at 22.30 hours.

➪ *For more information on* ***Prepositions****, see pages* 153.

7 There is, there are

➤ Both *there is* and *there are* are translated by **es gibt**.

Hier gibt es ein schönes Freibad.	There's a lovely open-air pool here.
In Stuttgart gibt es viele Parks.	There are lots of parks in Stuttgart.

8 The imperfect of modal verbs

➤ Modal verbs never have an umlaut in the imperfect tense.

können (can, to be able)	**konnte**
müssen (must, to have to)	**musste**
mögen (to like)	**mochte**
dürfen (to be allowed to)	**durfte**
sollen (to ought to)	**sollte**
wollen (to want)	**wollte**

➪ *For more information on* ***Modal verbs****, see page* 136.

9 Er/sie/es parts of strong verbs in the imperfect

➤ You do NOT add a **-t** to the **er/sie/es** parts of the imperfect tense of strong verbs.

Er/sie/es ging	He/she/it went
NOT	
Er/sie/es gingt	
Er/sie/es sang	He/she/it sang
NOT	
Er/sie/es sangt	

*For more information on the **Imperfect tense**, see page 118.*

10 Inseparable verbs in the perfect tense

➤ Inseparable verbs have no **ge-** added to the beginning of the past participle in the perfect tense. For example:

Das habe ich schon bezahlt.	I've already paid for that.
Er hat sich endlich entschlossen.	He's finally decided.

*For more information on **Inseparable verbs**, see page 109.*

11 Can, to be able

➤ If you want to say *could*, meaning *was able*, you use **konnte**, the imperfect form of **können**, you do NOT use the conditional form **könnte**.

Sie konnte nicht kommen.	She couldn't make it.
Er konnte das einfach nicht.	He just wasn't able to do it.

Alphabet

➤ The German alphabet is pronounced differently from the way it is pronounced in English. Use the list below to help you sound out the letters.

A, a	[aː]	(ah)	
B, b	[beː]	(bay)	
C, c	[tseː]	(tsay)	
D, d	[deː]	(day)	
E, e	[eː]	(ay)	
F, f	[ɛf]	(ef)	
G, g	[geː]	(gay)	
H, h	[haː]	(hah)	
I, i	[iː]	(ee)	
J, j	[jɔt]	(yot)	
K, k	[kaː]	(kah)	
L, l	[ɛl]	(el)	
M, m	[ɛm]	(em)	
N, n	[ɛn]	(en)	
O, o	[oː]	(oh)	
P, p	[peː]	(pay)	
Q, q	[kuː]	(koo)	
R, r	[ɛr]	(air)	
S, s	[ɛs]	(es)	
T, t	[teː]	(tay)	
U, u	[uː]	(oo)	
V, v	[fau]	(fow)	
W, w	[veː]	(vay)	
X, x	[ɪks]	(ix)	
Y, y	[ʏpsilɔn]	(üpsilon)	like 'ü' in 'über'
Z, z	[tsɛt]	(tset)	

For further explanation of grammatical terms, please see pages viii–xii.

Main Index

VERB TABLES

Introduction

The **Verb Tables** *in the following section contain 97 tables of German verbs (strong, weak and mixed) in alphabetical order. Each table shows you the following forms:* **Present, Perfect, Future, Present Subjunctive, Imperfect, Conditional, Imperative** *and the* **Present** *and* **Past Participles**. *For more information on these tenses, how they are formed, when they are used and so on, you should look at the section on* **Verbs** *in the main text on pages 91–152.*

In order to help you use the verbs shown in the **Verb Tables** *correctly, there are also a number of example phrases at the bottom of each page to show the verb as it is used in context.*

In German there are **weak** *verbs (their forms follow regular patterns),* **strong** *verbs (their forms follow irregular patterns) and* **mixed** *verbs (their forms follow a mixture of regular and irregular patterns). Two of the weak verbs in these tables are* **holen** *(to fetch) and* **machen** *(to do, to make). All weak, strong and mixed verbs are shown in full.*

The **Verb Index** at the end of this section contains around 1000 verbs, each of which is cross-referred to one of the verbs given in the Verb Tables. The table shows the patterns that the verb listed in the index follows.

annehmen (to accept)

strong, separable, *formed with* **haben**

PRESENT

ich	**nehme an**
du	**nimmst an**
er/sie/es	**nimmt an**
wir	**nehmen an**
ihr	**nehmt an**
sie/Sie	**nehmen an**

PERFECT

ich	**habe angenommen**
du	**hast angenommen**
er/sie/es	**hat angenommen**
wir	**haben angenommen**
ihr	**habt angenommen**
sie/Sie	**haben angenommen**

FUTURE

ich	**werde annehmen**
du	**wirst annehmen**
er/sie/es	**wird annehmen**
wir	**werden annehmen**
ihr	**werdet annehmen**
sie/Sie	**werden annehmen**

IMPERATIVE

nimm an!/nehmen wir an!/ nehmt an!/nehmen Sie an!

PRESENT SUBJUNCTIVE

ich	**nehme an**
du	**nehmest an**
er/sie/es	**nehme an**
wir	**nehmen an**
ihr	**nehmet an**
sie/Sie	**nehmen an**

IMPERFECT

ich	**nahm an**
du	**nahmst an**
er/sie/es	**nahm an**
wir	**nahmen an**
ihr	**nahmt an**
sie/Sie	**nahmen an**

CONDITIONAL

ich	**würde annehmen**
du	**würdest annehmen**
er/sie/es	**würde annehmen**
wir	**würden annehmen**
ihr	**würdet annehmen**
sie/Sie	**würden annehmen**

PAST PARTICIPLE

angenommen

PRESENT PARTICIPLE

annehmend

EXAMPLE PHRASES

Ich **nehme an**, dass er heute nicht mehr kommt. *I assume that he isn't coming today.*
Sie **hatte angenommen**, dass sie zu der Party gehen darf. *She had assumed that she was allowed to go to the party.*
Nehmen Sie unsere Einladung **an**? *Will you accept our invitation?*

arbeiten (to work)

weak, *formed with* **haben**

PRESENT

ich	**arbeite**
du	**arbeitest**
er/sie/es	**arbeitet**
wir	**arbeiten**
ihr	**arbeitet**
sie/Sie	**arbeiten**

PRESENT SUBJUNCTIVE

ich	**arbeite**
du	**arbeitest**
er/sie/es	**arbeite**
wir	**arbeiten**
ihr	**arbeitet**
sie/Sie	**arbeiten**

PERFECT

ich	**habe gearbeitet**
du	**hast gearbeitet**
er/sie/es	**hat gearbeitet**
wir	**haben gearbeitet**
ihr	**habt gearbeitet**
sie/Sie	**haben gearbeitet**

IMPERFECT

ich	**arbeitete**
du	**arbeitetest**
er/sie/es	**arbeitete**
wir	**arbeiteten**
ihr	**arbeitetet**
sie/Sie	**arbeiteten**

FUTURE

ich	**werde arbeiten**
du	**wirst arbeiten**
er/sie/es	**wird arbeiten**
wir	**werden arbeiten**
ihr	**werdet arbeiten**
sie/Sie	**werden arbeiten**

CONDITIONAL

ich	**würde arbeiten**
du	**würdest arbeiten**
er/sie/es	**würde arbeiten**
wir	**würden arbeiten**
ihr	**würdet arbeiten**
sie/Sie	**würden arbeiten**

IMPERATIVE

arbeite!/arbeiten wir!/arbeitet!/ arbeiten Sie!

PAST PARTICIPLE

gearbeitet

PRESENT PARTICIPLE

arbeitend

EXAMPLE PHRASES

Er **arbeitet** seit einem Jahr bei der Computerfirma. *He has been working for the computer firm for a year.*
Er **hat** früher als Elektriker **gearbeitet**. *He used to work as an electrician.*
Ich **würde** nicht gern sonntags **arbeiten**. *I wouldn't like to work on Sundays.*

atmen (to breathe)

weak, *formed with* **haben**

PRESENT

ich	**atme**
du	**atmest**
er/sie/es	**atmet**
wir	**atmen**
ihr	**atmet**
sie/Sie	**atmen**

PRESENT SUBJUNCTIVE

ich	**atme**
du	**atmest**
er/sie/es	**atme**
wir	**atmen**
ihr	**atmet**
sie/Sie	**atmen**

PERFECT

ich	**habe geatmet**
du	**hast geatmet**
er/sie/es	**hat geatmet**
wir	**haben geatmet**
ihr	**habt geatmet**
sie/Sie	**haben geatmet**

IMPERFECT

ich	**atmete**
du	**atmetest**
er/sie/es	**atmete**
wir	**atmeten**
ihr	**atmetet**
sie/Sie	**atmeten**

FUTURE

ich	**werde atmen**
du	**wirst atmen**
er/sie/es	**wird atmen**
wir	**werden atmen**
ihr	**werdet atmen**
sie/Sie	**werden atmen**

CONDITIONAL

ich	**würde atmen**
du	**würdest atmen**
er/sie/es	**würde atmen**
wir	**würden atmen**
ihr	**würdet atmen**
sie/Sie	**würden atmen**

IMPERATIVE

atme!/atmen wir!/atmet!/ atmen Sie!

PAST PARTICIPLE

geatmet

PRESENT PARTICIPLE

atmend

EXAMPLE PHRASES

Sie konnte wieder frei **atmen**. *She was able to breathe freely again.*
Wir **atmeten** tief ein und aus. *We took deep breaths.*
Er **hat** ganz normal **geatmet**. *He breathed normally.*

ich = I **du** = you **er** = he/it **sie** = she/it **es** = it/he/she **wir** = we **ihr** = you **sie** = they **Sie** = you

ausreichen (to be enough)

weak, separable, *formed with* **haben**

PRESENT

ich	**reiche aus**
du	**reichst aus**
er/sie/es	**reicht aus**
wir	**reichen aus**
ihr	**reicht aus**
sie/Sie	**reichen aus**

PRESENT SUBJUNCTIVE

ich	**reiche aus**
du	**reichest aus**
er/sie/es	**reiche aus**
wir	**reichen aus**
ihr	**reichet aus**
sie/Sie	**reichen aus**

PERFECT

ich	**habe ausgereicht**
du	**hast ausgereicht**
er/sie/es	**hat ausgereicht**
wir	**haben ausgereicht**
ihr	**habt ausgereicht**
sie/Sie	**haben ausgereicht**

IMPERFECT

ich	**reichte aus**
du	**reichtest aus**
er/sie/es	**reichte aus**
wir	**reichten aus**
ihr	**reichtet aus**
sie/Sie	**reichten aus**

FUTURE

ich	**werde ausreichen**
du	**wirst ausreichen**
er/sie/es	**wird ausreichen**
wir	**werden ausreichen**
ihr	**werdet ausreichen**
sie/Sie	**werden ausreichen**

CONDITIONAL

ich	**würde ausreichen**
du	**würdest ausreichen**
er/sie/es	**würde ausreichen**
wir	**würden ausreichen**
ihr	**würdet ausreichen**
sie/Sie	**würden ausreichen**

IMPERATIVE

reich(e) aus!/reichen wir aus!/ reicht aus!/reichen Sie aus!

PAST PARTICIPLE

ausgereicht

PRESENT PARTICIPLE

ausreichend

EXAMPLE PHRASES

Das Geld hat nicht **ausgereicht**. *There wasn't enough money.*
Reicht dir das **aus**? *Is that enough for you?*
Die Zeit **reichte** nie **aus**. *There was never enough time.*

beginnen (to begin)

strong, inseparable, *formed with* **haben**

PRESENT

ich	**beginne**
du	**beginnst**
er/sie/es	**beginnt**
wir	**beginnen**
ihr	**beginnt**
sie/Sie	**beginnen**

PRESENT SUBJUNCTIVE

ich	**beginne**
du	**beginnest**
er/sie/es	**beginne**
wir	**beginnen**
ihr	**beginnet**
sie/Sie	**beginnen**

PERFECT

ich	**habe begonnen**
du	**hast begonnen**
er/sie/es	**hat begonnen**
wir	**haben begonnen**
ihr	**habt begonnen**
sie/Sie	**haben begonnen**

IMPERFECT

ich	**begann**
du	**begannst**
er/sie/es	**begann**
wir	**begannen**
ihr	**begannt**
sie/Sie	**begannen**

FUTURE

ich	**werde beginnen**
du	**wirst beginnen**
er/sie/es	**wird beginnen**
wir	**werden beginnen**
ihr	**werdet beginnen**
sie/Sie	**werden beginnen**

CONDITIONAL

ich	**würde beginnen**
du	**würdest beginnen**
er/sie/es	**würde beginnen**
wir	**würden beginnen**
ihr	**würdet beginnen**
sie/Sie	**würden beginnen**

IMPERATIVE

beginn(e)!/beginnen wir!/ beginnt!/beginnen Sie!

PAST PARTICIPLE

begonnen

PRESENT PARTICIPLE

beginnend

EXAMPLE PHRASES

Sie **begann** mit der Arbeit. *She started working.*
Die Vorstellung **beginnt** gleich. *The performance is about to begin.*
Er **hat** als Lehrling **begonnen**. *He started off as an apprentice.*

beißen (to bite)

strong, *formed with* **haben**

PRESENT

ich	**beiße**
du	**beißt**
er/sie/es	**beißt**
wir	**beißen**
ihr	**beißt**
sie/Sie	**beißen**

PERFECT

ich	**habe gebissen**
du	**hast gebissen**
er/sie/es	**hat gebissen**
wir	**haben gebissen**
ihr	**habt gebissen**
sie/Sie	**haben gebissen**

FUTURE

ich	**werde beißen**
du	**wirst beißen**
er/sie/es	**wird beißen**
wir	**werden beißen**
ihr	**werdet beißen**
sie/Sie	**werden beißen**

IMPERATIVE

beiß(e)!/beißen wir!/beißt!/ beißen Sie!

PRESENT SUBJUNCTIVE

ich	**beiße**
du	**beißest**
er/sie/es	**beiße**
wir	**beißen**
ihr	**beißet**
sie/Sie	**beißen**

IMPERFECT

ich	**biss**
du	**bissest**
er/sie/es	**biss**
wir	**bissen**
ihr	**bisst**
sie/Sie	**bissen**

CONDITIONAL

ich	**würde beißen**
du	**würdest beißen**
er/sie/es	**würde beißen**
wir	**würden beißen**
ihr	**würdet beißen**
sie/Sie	**würden beißen**

PAST PARTICIPLE

gebissen

PRESENT PARTICIPLE

beißend

EXAMPLE PHRASES

Der Hund **hat** mich **gebissen**. *The dog bit me.*
Sie **biss** in den Apfel. *She bit into the apple.*
Rosa **beißt** sich mit Orange. *Pink clashes with orange.*

bestellen (to order)

weak, inseparable, *formed with* **haben**

PRESENT

ich	**bestelle**
du	**bestellst**
er/sie/es	**bestellt**
wir	**bestellen**
ihr	**bestellt**
sie/Sie	**bestellen**

PRESENT SUBJUNCTIVE

ich	**bestelle**
du	**bestellest**
er/sie/es	**bestelle**
wir	**bestellen**
ihr	**bestellet**
sie/Sie	**bestellen**

PERFECT

ich	**habe bestellt**
du	**hast bestellt**
er/sie/es	**hat bestellt**
wir	**haben bestellt**
ihr	**habt bestellt**
sie/Sie	**haben bestellt**

IMPERFECT

ich	**bestellte**
du	**bestelltest**
er/sie/es	**bestellte**
wir	**bestellten**
ihr	**bestelltet**
sie/Sie	**bestellten**

FUTURE

ich	**werde bestellen**
du	**wirst bestellen**
er/sie/es	**wird bestellen**
wir	**werden bestellen**
ihr	**werdet bestellen**
sie/Sie	**werden bestellen**

CONDITIONAL

ich	**würde bestellen**
du	**würdest bestellen**
er/sie/es	**würde bestellen**
wir	**würden bestellen**
ihr	**würdet bestellen**
sie/Sie	**würden bestellen**

IMPERATIVE

bestell(e)!/bestellen wir!/ bestellt!/bestellen Sie!

PAST PARTICIPLE

bestellt

PRESENT PARTICIPLE

bestellend

EXAMPLE PHRASES

Wir **bestellten** einen Tisch für zwei. *We reserved a table for two.*
Ich **würde** die Karten gern im Voraus **bestellen**. *I'd like to book the tickets in advance.*
Haben Sie schon **bestellt**? *Have you ordered yet?*

bieten (to offer)

strong, *formed with* **haben**

PRESENT

ich	**biete**
du	**bietest**
er/sie/es	**bietet**
wir	**bieten**
ihr	**bietet**
sie/Sie	**bieten**

PRESENT SUBJUNCTIVE

ich	**biete**
du	**bietest**
er/sie/es	**biete**
wir	**bieten**
ihr	**bietet**
sie/Sie	**bieten**

PERFECT

ich	**habe geboten**
du	**hast geboten**
er/sie/es	**hat geboten**
wir	**haben geboten**
ihr	**habt geboten**
sie/Sie	**haben geboten**

IMPERFECT

ich	**bot**
du	**bot(e)st**
er/sie/es	**bot**
wir	**boten**
ihr	**botet**
sie/Sie	**boten**

FUTURE

ich	**werde bieten**
du	**wirst bieten**
er/sie/es	**wird bieten**
wir	**werden bieten**
ihr	**werdet bieten**
sie/Sie	**werden bieten**

CONDITIONAL

ich	**würde bieten**
du	**würdest bieten**
er/sie/es	**würde bieten**
wir	**würden bieten**
ihr	**würdet bieten**
sie/Sie	**würden bieten**

IMPERATIVE

biet(e)!/bieten wir!/bietet!/ bieten Sie!

PAST PARTICIPLE

geboten

PRESENT PARTICIPLE

bietend

EXAMPLE PHRASES

Er **bot** ihm die Hand. *He held out his hand to him.*
Für das Bild **wurden** 2000 Euro **geboten**. *There was a bid of 2000 euros for the painting.*
Diese Stadt hat nichts zu **bieten**. *This town has nothing to offer.*

ich = I **du** = you **er** = he/it **sie** = she/it **es** = it/he/she **wir** = we **ihr** = you **sie** = they **Sie** = you

bitten (to request)

strong, *formed with* **haben**

PRESENT

ich	**bitte**
du	**bittest**
er/sie/es	**bittet**
wir	**bitten**
ihr	**bittet**
sie/Sie	**bitten**

PRESENT SUBJUNCTIVE

ich	**bitte**
du	**bittest**
er/sie/es	**bitte**
wir	**bitten**
ihr	**bittet**
sie/Sie	**bitten**

PERFECT

ich	**habe gebeten**
du	**hast gebeten**
er/sie/es	**hat gebeten**
wir	**haben gebeten**
ihr	**habt gebeten**
sie/Sie	**haben gebeten**

IMPERFECT

ich	**bat**
du	**bat(e)st**
er/sie/es	**bat**
wir	**baten**
ihr	**batet**
sie/Sie	**baten**

FUTURE

ich	**werde bitten**
du	**wirst bitten**
er/sie/es	**wird bitten**
wir	**werden bitten**
ihr	**werdet bitten**
sie/Sie	**werden bitten**

CONDITIONAL

ich	**würde bitten**
du	**würdest bitten**
er/sie/es	**würde bitten**
wir	**würden bitten**
ihr	**würdet bitten**
sie/Sie	**würden bitten**

IMPERATIVE

bitt(e)!/bitten wir!/bittet!/ bitten Sie!

PAST PARTICIPLE

gebeten

PRESENT PARTICIPLE

bittend

EXAMPLE PHRASES

Sie **bat** ihn um Hilfe. *She asked him for help.*
Herr Müller lässt **bitten**. *Mr Müller will see you now.*
Man **hat** die Bevölkerung um Mithilfe **gebeten**. *The public was asked for assistance.*

bleiben (to remain)

strong, *formed with* **sein**

PRESENT

ich	**bleibe**
du	**bleibst**
er/sie/es	**bleibt**
wir	**bleiben**
ihr	**bleibt**
sie/Sie	**bleiben**

PRESENT SUBJUNCTIVE

ich	**bleibe**
du	**bleibest**
er/sie/es	**bleibe**
wir	**bleiben**
ihr	**bleibet**
sie/Sie	**bleiben**

PERFECT

ich	**bin geblieben**
du	**bist geblieben**
er/sie/es	**ist geblieben**
wir	**sind geblieben**
ihr	**seid geblieben**
sie/Sie	**sind geblieben**

IMPERFECT

ich	**blieb**
du	**bliebst**
er/sie/es	**blieb**
wir	**blieben**
ihr	**bliebt**
sie/Sie	**blieben**

FUTURE

ich	**werde bleiben**
du	**wirst bleiben**
er/sie/es	**wird bleiben**
wir	**werden bleiben**
ihr	**werdet bleiben**
sie/Sie	**werden bleiben**

CONDITIONAL

ich	**würde bleiben**
du	**würdest bleiben**
er/sie/es	**würde bleiben**
wir	**würden bleiben**
ihr	**würdet bleiben**
sie/Sie	**würden bleiben**

IMPERATIVE

bleib(e)!/bleiben wir!/bleibt!/ bleiben Sie!

PAST PARTICIPLE

geblieben

PRESENT PARTICIPLE

bleibend

EXAMPLE PHRASES

Hoffentlich **bleibt** das Wetter schön. *I hope the weather will stay fine.*
Vom Kuchen **ist** nur noch ein Stück **geblieben**. *There's only one piece of cake left.*
Dieses Erlebnis **blieb** in meiner Erinnerung. *This experience stayed with me.*

brechen (to break)

strong, *formed with* **haben/sein***

PRESENT

ich	**breche**
du	**brichst**
er/sie/es	**bricht**
wir	**brechen**
ihr	**brecht**
sie/Sie	**brechen**

PRESENT SUBJUNCTIVE

ich	**breche**
du	**brechest**
er/sie/es	**breche**
wir	**brechen**
ihr	**brechet**
sie/Sie	**brechen**

PERFECT

ich	**habe gebrochen**
du	**hast gebrochen**
er/sie/es	**hat gebrochen**
wir	**haben gebrochen**
ihr	**habt gebrochen**
sie/Sie	**haben gebrochen**

IMPERFECT

ich	**brach**
du	**brachst**
er/sie/es	**brach**
wir	**brachen**
ihr	**bracht**
sie/Sie	**brachen**

FUTURE

ich	**werde brechen**
du	**wirst brechen**
er/sie/es	**wird brechen**
wir	**werden brechen**
ihr	**werdet brechen**
sie/Sie	**werden brechen**

CONDITIONAL

ich	**würde brechen**
du	**würdest brechen**
er/sie/es	**würde brechen**
wir	**würden brechen**
ihr	**würdet brechen**
sie/Sie	**würden brechen**

IMPERATIVE

brich!/brechen wir!/brecht!/ brechen Sie!

PAST PARTICIPLE

gebrochen

PRESENT PARTICIPLE

brechend

EXAMPLE PHRASES

Mir **bricht** das Herz. *It's breaking my heart.*
Der Sturz **brach** ihm fast den Arm. *The fall almost broke his arm.*
Sie **hat** ihr Versprechen **gebrochen**. *She broke her promise.*
Das Eis **ist gebrochen**. *The ice is broken.*

*When **brechen** is used with no direct object, it is formed with **sein**.

brennen (to burn)

mixed, *formed with* **haben**

PRESENT

ich	**brenne**
du	**brennst**
er/sie/es	**brennt**
wir	**brennen**
ihr	**brennt**
sie/Sie	**brennen**

PRESENT SUBJUNCTIVE

ich	**brenne**
du	**brennest**
er/sie/es	**brenne**
wir	**brennen**
ihr	**brennet**
sie/Sie	**brennen**

PERFECT

ich	**habe gebrannt**
du	**hast gebrannt**
er/sie/es	**hat gebrannt**
wir	**haben gebrannt**
ihr	**habt gebrannt**
sie/Sie	**haben gebrannt**

IMPERFECT

ich	**brannte**
du	**branntest**
er/sie/es	**brannte**
wir	**brannten**
ihr	**branntet**
sie/Sie	**brannten**

FUTURE

ich	**werde brennen**
du	**wirst brennen**
er/sie/es	**wird brennen**
wir	**werden brennen**
ihr	**werdet brennen**
sie/Sie	**werden brennen**

CONDITIONAL

ich	**würde brennen**
du	**würdest brennen**
er/sie/es	**würde brennen**
wir	**würden brennen**
ihr	**würdet brennen**
sie/Sie	**würden brennen**

IMPERATIVE

brenn(e)!/brennen wir!/brennt!/ brennen Sie!

PAST PARTICIPLE

gebrannt

PRESENT PARTICIPLE

brennend

EXAMPLE PHRASES

Das ganze Haus **brannte**. *The entire house was on fire.*
Wir **werden** diese CD zuerst **brennen**. *We'll burn this CD first.*
Das Streichholz **brennt** nicht. *The match won't light.*

ich = I **du** = you **er** = he/it **sie** = she/it **es** = it/he/she **wir** = we **ihr** = you **sie** = they **Sie** = you

bringen (to bring)

mixed, *formed with* **haben**

PRESENT

ich	**bringe**
du	**bringst**
er/sie/es	**bringt**
wir	**bringen**
ihr	**bringt**
sie/Sie	**bringen**

PRESENT SUBJUNCTIVE

ich	**bringe**
du	**bringest**
er/sie/es	**bringe**
wir	**bringen**
ihr	**bringet**
sie/Sie	**bringen**

PERFECT

ich	**habe gebracht**
du	**hast gebracht**
er/sie/es	**hat gebracht**
wir	**haben gebracht**
ihr	**habt gebracht**
sie/Sie	**haben gebracht**

IMPERFECT

ich	**brachte**
du	**brachtest**
er/sie/es	**brachte**
wir	**brachten**
ihr	**brachtet**
sie/Sie	**brachten**

FUTURE

ich	**werde bringen**
du	**wirst bringen**
er/sie/es	**wird bringen**
wir	**werden bringen**
ihr	**werdet bringen**
sie/Sie	**werden bringen**

CONDITIONAL

ich	**würde bringen**
du	**würdest bringen**
er/sie/es	**würde bringen**
wir	**würden bringen**
ihr	**würdet bringen**
sie/Sie	**würden bringen**

IMPERATIVE

bring(e)!/bringen wir!/bringt!/ bringen Sie!

PAST PARTICIPLE

gebracht

PRESENT PARTICIPLE

bringend

EXAMPLE PHRASES

Kannst du mich zum Flughafen **bringen**? *Can you take me to the airport?*
Max **hat** mir Blumen **gebracht**. *Max brought me flowers.*
Das **brachte** mich auf eine Idee. *It gave me an idea.*

denken (to think)

mixed, *formed with* **haben**

PRESENT

ich	**denke**
du	**denkst**
er/sie/es	**denkt**
wir	**denken**
ihr	**denkt**
sie/Sie	**denken**

PERFECT

ich	**habe gedacht**
du	**hast gedacht**
er/sie/es	**hat gedacht**
wir	**haben gedacht**
ihr	**habt gedacht**
sie/Sie	**haben gedacht**

FUTURE

ich	**werde denken**
du	**wirst denken**
er/sie/es	**wird denken**
wir	**werden denken**
ihr	**werdet denken**
sie/Sie	**werden denken**

IMPERATIVE

denk(e)!/denken wir!/denkt!/ denken Sie!

PRESENT SUBJUNCTIVE

ich	**denke**
du	**denkest**
er/sie/es	**denke**
wir	**denken**
ihr	**denket**
sie/Sie	**denken**

IMPERFECT

ich	**dachte**
du	**dachtest**
er/sie/es	**dachte**
wir	**dachten**
ihr	**dachtet**
sie/Sie	**dachten**

CONDITIONAL

ich	**würde denken**
du	**würdest denken**
er/sie/es	**würde denken**
wir	**würden denken**
ihr	**würdet denken**
sie/Sie	**würden denken**

PAST PARTICIPLE

gedacht

PRESENT PARTICIPLE

denkend

EXAMPLE PHRASES

Wie **denken** Sie darüber? *What do you think about it?*
Das **war** für ihn **gedacht**. *It was meant for him.*
Es war das Erste, woran ich **dachte**. *It was the first thing I thought of.*

durchsetzen (to enforce)

weak, separable, *formed with* **haben**

PRESENT

ich	**setze durch**
du	**setzt durch**
er/sie/es	**setzt durch**
wir	**setzen durch**
ihr	**setzt durch**
sie/Sie	**setzen durch**

PRESENT SUBJUNCTIVE

ich	**setze durch**
du	**setzest durch**
er/sie/es	**setze durch**
wir	**setzen durch**
ihr	**setzet durch**
sie/Sie	**setzen durch**

PERFECT

ich	**habe durchgesetzt**
du	**hast durchgesetzt**
er/sie/es	**hat durchgesetzt**
wir	**haben durchgesetzt**
ihr	**habt durchgesetzt**
sie/Sie	**haben durchgesetzt**

IMPERFECT

ich	**setzte durch**
du	**setztest durch**
er/sie/es	**setzte durch**
wir	**setzten durch**
ihr	**setztet durch**
sie/Sie	**setzten durch**

FUTURE

ich	**werde durchsetzen**
du	**wirst durchsetzen**
er/sie/es	**wird durchsetzen**
wir	**werden durchsetzen**
ihr	**werdet durchsetzen**
sie/Sie	**werden durchsetzen**

CONDITIONAL

ich	**würde durchsetzen**
du	**würdest durchsetzen**
er/sie/es	**würde durchsetzen**
wir	**würden durchsetzen**
ihr	**würdet durchsetzen**
sie/Sie	**würden durchsetzen**

IMPERATIVE

setz(e) durch!/setzen wir durch!/ setzt durch!/setzen Sie durch!

PAST PARTICIPLE

durchgesetzt

PRESENT PARTICIPLE

durchsetzend

EXAMPLE PHRASES

Sie **setzt** immer ihren Willen **durch**. *She always gets her own way.*
Er kann sich nicht **durchsetzen**. *He doesn't know how to assert himself.*
Ich **habe** mich mit meinem Vorschlag **durchgesetzt**. *They accepted my suggestion.*

dürfen (to be allowed to)

modal, *formed with* **haben**

PRESENT

ich	**darf**
du	**darfst**
er/sie/es	**darf**
wir	**dürfen**
ihr	**dürft**
sie/Sie	**dürfen**

PERFECT

ich	**habe gedurft/dürfen**
du	**hast gedurft/dürfen**
er/sie/es	**hat gedurft/dürfen**
wir	**haben gedurft/dürfen**
ihr	**habt gedurft/dürfen**
sie/Sie	**haben gedurft/dürfen**

FUTURE

ich	**werde dürfen**
du	**wirst dürfen**
er/sie/es	**wird dürfen**
wir	**werden dürfen**
ihr	**werdet dürfen**
sie/Sie	**werden dürfen**

PRESENT SUBJUNCTIVE

ich	**dürfe**
du	**dürfest**
er/sie/es	**dürfe**
wir	**dürfen**
ihr	**dürfet**
sie/Sie	**dürfen**

IMPERFECT

ich	**durfte**
du	**durftest**
er/sie/es	**durfte**
wir	**durften**
ihr	**durftet**
sie/Sie	**durften**

CONDITIONAL

ich	**würde dürfen**
du	**würdest dürfen**
er/sie/es	**würde dürfen**
wir	**würden dürfen**
ihr	**würdet dürfen**
sie/Sie	**würden dürfen**

PAST PARTICIPLE

gedurft/dürfen*

PRESENT PARTICIPLE

dürfend

**This form is used when combined with another infinitive.*

EXAMPLE PHRASES

Darf ich ins Kino? *Can I go to the cinema?*
Das **würde** ich zu Hause nicht **dürfen**. *I wouldn't be allowed to do that at home.*
Das **dürfen** Sie mir glauben. *You can take my word for it.*

empfehlen (to recommend) strong, inseparable, *formed with* **haben**

PRESENT

ich	**empfehle**
du	**empfiehlst**
er/sie/es	**empfiehlt**
wir	**empfehlen**
ihr	**empfehlt**
sie/Sie	**empfehlen**

PERFECT

ich	**habe empfohlen**
du	**hast empfohlen**
er/sie/es	**hat empfohlen**
wir	**haben empfohlen**
ihr	**habt empfohlen**
sie/Sie	**haben empfohlen**

FUTURE

ich	**werde empfehlen**
du	**wirst empfehlen**
er/sie/es	**wird empfehlen**
wir	**werden empfehlen**
ihr	**werdet empfehlen**
sie/Sie	**werden empfehlen**

IMPERATIVE

empfiehl!/empfehlen wir!/ empfehlt!/empfehlen Sie!

PRESENT SUBJUNCTIVE

ich	**empfehle**
du	**empfehlest**
er/sie/es	**empfehle**
wir	**empfehlen**
ihr	**empfehlet**
sie/Sie	**empfehlen**

IMPERFECT

ich	**empfahl**
du	**empfahlst**
er/sie/es	**empfahl**
wir	**empfahlen**
ihr	**empfahlt**
sie/Sie	**empfahlen**

CONDITIONAL

ich	**würde empfehlen**
du	**würdest empfehlen**
er/sie/es	**würde empfehlen**
wir	**würden empfehlen**
ihr	**würdet empfehlen**
sie/Sie	**würden empfehlen**

PAST PARTICIPLE

empfohlen

PRESENT PARTICIPLE

empfehlend

EXAMPLE PHRASES

Ich **würde** Ihnen **empfehlen**, zu gehen. *I would advise you to go.*
Was **empfiehlst** du mir zu tun? *What would you recommend I do?*
Dieses Restaurant **wurde** uns **empfohlen**. *This restaurant has been recommended to us.*

entdecken (to discover)

weak, inseparable, *formed with* **haben**

PRESENT

ich	**entdecke**
du	**entdeckst**
er/sie/es	**entdeckt**
wir	**entdecken**
ihr	**entdeckt**
sie/Sie	**entdecken**

PRESENT SUBJUNCTIVE

ich	**entdecke**
du	**entdeckest**
er/sie/es	**entdecke**
wir	**entdecken**
ihr	**entdecket**
sie/Sie	**entdecken**

PERFECT

ich	**habe entdeckt**
du	**hast entdeckt**
er/sie/es	**hat entdeckt**
wir	**haben entdeckt**
ihr	**habt entdeckt**
sie/Sie	**haben entdeckt**

IMPERFECT

ich	**entdeckte**
du	**entdecktest**
er/sie/es	**entdeckte**
wir	**entdeckten**
ihr	**entdecktet**
sie/Sie	**entdeckten**

FUTURE

ich	**werde entdecken**
du	**wirst entdecken**
er/sie/es	**wird entdecken**
wir	**werden entdecken**
ihr	**werdet entdecken**
sie/Sie	**werden entdecken**

CONDITIONAL

ich	**würde entdecken**
du	**würdest entdecken**
er/sie/es	**würde entdecken**
wir	**würden entdecken**
ihr	**würdet entdecken**
sie/Sie	**würden entdecken**

IMPERATIVE

entdeck(e)!/entdecken wir!/ entdeckt!/entdecken Sie!

PAST PARTICIPLE

entdeckt

PRESENT PARTICIPLE

entdeckend

EXAMPLE PHRASES

Kolumbus **hat** Amerika **entdeckt**. *Columbus discovered America.*
Ich **entdecke** im Park oft neue Insekten. *I often discover new insects in the park.*
Er **entdeckte** sie in der Menge. *He spotted her in the crowd.*

ich = I **du** = you **er** = he/it **sie** = she/it **es** = it/he/she **wir** = we **ihr** = you **sie** = they **Sie** = you

erzählen (to tell)

weak, inseparable, *formed with* **haben**

PRESENT

ich	**erzähle**
du	**erzählst**
er/sie/es	**erzählt**
wir	**erzählen**
ihr	**erzählt**
sie/Sie	**erzählen**

PRESENT SUBJUNCTIVE

ich	**erzähle**
du	**erzählest**
er/sie/es	**erzähle**
wir	**erzählen**
ihr	**erzählet**
sie/Sie	**erzählen**

PERFECT

ich	**habe erzählt**
du	**hast erzählt**
er/sie/es	**hat erzählt**
wir	**haben erzählt**
ihr	**habt erzählt**
sie/Sie	**haben erzählt**

IMPERFECT

ich	**erzählte**
du	**erzähltest**
er/sie/es	**erzählte**
wir	**erzählten**
ihr	**erzähltet**
sie/Sie	**erzählten**

FUTURE

ich	**werde erzählen**
du	**wirst erzählen**
er/sie/es	**wird erzählen**
wir	**werden erzählen**
ihr	**werdet erzählen**
sie/Sie	**werden erzählen**

CONDITIONAL

ich	**würde erzählen**
du	**würdest erzählen**
er/sie/es	**würde erzählen**
wir	**würden erzählen**
ihr	**würdet erzählen**
sie/Sie	**würden erzählen**

IMPERATIVE

erzähl(e)!/erzählen wir!/ erzählt!/erzählen Sie!

PAST PARTICIPLE

erzählt

PRESENT PARTICIPLE

erzählend

EXAMPLE PHRASES

Er **hat** mir **erzählt**, dass er schon oft in dieser Pizzeria war. *He told me that he has often been to this pizzeria.*
Sie **erzählte** uns ihren Traum. *She told us about her dream.*
Man **erzählt** sich, dass er Millionär ist. *People say that he is a millionaire.*

essen (to eat)

strong, *formed with* **haben**

PRESENT

ich	**esse**
du	**isst**
er/sie/es	**isst**
wir	**essen**
ihr	**esst**
sie/Sie	**essen**

PRESENT SUBJUNCTIVE

ich	**esse**
du	**essest**
er/sie/es	**esse**
wir	**essen**
ihr	**esset**
sie/Sie	**essen**

PERFECT

ich	**habe gegessen**
du	**hast gegessen**
er/sie/es	**hat gegessen**
wir	**haben gegessen**
ihr	**habt gegessen**
sie/Sie	**haben gegessen**

IMPERFECT

ich	**aß**
du	**aßest**
er/sie/es	**aß**
wir	**aßen**
ihr	**aßt**
sie/Sie	**aßen**

FUTURE

ich	**werde essen**
du	**wirst essen**
er/sie/es	**wird essen**
wir	**werden essen**
ihr	**werdet essen**
sie/Sie	**werden essen**

CONDITIONAL

ich	**würde essen**
du	**würdest essen**
er/sie/es	**würde essen**
wir	**würden essen**
ihr	**würdet essen**
sie/Sie	**würden essen**

IMPERATIVE

iss!/essen wir!/esst!/essen Sie!

PAST PARTICIPLE

gegessen

PRESENT PARTICIPLE

essend

EXAMPLE PHRASES

Ich **esse** kein Fleisch. *I don't eat meat.*
Wir **haben** nichts **gegessen**. *We haven't had anything to eat.*
Ich möchte etwas **essen**. *I'd like something to eat.*

fahren (to drive; to go)

strong, *formed with* **haben/sein***

PRESENT

ich	**fahre**
du	**fährst**
er/sie/es	**fährt**
wir	**fahren**
ihr	**fahrt**
sie/Sie	**fahren**

PERFECT

ich	**bin gefahren**
du	**bist gefahren**
er/sie/es	**ist gefahren**
wir	**sind gefahren**
ihr	**seid gefahren**
sie/Sie	**sind gefahren**

FUTURE

ich	**werde fahren**
du	**wirst fahren**
er/sie/es	**wird fahren**
wir	**werden fahren**
ihr	**werdet fahren**
sie/Sie	**werden fahren**

IMPERATIVE

fahr(e)!/fahren wir!/fahrt!/ fahren Sie!

PRESENT SUBJUNCTIVE

ich	**fahre**
du	**fahrest**
er/sie/es	**fahre**
wir	**fahren**
ihr	**fahret**
sie/Sie	**fahren**

IMPERFECT

ich	**fuhr**
du	**fuhrst**
er/sie/es	**fuhr**
wir	**fuhren**
ihr	**fuhrt**
sie/Sie	**fuhren**

CONDITIONAL

ich	**würde fahren**
du	**würdest fahren**
er/sie/es	**würde fahren**
wir	**würden fahren**
ihr	**würdet fahren**
sie/Sie	**würden fahren**

PAST PARTICIPLE

gefahren

PRESENT PARTICIPLE

fahrend

EXAMPLE PHRASES

Sie **fahren** mit dem Bus in die Schule. *They go to school by bus.*
Rechts **fahren**! *Drive on the right!*
Ich **bin** mit der Familie nach Spanien **gefahren**. *I went to Spain with my family.*
Sie **hat** das Auto **gefahren**. *She drove the car.*

*When **fahren** is used with a direct object, it is formed with **haben**.

ich = I **du** = you **er** = he/it **sie** = she/it **es** = it/he/she **wir** = we **ihr** = you **sie** = they **Sie** = you

fallen (to fall)

strong, *formed with* **sein**

PRESENT

ich	**falle**
du	**fällst**
er/sie/es	**fällt**
wir	**fallen**
ihr	**fallt**
sie/Sie	**fallen**

PERFECT

ich	**bin gefallen**
du	**bist gefallen**
er/sie/es	**ist gefallen**
wir	**sind gefallen**
ihr	**seid gefallen**
sie/Sie	**sind gefallen**

FUTURE

ich	**werde fallen**
du	**wirst fallen**
er/sie/es	**wird fallen**
wir	**werden fallen**
ihr	**werdet fallen**
sie/Sie	**werden fallen**

IMPERATIVE

fall(e)!/fallen wir!/fallt!/ fallen Sie!

PRESENT SUBJUNCTIVE

ich	**falle**
du	**fallest**
er/sie/es	**falle**
wir	**fallen**
ihr	**fallet**
sie/Sie	**fallen**

IMPERFECT

ich	**fiel**
du	**fielst**
er/sie/es	**fiel**
wir	**fielen**
ihr	**fielt**
sie/Sie	**fielen**

CONDITIONAL

ich	**würde fallen**
du	**würdest fallen**
er/sie/es	**würde fallen**
wir	**würden fallen**
ihr	**würdet fallen**
sie/Sie	**würden fallen**

PAST PARTICIPLE

gefallen

PRESENT PARTICIPLE

fallend

EXAMPLE PHRASES

Er **fiel** vom Fahrrad. *He fell off his bike.*
Ich **bin** durch die Prüfung **gefallen**. *I failed my exam.*
Die Aktien **fielen** im Kurs. *Share prices fell.*

fangen (to catch)

strong, *formed with* **haben**

PRESENT

ich	**fange**
du	**fängst**
er/sie/es	**fängt**
wir	**fangen**
ihr	**fangt**
sie/Sie	**fangen**

PRESENT SUBJUNCTIVE

ich	**fange**
du	**fangest**
er/sie/es	**fange**
wir	**fangen**
ihr	**fanget**
sie/Sie	**fangen**

PERFECT

ich	**habe gefangen**
du	**hast gefangen**
er/sie/es	**hat gefangen**
wir	**haben gefangen**
ihr	**habt gefangen**
sie/Sie	**haben gefangen**

IMPERFECT

ich	**fing**
du	**fingst**
er/sie/es	**fing**
wir	**fingen**
ihr	**fingt**
sie/Sie	**fingen**

FUTURE

ich	**werde fangen**
du	**wirst fangen**
er/sie/es	**wird fangen**
wir	**werden fangen**
ihr	**werdet fangen**
sie/Sie	**werden fangen**

CONDITIONAL

ich	**würde fangen**
du	**würdest fangen**
er/sie/es	**würde fangen**
wir	**würden fangen**
ihr	**würdet fangen**
sie/Sie	**würden fangen**

IMPERATIVE

fang(e)!/fangen wir!/ fangt!/fangen Sie!

PAST PARTICIPLE

gefangen

PRESENT PARTICIPLE

fangend

EXAMPLE PHRASES

Ich **fing** den Ball. *I caught the ball.*
Die Polizei **hat** die Verbrecher **gefangen**. *The police caught the criminals.*
Die Katze **fing** die Maus. *The cat caught the mouse.*

finden (to find)

strong, *formed with* **haben**

PRESENT

ich	**finde**
du	**findest**
er/sie/es	**findet**
wir	**finden**
ihr	**findet**
sie/Sie	**finden**

PRESENT SUBJUNCTIVE

ich	**finde**
du	**findest**
er/sie/es	**finde**
wir	**finden**
ihr	**findet**
sie/Sie	**finden**

PERFECT

ich	**habe gefunden**
du	**hast gefunden**
er/sie/es	**hat gefunden**
wir	**haben gefunden**
ihr	**habt gefunden**
sie/Sie	**haben gefunden**

IMPERFECT

ich	**fand**
du	**fand(e)st**
er/sie/es	**fand**
wir	**fanden**
ihr	**fandet**
sie/Sie	**fanden**

FUTURE

ich	**werde finden**
du	**wirst finden**
er/sie/es	**wird finden**
wir	**werden finden**
ihr	**werdet finden**
sie/Sie	**werden finden**

CONDITIONAL

ich	**würde finden**
du	**würdest finden**
er/sie/es	**würde finden**
wir	**würden finden**
ihr	**würdet finden**
sie/Sie	**würden finden**

IMPERATIVE

find(e)!/finden wir!/findet!/ finden Sie!

PAST PARTICIPLE

gefunden

PRESENT PARTICIPLE

findend

EXAMPLE PHRASES

Hast du deine Brieftasche **gefunden**? *Have you found your wallet?*
Er **fand** den Mut, sie zu fragen. *He found the courage to ask her.*
Ich **finde**, sie ist eine gute Lehrerin. *I think she's a good teacher.*

fliegen (to fly)

strong, *formed with* **haben/sein***

PRESENT

ich	**fliege**
du	**fliegst**
er/sie/es	**fliegt**
wir	**fliegen**
ihr	**fliegt**
sie/Sie	**fliegen**

PERFECT

ich	**bin geflogen**
du	**bist geflogen**
er/sie/es	**ist geflogen**
wir	**sind geflogen**
ihr	**seid geflogen**
sie/Sie	**sind geflogen**

FUTURE

ich	**werde fliegen**
du	**wirst fliegen**
er/sie/es	**wird fliegen**
wir	**werden fliegen**
ihr	**werdet fliegen**
sie/Sie	**werden fliegen**

IMPERATIVE

flieg(e)!/fliegen wir!/fliegt!/ fliegen Sie!

PRESENT SUBJUNCTIVE

ich	**fliege**
du	**fliegest**
er/sie/es	**fliege**
wir	**fliegen**
ihr	**flieget**
sie/Sie	**fliegen**

IMPERFECT

ich	**flog**
du	**flogst**
er/sie/es	**flog**
wir	**flogen**
ihr	**flogt**
sie/Sie	**flogen**

CONDITIONAL

ich	**würde fliegen**
du	**würdest fliegen**
er/sie/es	**würde fliegen**
wir	**würden fliegen**
ihr	**würdet fliegen**
sie/Sie	**würden fliegen**

PAST PARTICIPLE

geflogen

PRESENT PARTICIPLE

fliegend

EXAMPLE PHRASES

Wir **flogen** zusammen nach Spanien. *We flew together to Spain.*
Die Zeit **fliegt**. *Time flies.*
Er **ist** von der Schule **geflogen**. *He was thrown out of school.*

*When **fliegen** is used with a direct object, it is formed with **haben**.

fliehen (to flee)

strong, *formed with* **haben/sein***

PRESENT

ich	**fliehe**
du	**fliehst**
er/sie/es	**flieht**
wir	**fliehen**
ihr	**flieht**
sie/Sie	**fliehen**

PRESENT SUBJUNCTIVE

ich	**fliehe**
du	**fliehest**
er/sie/es	**fliehe**
wir	**fliehen**
ihr	**fliehet**
sie/Sie	**fliehen**

PERFECT

ich	**bin geflohen**
du	**bist geflohen**
er/sie/es	**ist geflohen**
wir	**sind geflohen**
ihr	**seid geflohen**
sie/Sie	**sind geflohen**

IMPERFECT

ich	**floh**
du	**flohst**
er/sie/es	**floh**
wir	**flohen**
ihr	**floht**
sie/Sie	**flohen**

FUTURE

ich	**werde fliehen**
du	**wirst fliehen**
er/sie/es	**wird fliehen**
wir	**werden fliehen**
ihr	**werdet fliehen**
sie/Sie	**werden fliehen**

CONDITIONAL

ich	**würde fliehen**
du	**würdest fliehen**
er/sie/es	**würde fliehen**
wir	**würden fliehen**
ihr	**würdet fliehen**
sie/Sie	**würden fliehen**

IMPERATIVE

flieh(e)!/fliehen wir!/flieht!/ fliehen Sie!

PAST PARTICIPLE

geflohen

PRESENT PARTICIPLE

fliehend

EXAMPLE PHRASES

Sie **floh** vor der Polizei. *She fled from the police.*
Es gelang ihm, aus dem Gefängnis zu **fliehen**. *He managed to escape from prison.*
Sie **sind** aus Afghanistan **geflohen**. *They are refugees from Afghanistan.*

*When **fliehen** is used with a direct object, it is formed with **haben**.

ich = I **du** = you **er** = he/it **sie** = she/it **es** = it/he/she **wir** = we **ihr** = you **sie** = they **Sie** = you

fließen (to flow)

strong, *formed with* **sein**

PRESENT

ich	**fließe**
du	**fließt**
er/sie/es	**fließt**
wir	**fließen**
ihr	**fließt**
sie/Sie	**fließen**

PRESENT SUBJUNCTIVE

ich	**fließe**
du	**fließest**
er/sie/es	**fließe**
wir	**fließen**
ihr	**fließet**
sie/Sie	**fließen**

PERFECT

ich	**bin geflossen**
du	**bist geflossen**
er/sie/es	**ist geflossen**
wir	**sind geflossen**
ihr	**seid geflossen**
sie/Sie	**sind geflossen**

IMPERFECT

ich	**floss**
du	**flossest**
er/sie/es	**floss**
wir	**flossen**
ihr	**flosst**
sie/Sie	**flossen**

FUTURE

ich	**werde fließen**
du	**wirst fließen**
er/sie/es	**wird fließen**
wir	**werden fließen**
ihr	**werdet fließen**
sie/Sie	**werden fließen**

CONDITIONAL

ich	**würde fließen**
du	**würdest fließen**
er/sie/es	**würde fließen**
wir	**würden fließen**
ihr	**würdet fließen**
sie/Sie	**würden fließen**

IMPERATIVE

fließ(e)!/fließen wir!/fließt!/ fließen Sie!

PAST PARTICIPLE

geflossen

PRESENT PARTICIPLE

fließend

EXAMPLE PHRASES

Welcher Fluss **fließt** durch Hamburg? *Which river flows through Hamburg?*
Die Tränen **flossen** in Strömen. *There were floods of tears.*
Es **ist** genug Blut **geflossen**. *Enough blood has been spilled.*

ich = I **du** = you **er** = he/it **sie** = she/it **es** = it/he/she **wir** = we **ihr** = you **sie** = they **Sie** = you

geben (to give)

strong, *formed with* **haben**

PRESENT

ich	**gebe**
du	**gibst**
er/sie/es	**gibt**
wir	**geben**
ihr	**gebt**
sie/Sie	**geben**

PRESENT SUBJUNCTIVE

ich	**gebe**
du	**gebest**
er/sie/es	**gebe**
wir	**geben**
ihr	**gebet**
sie/Sie	**geben**

PERFECT

ich	**habe gegeben**
du	**hast gegeben**
er/sie/es	**hat gegeben**
wir	**haben gegeben**
ihr	**habt gegeben**
sie/Sie	**haben gegeben**

IMPERFECT

ich	**gab**
du	**gabst**
er/sie/es	**gab**
wir	**gaben**
ihr	**gabt**
sie/Sie	**gaben**

FUTURE

ich	**werde geben**
du	**wirst geben**
er/sie/es	**wird geben**
wir	**werden geben**
ihr	**werdet geben**
sie/Sie	**werden geben**

CONDITIONAL

ich	**würde geben**
du	**würdest geben**
er/sie/es	**würde geben**
wir	**würden geben**
ihr	**würdet geben**
sie/Sie	**würden geben**

IMPERATIVE

gib!/geben wir!/gebt!/
geben Sie!

PAST PARTICIPLE

gegeben

PRESENT PARTICIPLE

gebend

EXAMPLE PHRASES

Er **gab** mir das Geld für den Laptop. *He gave me the money for the laptop.*
Was **gibt** es im Kino? *What's on at the cinema?*
Wir **würden** alles darum **geben**, ins Finale zu kommen. *We would give anything to reach the finals.*

gehen (to go)

strong, *formed with* **sein**

PRESENT

ich	**gehe**
du	**gehst**
er/sie/es	**geht**
wir	**gehen**
ihr	**geht**
sie/Sie	**gehen**

PRESENT SUBJUNCTIVE

ich	**gehe**
du	**gehest**
er/sie/es	**gehe**
wir	**gehen**
ihr	**gehet**
sie/Sie	**gehen**

PERFECT

ich	**bin gegangen**
du	**bist gegangen**
er/sie/es	**ist gegangen**
wir	**sind gegangen**
ihr	**seid gegangen**
sie/Sie	**sind gegangen**

IMPERFECT

ich	**ging**
du	**gingst**
er/sie/es	**ging**
wir	**gingen**
ihr	**gingt**
sie/Sie	**gingen**

FUTURE

ich	**werde gehen**
du	**wirst gehen**
er/sie/es	**wird gehen**
wir	**werden gehen**
ihr	**werdet gehen**
sie/Sie	**werden gehen**

CONDITIONAL

ich	**würde gehen**
du	**würdest gehen**
er/sie/es	**würde gehen**
wir	**würden gehen**
ihr	**würdet gehen**
sie/Sie	**würden gehen**

IMPERATIVE

geh(e)!/gehen wir!/geht!/ gehen Sie!

PAST PARTICIPLE

gegangen

PRESENT PARTICIPLE

gehend

EXAMPLE PHRASES

Die Kinder **gingen** ins Haus. *The children went into the house.*
Wie **geht** es dir? *How are you?*
Wir **sind** gestern schwimmen **gegangen**. *We went swimming yesterday.*

ich = I **du** = you **er** = he/it **sie** = she/it **es** = it/he/she **wir** = we **ihr** = you **sie** = they **Sie** = you

gewinnen (to win)

strong, inseparable, *formed with* **haben**

PRESENT

ich	**gewinne**
du	**gewinnst**
er/sie/es	**gewinnt**
wir	**gewinnen**
ihr	**gewinnt**
sie/Sie	**gewinnen**

PRESENT SUBJUNCTIVE

ich	**gewinne**
du	**gewinnest**
er/sie/es	**gewinne**
wir	**gewinnen**
ihr	**gewinnet**
sie/Sie	**gewinnen**

PERFECT

ich	**habe gewonnen**
du	**hast gewonnen**
er/sie/es	**hat gewonnen**
wir	**haben gewonnen**
ihr	**habt gewonnen**
sie/Sie	**haben gewonnen**

IMPERFECT

ich	**gewann**
du	**gewannst**
er/sie/es	**gewann**
wir	**gewannen**
ihr	**gewannt**
sie/Sie	**gewannen**

FUTURE

ich	**werde gewinnen**
du	**wirst gewinnen**
er/sie/es	**wird gewinnen**
wir	**werden gewinnen**
ihr	**werdet gewinnen**
sie/Sie	**werden gewinnen**

CONDITIONAL

ich	**würde gewinnen**
du	**würdest gewinnen**
er/sie/es	**würde gewinnen**
wir	**würden gewinnen**
ihr	**würdet gewinnen**
sie/Sie	**würden gewinnen**

IMPERATIVE

gewinn(e)!/gewinnen wir!/ gewinnt!/gewinnen Sie!

PAST PARTICIPLE

gewonnen

PRESENT PARTICIPLE

gewinnend

EXAMPLE PHRASES

Er **hat** den ersten Preis **gewonnen**. *He won first prize.*
Am liebsten **würde** ich im Lotto **gewinnen**. *What I'd love most is to win the lottery.*
Das Flugzeug **gewann** an Höhe. *The plane gained altitude.*

grüßen (to greet)

weak, *formed with* **haben**

PRESENT

ich	**grüße**
du	**grüßt**
er/sie/es	**grüßt**
wir	**grüßen**
ihr	**grüßt**
sie/Sie	**grüßen**

PRESENT SUBJUNCTIVE

ich	**grüße**
du	**grüßest**
er/sie/es	**grüße**
wir	**grüßen**
ihr	**grüßet**
sie/Sie	**grüßen**

PERFECT

ich	**habe gegrüßt**
du	**hast gegrüßt**
er/sie/es	**hat gegrüßt**
wir	**haben gegrüßt**
ihr	**habt gegrüßt**
sie/Sie	**haben gegrüßt**

IMPERFECT

ich	**grüßte**
du	**grüßtest**
er/sie/es	**grüßte**
wir	**grüßten**
ihr	**grüßtet**
sie/Sie	**grüßten**

FUTURE

ich	**werde grüßen**
du	**wirst grüßen**
er/sie/es	**wird grüßen**
wir	**werden grüßen**
ihr	**werdet grüßen**
sie/Sie	**werden grüßen**

CONDITIONAL

ich	**würde grüßen**
du	**würdest grüßen**
er/sie/es	**würde grüßen**
wir	**würden grüßen**
ihr	**würdet grüßen**
sie/Sie	**würden grüßen**

IMPERATIVE

grüß(e)!/grüßen wir!/grüßt!/ grüßen Sie!

PAST PARTICIPLE

gegrüßt

PRESENT PARTICIPLE

grüßend

EXAMPLE PHRASES

Unsere Nachbarin **grüßt** uns jeden Morgen. *Our neighbour greets us every morning.*
Er **hat** mich nicht **gegrüßt**. *He didn't say hello to me.*
Oliver lässt dich **grüßen**. *Oliver sends his regards.*

haben (to have)

strong, *formed with* **haben**

PRESENT

ich	**habe**
du	**hast**
er/sie/es	**hat**
wir	**haben**
ihr	**habt**
sie/Sie	**haben**

PRESENT SUBJUNCTIVE

ich	**habe**
du	**habest**
er/sie/es	**habe**
wir	**haben**
ihr	**habet**
sie/Sie	**haben**

PERFECT

ich	**habe gehabt**
du	**hast gehabt**
er/sie/es	**hat gehabt**
wir	**haben gehabt**
ihr	**habt gehabt**
sie/Sie	**haben gehabt**

IMPERFECT

ich	**hatte**
du	**hattest**
er/sie/es	**hatte**
wir	**hatten**
ihr	**hattet**
sie/Sie	**hatten**

FUTURE

ich	**werde haben**
du	**wirst haben**
er/sie/es	**wird haben**
wir	**werden haben**
ihr	**werdet haben**
sie/Sie	**werden haben**

CONDITIONAL

ich	**würde haben**
du	**würdest haben**
er/sie/es	**würde haben**
wir	**würden haben**
ihr	**würdet haben**
sie/Sie	**würden haben**

IMPERATIVE

hab(e)!/haben wir!/habt!/ haben Sie!

PAST PARTICIPLE

gehabt

PRESENT PARTICIPLE

habend

EXAMPLE PHRASES

Hast du eine Schwester? *Have you got a sister?*
Er **hatte** Hunger. *He was hungry.*
Sie **hat** heute Geburtstag. *It's her birthday today.*

halten (to hold)

strong, *formed with* **haben**

PRESENT

ich	**halte**
du	**hältst**
er/sie/es	**hält**
wir	**halten**
ihr	**haltet**
sie/Sie	**halten**

PRESENT SUBJUNCTIVE

ich	**halte**
du	**haltest**
er/sie/es	**halte**
wir	**halten**
ihr	**haltet**
sie/Sie	**halten**

PERFECT

ich	**habe gehalten**
du	**hast gehalten**
er/sie/es	**hat gehalten**
wir	**haben gehalten**
ihr	**habt gehalten**
sie/Sie	**haben gehalten**

IMPERFECT

ich	**hielt**
du	**hielt(e)st**
er/sie/es	**hielt**
wir	**hielten**
ihr	**hieltet**
sie/Sie	**hielten**

FUTURE

ich	**werde halten**
du	**wirst halten**
er/sie/es	**wird halten**
wir	**werden halten**
ihr	**werdet halten**
sie/Sie	**werden halten**

CONDITIONAL

ich	**würde halten**
du	**würdest halten**
er/sie/es	**würde halten**
wir	**würden halten**
ihr	**würdet halten**
sie/Sie	**würden halten**

IMPERATIVE

halt(e)!/halten wir!/haltet!/ halten Sie!

PAST PARTICIPLE

gehalten

PRESENT PARTICIPLE

haltend

EXAMPLE PHRASES

Kannst du das mal **halten**? *Can you hold that for a moment?*
Der Bus **hielt** vor dem Rathaus. *The bus stopped in front of the town hall.*
Ich **habe** sie für deine Mutter **gehalten**. *I took her for your mother.*

ich = I **du** = you **er** = he/it **sie** = she/it **es** = it/he/she **wir** = we **ihr** = you **sie** = they **Sie** = you

handeln (to trade; to act)

weak, *formed with* **haben**

PRESENT

ich	**handle**
du	**handelst**
er/sie/es	**handelt**
wir	**handeln**
ihr	**handelt**
sie/Sie	**handeln**

PRESENT SUBJUNCTIVE

ich	**handle**
du	**handelst**
er/sie/es	**hand(e)le**
wir	**handeln**
ihr	**handelt**
sie/Sie	**handeln**

PERFECT

ich	**habe gehandelt**
du	**hast gehandelt**
er/sie/es	**hat gehandelt**
wir	**haben gehandelt**
ihr	**habt gehandelt**
sie/Sie	**haben gehandelt**

IMPERFECT

ich	**handelte**
du	**handeltest**
er/sie/es	**handelte**
wir	**handelten**
ihr	**handeltet**
sie/Sie	**handelten**

FUTURE

ich	**werde handeln**
du	**wirst handeln**
er/sie/es	**wird handeln**
wir	**werden handeln**
ihr	**werdet handeln**
sie/Sie	**werden handeln**

CONDITIONAL

ich	**würde handeln**
du	**würdest handeln**
er/sie/es	**würde handeln**
wir	**würden handeln**
ihr	**würdet handeln**
sie/Sie	**würden handeln**

IMPERATIVE

handle!/handeln wir!/handelt!/ handeln Sie

PAST PARTICIPLE

gehandelt

PRESENT PARTICIPLE

handelnd

EXAMPLE PHRASES

Die Geschichte **handelte** von einem alten Mann. *The story was about an old man.*
Wir müssen schnell **handeln**. *We must act quickly.*
Er **hat** früher in Gebrauchtwagen **gehandelt**. *He used to deal in used cars.*

ich = I **du** = you **er** = he/it **sie** = she/it **es** = it/he/she **wir** = we **ihr** = you **sie** = they **Sie** = you

hängen* (to hang)

strong, *formed with* **haben**

PRESENT

ich	**hänge**
du	**hängst**
er/sie/es	**hängt**
wir	**hängen**
ihr	**hängt**
sie/Sie	**hängen**

PRESENT SUBJUNCTIVE

ich	**hänge**
du	**hängest**
er/sie/es	**hänge**
wir	**hängen**
ihr	**hänget**
sie/Sie	**hängen**

PERFECT

ich	**habe gehangen/gehängt**
du	**hast gehangen/gehängt**
er/sie/es	**hat gehangen/gehängt**
wir	**haben gehangen/gehängt**
ihr	**habt gehangen/gehängt**
sie/Sie	**haben gehangen/gehängt**

IMPERFECT

ich	**hing**
du	**hingst**
er/sie/es	**hing**
wir	**hingen**
ihr	**hingt**
sie/Sie	**hingen**

FUTURE

ich	**werde hängen**
du	**wirst hängen**
er/sie/es	**wird hängen**
wir	**werden hängen**
ihr	**werdet hängen**
sie/Sie	**werden hängen**

CONDITIONAL

ich	**würde hängen**
du	**würdest hängen**
er/sie/es	**würde hängen**
wir	**würden hängen**
ihr	**würdet hängen**
sie/Sie	**würden hängen**

IMPERATIVE

häng(e)!/hängen wir!/hängt!/ hängen Sie!

PAST PARTICIPLE

gehangen/gehängt

PRESENT PARTICIPLE

hängend

EXAMPLE PHRASES

Sie **hat** sehr an ihrem Vater **gehangen**. *She was very attached to her father.*
Er **hängt** an seinem Beruf. *He loves his job.*
Er **hat** das Bild an die Wand **gehängt**. *He hung the picture on the wall.*

*__hängen__ is conjugated as a weak verb when it has a direct object.

heizen (to heat)

weak, *formed with* **haben**

PRESENT

ich	**heize**
du	**heizt**
er/sie/es	**heizt**
wir	**heizen**
ihr	**heizt**
sie/Sie	**heizen**

PRESENT SUBJUNCTIVE

ich	**heize**
du	**heizest**
er/sie/es	**heize**
wir	**heizen**
ihr	**heizet**
sie/Sie	**heizen**

PERFECT

ich	**habe geheizt**
du	**hast geheizt**
er/sie/es	**hat geheizt**
wir	**haben geheizt**
ihr	**habt geheizt**
sie/Sie	**haben geheizt**

IMPERFECT

ich	**heizte**
du	**heiztest**
er/sie/es	**heizte**
wir	**heizten**
ihr	**heiztet**
sie/Sie	**heizten**

FUTURE

ich	**werde heizen**
du	**wirst heizen**
er/sie/es	**wird heizen**
wir	**werden heizen**
ihr	**werdet heizen**
sie/Sie	**werden heizen**

CONDITIONAL

ich	**würde heizen**
du	**würdest heizen**
er/sie/es	**würde heizen**
wir	**würden heizen**
ihr	**würdet heizen**
sie/Sie	**würden heizen**

IMPERATIVE

heiz(e)!/heizen wir!/heizt!/ heizen Sie!

PAST PARTICIPLE

geheizt

PRESENT PARTICIPLE

heizend

EXAMPLE PHRASES

Der Ofen **heizt** gut. *The stove gives off a good heat.*
Wir **heizen** mit Holz. *We use wood for heating.*
Ab Oktober wird **geheizt**. *The heating is put on in October.*

helfen (to help)

strong, *formed with* **haben**

PRESENT

ich	**helfe**
du	**hilfst**
er/sie/es	**hilft**
wir	**helfen**
ihr	**helft**
sie/Sie	**helfen**

PRESENT SUBJUNCTIVE

ich	**helfe**
du	**helfest**
er/sie/es	**helfe**
wir	**helfen**
ihr	**helfet**
sie/Sie	**helfen**

PERFECT

ich	**habe geholfen**
du	**hast geholfen**
er/sie/es	**hat geholfen**
wir	**haben geholfen**
ihr	**habt geholfen**
sie/Sie	**haben geholfen**

IMPERFECT

ich	**half**
du	**halfst**
er/sie/es	**half**
wir	**halfen**
ihr	**halft**
sie/Sie	**halfen**

FUTURE

ich	**werde helfen**
du	**wirst helfen**
er/sie/es	**wird helfen**
wir	**werden helfen**
ihr	**werdet helfen**
sie/Sie	**werden helfen**

CONDITIONAL

ich	**würde helfen**
du	**würdest helfen**
er/sie/es	**würde helfen**
wir	**würden helfen**
ihr	**würdet helfen**
sie/Sie	**würden helfen**

IMPERATIVE

hilf!/helfen wir!/helft!/ helfen Sie!

PAST PARTICIPLE

geholfen

PRESENT PARTICIPLE

helfend

EXAMPLE PHRASES

Er **hat** mir dabei **geholfen**. *He helped me with it.*
Dieses Medikament **hilft** gegen Kopfschmerzen. *This medicine is good for headaches.*
Sein Vorschlag **half** mir wenig. *His suggestion was not much help to me.*

holen (to fetch)

weak, *formed with* **haben**

PRESENT

ich	**hole**
du	**holst**
er/sie/es	**holt**
wir	**holen**
ihr	**holt**
sie/Sie	**holen**

PRESENT SUBJUNCTIVE

ich	**hole**
du	**holest**
er/sie/es	**hole**
wir	**holen**
ihr	**holet**
sie/Sie	**holen**

PERFECT

ich	**habe geholt**
du	**hast geholt**
er/sie/es	**hat geholt**
wir	**haben geholt**
ihr	**habt geholt**
sie/Sie	**haben geholt**

IMPERFECT

ich	**holte**
du	**holtest**
er/sie/es	**holte**
wir	**holten**
ihr	**holtet**
sie/Sie	**holten**

FUTURE

ich	**werde holen**
du	**wirst holen**
er/sie/es	**wird holen**
wir	**werden holen**
ihr	**werdet holen**
sie/Sie	**werden holen**

CONDITIONAL

ich	**würde holen**
du	**würdest holen**
er/sie/es	**würde holen**
wir	**würden holen**
ihr	**würdet holen**
sie/Sie	**würden holen**

IMPERATIVE

hol(e)!/holen wir!/holt!/holen Sie!

PAST PARTICIPLE

geholt

PRESENT PARTICIPLE

holend

EXAMPLE PHRASES

Er **holt** jeden Tag frische Brötchen vom Supermarkt. *He fetches fresh rolls from the supermarket every day.*
Soll ich ihn ans Telefon **holen**? *Shall I get him to come to the phone?*
Ich **habe** mir eine Erkältung **geholt**. *I caught a cold.*

kennen (to know) *(be acquainted with)*

mixed, formed with **haben**

PRESENT

ich	**kenne**
du	**kennst**
er/sie/es	**kennt**
wir	**kennen**
ihr	**kennt**
sie/Sie	**kennen**

PRESENT SUBJUNCTIVE

ich	**kenne**
du	**kennest**
er/sie/es	**kenne**
wir	**kennen**
ihr	**kennet**
sie/Sie	**kennen**

PERFECT

ich	**habe gekannt**
du	**hast gekannt**
er/sie/es	**hat gekannt**
wir	**haben gekannt**
ihr	**habt gekannt**
sie/Sie	**haben gekannt**

IMPERFECT

ich	**kannte**
du	**kanntest**
er/sie/es	**kannte**
wir	**kannten**
ihr	**kanntet**
sie/Sie	**kannten**

FUTURE

ich	**werde kennen**
du	**wirst kennen**
er/sie/es	**wird kennen**
wir	**werden kennen**
ihr	**werdet kennen**
sie/Sie	**werden kennen**

CONDITIONAL

ich	**würde kennen**
du	**würdest kennen**
er/sie/es	**würde kennen**
wir	**würden kennen**
ihr	**würdet kennen**
sie/Sie	**würden kennen**

IMPERATIVE

kenn(e)!/kennen wir!/kennt!/ kennen Sie!

PAST PARTICIPLE

gekannt

PRESENT PARTICIPLE

kennend

EXAMPLE PHRASES

Ich **kenne** ihn nicht. *I don't know him.*
Er **kannte** kein Erbarmen. *He knew no mercy.*
Kennst du mich noch? *Do you remember me?*

kommen (to come)

strong, *formed with* **sein**

PRESENT

ich	**komme**
du	**kommst**
er/sie/es	**kommt**
wir	**kommen**
ihr	**kommt**
sie/Sie	**kommen**

PERFECT

ich	**bin gekommen**
du	**bist gekommen**
er/sie/es	**ist gekommen**
wir	**sind gekommen**
ihr	**seid gekommen**
sie/Sie	**sind gekommen**

FUTURE

ich	**werde kommen**
du	**wirst kommen**
er/sie/es	**wird kommen**
wir	**werden kommen**
ihr	**werdet kommen**
sie/Sie	**werden kommen**

IMPERATIVE

komm(e)!/kommen wir!/ kommt!/kommen Sie!

PRESENT SUBJUNCTIVE

ich	**komme**
du	**kommest**
er/sie/es	**komme**
wir	**kommen**
ihr	**kommet**
sie/Sie	**kommen**

IMPERFECT

ich	**kam**
du	**kamst**
er/sie/es	**kam**
wir	**kamen**
ihr	**kamt**
sie/Sie	**kamen**

CONDITIONAL

ich	**würde kommen**
du	**würdest kommen**
er/sie/es	**würde kommen**
wir	**würden kommen**
ihr	**würdet kommen**
sie/Sie	**würden kommen**

PAST PARTICIPLE

gekommen

PRESENT PARTICIPLE

kommend

EXAMPLE PHRASES

Er **kam** die Straße entlang. *He was coming along the street.*
Ich **komme** zu deiner Party. *I'm coming to your party.*
Woher **kommst** du? *Where do you come from?*

können (to be able to)

modal, *formed with* **haben**

PRESENT

ich	**kann**
du	**kannst**
er/sie/es	**kann**
wir	**können**
ihr	**könnt**
sie/Sie	**können**

PRESENT SUBJUNCTIVE

ich	**könne**
du	**könnest**
er/sie/es	**könne**
wir	**können**
ihr	**könnet**
sie/Sie	**können**

PERFECT

ich	**habe gekonnt/können**
du	**hast gekonnt/können**
er/sie/es	**hat gekonnt/können**
wir	**haben gekonnt/können**
ihr	**habt gekonnt/können**
sie/Sie	**haben gekonnt/können**

IMPERFECT

ich	**konnte**
du	**konntest**
er/sie/es	**konnte**
wir	**konnten**
ihr	**konntet**
sie/Sie	**konnten**

FUTURE

ich	**werde können**
du	**wirst können**
er/sie/es	**wird können**
wir	**werden können**
ihr	**werdet können**
sie/Sie	**werden können**

CONDITIONAL

ich	**würde können**
du	**würdest können**
er/sie/es	**würde können**
wir	**würden können**
ihr	**würdet können**
sie/Sie	**würden können**

PAST PARTICIPLE

gekonnt/können*

PRESENT PARTICIPLE

könnend

**This form is used when combined with another infinitive.*

EXAMPLE PHRASES

Er **kann** gut schwimmen. *He can swim well.*
Sie **konnte** kein Wort Deutsch. *She couldn't speak a word of German.*
Kann ich gehen? *Can I go?*

lassen (to leave; to allow)

strong, *formed with* **haben**

PRESENT

ich	**lasse**
du	**lässt**
er/sie/es	**lässt**
wir	**lassen**
ihr	**lasst**
sie/Sie	**lassen**

PRESENT SUBJUNCTIVE

ich	**lasse**
du	**lassest**
er/sie/es	**lasse**
wir	**lassen**
ihr	**lasset**
sie/Sie	**lassen**

PERFECT

ich	**habe gelassen/lassen**
du	**hast gelassen/lassen**
er/sie/es	**hat gelassen/lassen**
wir	**haben gelassen/lassen**
ihr	**habt gelassen/lassen**
sie/Sie	**haben gelassen/lassen**

IMPERFECT

ich	**ließ**
du	**ließest**
er/sie/es	**ließ**
wir	**ließen**
ihr	**ließt**
sie/Sie	**ließen**

FUTURE

ich	**werde lassen**
du	**wirst lassen**
er/sie/es	**wird lassen**
wir	**werden lassen**
ihr	**werdet lassen**
sie/Sie	**werden lassen**

CONDITIONAL

ich	**würde lassen**
du	**würdest lassen**
er/sie/es	**würde lassen**
wir	**würden lassen**
ihr	**würdet lassen**
sie/Sie	**würden lassen**

IMPERATIVE

lass(e)!/lassen wir!/lasst!/ lassen Sie!

PAST PARTICIPLE

gelassen/lassen*

PRESENT PARTICIPLE

lassend

**This form is used when combined with another infinitive.*

EXAMPLE PHRASES

Sie **ließ** uns warten. *She kept us waiting.*
Ich **lasse** den Hund nicht auf das Sofa. *I won't let the dog on the sofa.*
Sie **haben** ihn allein im Auto **gelassen**. *They left him alone in the car.*

ich = I **du** = you **er** = he/it **sie** = she/it **es** = it/he/she **wir** = we **ihr** = you **sie** = they **Sie** = you

laufen (to run)

strong, *formed with* **sein**

PRESENT

ich	**laufe**
du	**läufst**
er/sie/es	**läuft**
wir	**laufen**
ihr	**lauft**
sie/Sie	**laufen**

PERFECT

ich	**bin gelaufen**
du	**bist gelaufen**
er/sie/es	**ist gelaufen**
wir	**sind gelaufen**
ihr	**seid gelaufen**
sie/Sie	**sind gelaufen**

FUTURE

ich	**werde laufen**
du	**wirst laufen**
er/sie/es	**wird laufen**
wir	**werden laufen**
ihr	**werdet laufen**
sie/Sie	**werden laufen**

IMPERATIVE

lauf(e)!/laufen wir!/lauft!/ laufen Sie!

PRESENT SUBJUNCTIVE

ich	**laufe**
du	**laufest**
er/sie/es	**laufe**
wir	**laufen**
ihr	**laufet**
sie/Sie	**laufen**

IMPERFECT

ich	**lief**
du	**liefst**
er/sie/es	**lief**
wir	**liefen**
ihr	**lieft**
sie/Sie	**liefen**

CONDITIONAL

ich	**würde laufen**
du	**würdest laufen**
er/sie/es	**würde laufen**
wir	**würden laufen**
ihr	**würdet laufen**
sie/Sie	**würden laufen**

PAST PARTICIPLE

gelaufen

PRESENT PARTICIPLE

laufend

EXAMPLE PHRASES

Er **lief** so schnell er konnte. *He ran as fast as he could.*
Sie **läuft** ständig ins Fitnessstudio. *She's always going to the gym.*
Das Schiff **ist** auf Grund **gelaufen**. *The ship ran aground.*

leiden (to suffer)

strong, *formed with* **haben**

PRESENT

ich	**leide**
du	**leidest**
er/sie/es	**leidet**
wir	**leiden**
ihr	**leidet**
sie/Sie	**leiden**

PERFECT

ich	**habe gelitten**
du	**hast gelitten**
er/sie/es	**hat gelitten**
wir	**haben gelitten**
ihr	**habt gelitten**
sie/Sie	**haben gelitten**

FUTURE

ich	**werde leiden**
du	**wirst leiden**
er/sie/es	**wird leiden**
wir	**werden leiden**
ihr	**werdet leiden**
sie/Sie	**werden leiden**

IMPERATIVE

leid(e)!/leiden wir!/leidet!/ leiden Sie!

PRESENT SUBJUNCTIVE

ich	**leide**
du	**leidest**
er/sie/es	**leide**
wir	**leiden**
ihr	**leidet**
sie/Sie	**leiden**

IMPERFECT

ich	**litt**
du	**litt(e)st**
er/sie/es	**litt**
wir	**litten**
ihr	**littet**
sie/Sie	**litten**

CONDITIONAL

ich	**würde leiden**
du	**würdest leiden**
er/sie/es	**würde leiden**
wir	**würden leiden**
ihr	**würdet leiden**
sie/Sie	**würden leiden**

PAST PARTICIPLE

gelitten

PRESENT PARTICIPLE

leidend

EXAMPLE PHRASES

Sie **litt** an Asthma. *She suffered from asthma.*
Wir **haben** unter der Hitze **gelitten**. *We suffered in the heat.*
Ich kann ihn nicht **leiden**. *I can't stand him.*

lesen (to read)

strong, *formed with* **haben**

PRESENT

ich	**lese**
du	**liest**
er/sie/es	**liest**
wir	**lesen**
ihr	**lest**
sie/Sie	**lesen**

PRESENT SUBJUNCTIVE

ich	**lese**
du	**lesest**
er/sie/es	**lese**
wir	**lesen**
ihr	**leset**
sie/Sie	**lesen**

PERFECT

ich	**habe gelesen**
du	**hast gelesen**
er/sie/es	**hat gelesen**
wir	**haben gelesen**
ihr	**habt gelesen**
sie/Sie	**haben gelesen**

IMPERFECT

ich	**las**
du	**lasest**
er/sie/es	**las**
wir	**lasen**
ihr	**last**
sie/Sie	**lasen**

FUTURE

ich	**werde lesen**
du	**wirst lesen**
er/sie/es	**wird lesen**
wir	**werden lesen**
ihr	**werdet lesen**
sie/Sie	**werden lesen**

CONDITIONAL

ich	**würde lesen**
du	**würdest lesen**
er/sie/es	**würde lesen**
wir	**würden lesen**
ihr	**würdet lesen**
sie/Sie	**würden lesen**

IMPERATIVE

lies!/lesen wir!/lest!/lesen Sie!

PAST PARTICIPLE

gelesen

PRESENT PARTICIPLE

lesend

EXAMPLE PHRASES

Das **habe** ich in der Zeitung **gelesen**. *I read it in the newspaper.*
Es war in ihrem Gesicht zu **lesen**. *It was written all over her face.*
Dieses Buch **liest** sich gut. *This book is a good read.*

ich = I **du** = you **er** = he/it **sie** = she/it **es** = it/he/she **wir** = we **ihr** = you **sie** = they **Sie** = you

liegen (to lie)

strong, *formed with* **haben**

PRESENT

ich	**liege**
du	**liegst**
er/sie/es	**liegt**
wir	**liegen**
ihr	**liegt**
sie/Sie	**liegen**

PRESENT SUBJUNCTIVE

ich	**liege**
du	**liegest**
er/sie/es	**liege**
wir	**liegen**
ihr	**lieget**
sie/Sie	**liegen**

PERFECT

ich	**habe gelegen**
du	**hast gelegen**
er/sie/es	**hat gelegen**
wir	**haben gelegen**
ihr	**habt gelegen**
sie/Sie	**haben gelegen**

IMPERFECT

ich	**lag**
du	**lagst**
er/sie/es	**lag**
wir	**lagen**
ihr	**lagt**
sie/Sie	**lagen**

FUTURE

ich	**werde liegen**
du	**wirst liegen**
er/sie/es	**wird liegen**
wir	**werden liegen**
ihr	**werdet liegen**
sie/Sie	**werden liegen**

CONDITIONAL

ich	**würde liegen**
du	**würdest liegen**
er/sie/es	**würde liegen**
wir	**würden liegen**
ihr	**würdet liegen**
sie/Sie	**würden liegen**

IMPERATIVE

lieg(e)!/liegen wir!/liegt!/ liegen Sie!

PAST PARTICIPLE

gelegen

PRESENT PARTICIPLE

liegend

EXAMPLE PHRASES

Wir **lagen** den ganzen Tag am Strand. *We lay on the beach all day.*
Köln **liegt** am Rhein. *Cologne is on the Rhine.*
Es **hat** daran **gelegen**, dass ich krank war. *It was because I was ill.*

lügen (to (tell a) lie)

strong, *formed with* **haben**

PRESENT

ich	**lüge**
du	**lügst**
er/sie/es	**lügt**
wir	**lügen**
ihr	**lügt**
sie/Sie	**lügen**

PRESENT SUBJUNCTIVE

ich	**lüge**
du	**lügest**
er/sie/es	**lüge**
wir	**lügen**
ihr	**lüget**
sie/Sie	**lügen**

PERFECT

ich	**habe gelogen**
du	**hast gelogen**
er/sie/es	**hat gelogen**
wir	**haben gelogen**
ihr	**habt gelogen**
sie/Sie	**haben gelogen**

IMPERFECT

ich	**log**
du	**logst**
er/sie/es	**log**
wir	**logen**
ihr	**logt**
sie/Sie	**logen**

FUTURE

ich	**werde lügen**
du	**wirst lügen**
er/sie/es	**wird lügen**
wir	**werden lügen**
ihr	**werdet lügen**
sie/Sie	**werden lügen**

CONDITIONAL

ich	**würde lügen**
du	**würdest lügen**
er/sie/es	**würde lügen**
wir	**würden lügen**
ihr	**würdet lügen**
sie/Sie	**würden lügen**

IMPERATIVE

lüg(e)!/lügen wir!/lügt!/ lügen Sie!

PAST PARTICIPLE

gelogen

PRESENT PARTICIPLE

lügend

EXAMPLE PHRASES

Er **log** ständig. *He was always telling lies.*
Ich **würde lügen**, wenn ich das sagen würde. *I would be lying if I said that.*
Das ist **gelogen**! *That's a lie!*

ich = I **du** = you **er** = he/it **sie** = she/it **es** = it/he/she **wir** = we **ihr** = you **sie** = they **Sie** = you

machen (to do; to make)

weak, *formed with* **haben**

PRESENT

ich	**mache**
du	**machst**
er/sie/es	**macht**
wir	**machen**
ihr	**macht**
sie/Sie	**machen**

PERFECT

ich	**habe gemacht**
du	**hast gemacht**
er/sie/es	**hat gemacht**
wir	**haben gemacht**
ihr	**habt gemacht**
sie/Sie	**haben gemacht**

FUTURE

ich	**werde machen**
du	**wirst machen**
er/sie/es	**wird machen**
wir	**werden machen**
ihr	**werdet machen**
sie/Sie	**werden machen**

IMPERATIVE

mach!/machen wir!/macht!/ machen Sie!

PRESENT SUBJUNCTIVE

ich	**mache**
du	**machest**
er/sie/es	**mache**
wir	**machen**
ihr	**machet**
sie/Sie	**machen**

IMPERFECT

ich	**machte**
du	**machtest**
er/sie/es	**machte**
wir	**machten**
ihr	**machtet**
sie/Sie	**machten**

CONDITIONAL

ich	**würde machen**
du	**würdest machen**
er/sie/es	**würde machen**
wir	**würden machen**
ihr	**würdet machen**
sie/Sie	**würden machen**

PAST PARTICIPLE

gemacht

PRESENT PARTICIPLE

machend

EXAMPLE PHRASES

Was **machst** du? *What are you doing?*
Ich **habe** die Betten **gemacht**. *I made the beds.*
Ich **werde** es morgen **machen**. *I'll do it tomorrow.*

misstrauen (to mistrust)

weak, inseparable, *formed with* **haben**

PRESENT

ich	**misstraue**
du	**misstraust**
er/sie/es	**misstraut**
wir	**misstrauen**
ihr	**misstraut**
sie/Sie	**misstrauen**

PRESENT SUBJUNCTIVE

ich	**misstraue**
du	**misstrauest**
er/sie/es	**misstraue**
wir	**misstrauen**
ihr	**misstrauet**
sie/Sie	**misstrauen**

PERFECT

ich	**habe misstraut**
du	**hast misstraut**
er/sie/es	**hat misstraut**
wir	**haben misstraut**
ihr	**habt misstraut**
sie/Sie	**haben misstraut**

IMPERFECT

ich	**misstraute**
du	**misstrautest**
er/sie/es	**misstraute**
wir	**misstrauten**
ihr	**misstrautet**
sie/Sie	**misstrauten**

FUTURE

ich	**werde misstrauen**
du	**wirst misstrauen**
er/sie/es	**wird misstrauen**
wir	**werden misstrauen**
ihr	**werdet misstrauen**
sie/Sie	**werden misstrauen**

CONDITIONAL

ich	**würde misstrauen**
du	**würdest misstrauen**
er/sie/es	**würde misstrauen**
wir	**würden misstrauen**
ihr	**würdet misstrauen**
sie/Sie	**würden misstrauen**

IMPERATIVE

misstrau(e)!/misstrauen wir!/ misstraut!/misstrauen Sie!

PAST PARTICIPLE

misstraut

PRESENT PARTICIPLE

misstrauend

EXAMPLE PHRASES

Sie **misstraute** ihrem Gedächtnis. *She didn't trust her memory.*
Ich **würde** seinen Ratschlägen **misstrauen**. *I would not trust his advice.*
Ich **habe** ihr von Anfang an **misstraut**. *I didn't trust her from the start.*

mögen (to like)

modal, *formed with* **haben**

PRESENT

ich	**mag**
du	**magst**
er/sie/es	**mag**
wir	**mögen**
ihr	**mögt**
sie/Sie	**mögen**

PRESENT SUBJUNCTIVE

ich	**möge**
du	**mögest**
er/sie/es	**möge**
wir	**mögen**
ihr	**möget**
sie/Sie	**mögen**

PERFECT

ich	**habe gemocht/mögen**
du	**hast gemocht/mögen**
er/sie/es	**hat gemocht/mögen**
wir	**haben gemocht/mögen**
ihr	**habt gemocht/mögen**
sie/Sie	**haben gemocht/mögen**

IMPERFECT

ich	**mochte**
du	**mochtest**
er/sie/es	**mochte**
wir	**mochten**
ihr	**mochtet**
sie/Sie	**mochten**

FUTURE

ich	**werde mögen**
du	**wirst mögen**
er/sie/es	**wird mögen**
wir	**werden mögen**
ihr	**werdet mögen**
sie/Sie	**werden mögen**

CONDITIONAL

ich	**würde mögen**
du	**würdest mögen**
er/sie/es	**würde mögen**
wir	**würden mögen**
ihr	**würdet mögen**
sie/Sie	**würden mögen**

PAST PARTICIPLE

gemocht/mögen*

PRESENT PARTICIPLE

mögend

**This form is used when combined with another infinitive.*

EXAMPLE PHRASES

Ich **mag** gern Vanilleeis. *I like vanilla ice cream.*
Er **mochte** sie nicht danach fragen. *He didn't want to ask her about it.*
Ich **habe** ihn noch nie **gemocht**. *I never liked him.*

müssen (to have to)

modal, *formed with* **haben**

PRESENT

ich	**muss**
du	**musst**
er/sie/es	**muss**
wir	**müssen**
ihr	**müsst**
sie/Sie	**müssen**

PRESENT SUBJUNCTIVE

ich	**müsse**
du	**müssest**
er/sie/es	**müsse**
wir	**müssen**
ihr	**müsset**
sie/Sie	**müssen**

PERFECT

ich	**habe gemusst/müssen**
du	**hast gemusst/müssen**
er/sie/es	**hat gemusst/müssen**
wir	**haben gemusst/müssen**
ihr	**habt gemusst/müssen**
sie/Sie	**haben gemusst/müssen**

IMPERFECT

ich	**musste**
du	**musstest**
er/sie/es	**musste**
wir	**mussten**
ihr	**musstet**
sie/Sie	**mussten**

FUTURE

ich	**werde müssen**
du	**wirst müssen**
er/sie/es	**wird müssen**
wir	**werden müssen**
ihr	**werdet müssen**
sie/Sie	**werden müssen**

CONDITIONAL

ich	**würde müssen**
du	**würdest müssen**
er/sie/es	**würde müssen**
wir	**würden müssen**
ihr	**würdet müssen**
sie/Sie	**würden müssen**

PAST PARTICIPLE

gemusst/müssen*

PRESENT PARTICIPLE

müssend

**This form is used when combined with another infinitive.*

EXAMPLE PHRASES

Ich **muss** auf die Toilette. *I must go to the loo.*
Wir **müssen** jeden Abend unsere Hausaufgaben machen. *We have to do our homework every night.*
Sie **hat** abwaschen **müssen**. *She had to wash up.*

nehmen (to take)

strong, *formed with* **haben**

PRESENT

ich	**nehme**
du	**nimmst**
er/sie/es	**nimmt**
wir	**nehmen**
ihr	**nehmt**
sie/Sie	**nehmen**

PRESENT SUBJUNCTIVE

ich	**nehme**
du	**nehmest**
er/sie/es	**nehme**
wir	**nehmen**
ihr	**nehmet**
sie/Sie	**nehmen**

PERFECT

ich	**habe genommen**
du	**hast genommen**
er/sie/es	**hat genommen**
wir	**haben genommen**
ihr	**habt genommen**
sie/Sie	**haben genommen**

IMPERFECT

ich	**nahm**
du	**nahmst**
er/sie/es	**nahm**
wir	**nahmen**
ihr	**nahmt**
sie/Sie	**nahmen**

FUTURE

ich	**werde nehmen**
du	**wirst nehmen**
er/sie/es	**wird nehmen**
wir	**werden nehmen**
ihr	**werdet nehmen**
sie/Sie	**werden nehmen**

CONDITIONAL

ich	**würde nehmen**
du	**würdest nehmen**
er/sie/es	**würde nehmen**
wir	**würden nehmen**
ihr	**würdet nehmen**
sie/Sie	**würden nehmen**

IMPERATIVE

nimm!/nehmen wir!/nehmt!/ nehmen Sie!

PAST PARTICIPLE

genommen

PRESENT PARTICIPLE

nehmend

EXAMPLE PHRASES

Hast du den Bus in die Stadt **genommen**? *Did you take the bus into town?*
Wie viel **nimmst** du dafür? *How much will you take for it?*
Er **nahm** sich vom Brot. *He helped himself to bread.*

ich = I **du** = you **er** = he/it **sie** = she/it **es** = it/he/she **wir** = we **ihr** = you **sie** = they **Sie** = you

rechnen (to calculate)

weak, *formed with* **haben**

PRESENT

ich	**rechne**
du	**rechnest**
er/sie/es	**rechnet**
wir	**rechnen**
ihr	**rechnet**
sie/Sie	**rechnen**

PRESENT SUBJUNCTIVE

ich	**rechne**
du	**rechnest**
er/sie/es	**rechne**
wir	**rechnen**
ihr	**rechnet**
sie/Sie	**rechnen**

PERFECT

ich	**habe gerechnet**
du	**hast gerechnet**
er/sie/es	**hat gerechnet**
wir	**haben gerechnet**
ihr	**habt gerechnet**
sie/Sie	**haben gerechnet**

IMPERFECT

ich	**rechnete**
du	**rechnetest**
er/sie/es	**rechnete**
wir	**rechneten**
ihr	**rechnetet**
sie/Sie	**rechneten**

FUTURE

ich	**werde rechnen**
du	**wirst rechnen**
er/sie/es	**wird rechnen**
wir	**werden rechnen**
ihr	**werdet rechnen**
sie/Sie	**werden rechnen**

CONDITIONAL

ich	**würde rechnen**
du	**würdest rechnen**
er/sie/es	**würde rechnen**
wir	**würden rechnen**
ihr	**würdet rechnen**
sie/Sie	**würden rechnen**

IMPERATIVE

rechne!/rechnen wir!/rechnet!/ rechnen Sie!

PAST PARTICIPLE

gerechnet

PRESENT PARTICIPLE

rechnend

EXAMPLE PHRASES

Lass mich **rechnen**, wie viel das wird. *Let me work out how much that's going to be.*
Emma kann gut **rechnen**. *Emma is good at arithmetic.*
Damit **habe** ich nicht **gerechnet**. *I wasn't expecting that.*

reden (to talk)

weak, *formed with* **haben**

PRESENT

ich	**rede**
du	**redest**
er/sie/es	**redet**
wir	**reden**
ihr	**redet**
sie/Sie	**reden**

PRESENT SUBJUNCTIVE

ich	**rede**
du	**redest**
er/sie/es	**rede**
wir	**reden**
ihr	**redet**
sie/Sie	**reden**

PERFECT

ich	**habe geredet**
du	**hast geredet**
er/sie/es	**hat geredet**
wir	**haben geredet**
ihr	**habt geredet**
sie/Sie	**haben geredet**

IMPERFECT

ich	**redete**
du	**redetest**
er/sie/es	**redete**
wir	**redeten**
ihr	**redetet**
sie/Sie	**redeten**

FUTURE

ich	**werde reden**
du	**wirst reden**
er/sie/es	**wird reden**
wir	**werden reden**
ihr	**werdet reden**
sie/Sie	**werden reden**

CONDITIONAL

ich	**würde reden**
du	**würdest reden**
er/sie/es	**würde reden**
wir	**würden reden**
ihr	**würdet reden**
sie/Sie	**würden reden**

IMPERATIVE

red(e)!/reden wir!/redet!/ reden Sie!

PAST PARTICIPLE

geredet

PRESENT PARTICIPLE

redend

EXAMPLE PHRASES

Man kann überhaupt nicht mit ihr **reden**. *You can't talk to her at all.*
Er **redete** ständig von seinem Hund. *He kept talking about his dog.*
Ich **werde** mit deinem Vater **reden**. *I'll speak to your father.*

rennen (to run)

mixed, *formed with* **sein**

PRESENT

ich	**renne**
du	**rennst**
er/sie/es	**rennt**
wir	**rennen**
ihr	**rennt**
sie/Sie	**rennen**

PRESENT SUBJUNCTIVE

ich	**renne**
du	**rennest**
er/sie/es	**renne**
wir	**rennen**
ihr	**rennet**
sie/Sie	**rennen**

PERFECT

ich	**bin gerannt**
du	**bist gerannt**
er/sie/es	**ist gerannt**
wir	**sind gerannt**
ihr	**seid gerannt**
sie/Sie	**sind gerannt**

IMPERFECT

ich	**rannte**
du	**ranntest**
er/sie/es	**rannte**
wir	**rannten**
ihr	**ranntet**
sie/Sie	**rannten**

FUTURE

ich	**werde rennen**
du	**wirst rennen**
er/sie/es	**wird rennen**
wir	**werden rennen**
ihr	**werdet rennen**
sie/Sie	**werden rennen**

CONDITIONAL

ich	**würde rennen**
du	**würdest rennen**
er/sie/es	**würde rennen**
wir	**würden rennen**
ihr	**würdet rennen**
sie/Sie	**würden rennen**

IMPERATIVE

renn(e)!/rennen wir!/rennt!/ rennen Sie!

PAST PARTICIPLE

gerannt

PRESENT PARTICIPLE

rennend

EXAMPLE PHRASES

Sie **rannte** schnell weg. *She ran away fast.*
Er **rennt** dauernd zum Chef. *He keeps running to the boss.*
Ich **bin** mit dem Kopf gegen die Wand **gerannt**. *I bumped my head against the wall.*

rufen (to shout; call)

strong, *formed with* **haben**

PRESENT

ich	**rufe**
du	**rufst**
er/sie/es	**ruft**
wir	**rufen**
ihr	**ruft**
sie/Sie	**rufen**

PRESENT SUBJUNCTIVE

ich	**rufe**
du	**rufest**
er/sie/es	**rufe**
wir	**rufen**
ihr	**rufet**
sie/Sie	**rufen**

PERFECT

ich	**habe gerufen**
du	**hast gerufen**
er/sie/es	**hat gerufen**
wir	**haben gerufen**
ihr	**habt gerufen**
sie/Sie	**haben gerufen**

IMPERFECT

ich	**rief**
du	**riefst**
er/sie/es	**rief**
wir	**riefen**
ihr	**rieft**
sie/Sie	**riefen**

FUTURE

ich	**werde rufen**
du	**wirst rufen**
er/sie/es	**wird rufen**
wir	**werden rufen**
ihr	**werdet rufen**
sie/Sie	**werden rufen**

CONDITIONAL

ich	**würde rufen**
du	**würdest rufen**
er/sie/es	**würde rufen**
wir	**würden rufen**
ihr	**würdet rufen**
sie/Sie	**würden rufen**

IMPERATIVE

ruf(e)!/rufen wir!/ruft!/ rufen Sie!

PAST PARTICIPLE

gerufen

PRESENT PARTICIPLE

rufend

EXAMPLE PHRASES

Sie **riefen** um Hilfe. *They shouted for help.*
Ich **habe** dir ein Taxi **gerufen**. *I called you a taxi.*
Er **rief** seine Schwester zu sich. *He sent for his sister.*

scheinen (to shine; to seem)

strong, *formed with* **haben**

PRESENT

ich	**scheine**
du	**scheinst**
er/sie/es	**scheint**
wir	**scheinen**
ihr	**scheint**
sie/Sie	**scheinen**

PRESENT SUBJUNCTIVE

ich	**scheine**
du	**scheinest**
er/sie/es	**scheine**
wir	**scheinen**
ihr	**scheinet**
sie/Sie	**scheinen**

PERFECT

ich	**habe geschienen**
du	**hast geschienen**
er/sie/es	**hat geschienen**
wir	**haben geschienen**
ihr	**habt geschienen**
sie/Sie	**haben geschienen**

IMPERFECT

ich	**schien**
du	**schienst**
er/sie/es	**schien**
wir	**schienen**
ihr	**schient**
sie/Sie	**schienen**

FUTURE

ich	**werde scheinen**
du	**wirst scheinen**
er/sie/es	**wird scheinen**
wir	**werden scheinen**
ihr	**werdet scheinen**
sie/Sie	**werden scheinen**

CONDITIONAL

ich	**würde scheinen**
du	**würdest scheinen**
er/sie/es	**würde scheinen**
wir	**würden scheinen**
ihr	**würdet scheinen**
sie/Sie	**würden scheinen**

IMPERATIVE

schein(e)!/scheinen wir!/ scheint!/scheinen Sie!

PAST PARTICIPLE

geschienen

PRESENT PARTICIPLE

scheinend

EXAMPLE PHRASES

Die Sonne **schien**. *The sun was shining.*
Es **scheint**, als ob du recht hast. *It appears as if you're right.*
Sie **schienen** glücklich zu sein. *They seemed to be happy.*

ich = I **du** = you **er** = he/it **sie** = she/it **es** = it/he/she **wir** = we **ihr** = you **sie** = they **Sie** = you

schlafen (to sleep)

strong, *formed with* **haben**

PRESENT

ich	**schlafe**
du	**schläfst**
er/sie/es	**schläft**
wir	**schlafen**
ihr	**schlaft**
sie/Sie	**schlafen**

PRESENT SUBJUNCTIVE

ich	**schlafe**
du	**schlafest**
er/sie/es	**schlafe**
wir	**schlafen**
ihr	**schlafet**
sie/Sie	**schlafen**

PERFECT

ich	**habe geschlafen**
du	**hast geschlafen**
er/sie/es	**hat geschlafen**
wir	**haben geschlafen**
ihr	**habt geschlafen**
sie/Sie	**haben geschlafen**

IMPERFECT

ich	**schlief**
du	**schliefst**
er/sie/es	**schlief**
wir	**schliefen**
ihr	**schlieft**
sie/Sie	**schliefen**

FUTURE

ich	**werde schlafen**
du	**wirst schlafen**
er/sie/es	**wird schlafen**
wir	**werden schlafen**
ihr	**werdet schlafen**
sie/Sie	**werden schlafen**

CONDITIONAL

ich	**würde schlafen**
du	**würdest schlafen**
er/sie/es	**würde schlafen**
wir	**würden schlafen**
ihr	**würdet schlafen**
sie/Sie	**würden schlafen**

IMPERATIVE

**schlaf(e)!/schlafen wir!/
schlaft!/ schlafen Sie!**

PAST PARTICIPLE

geschlafen

PRESENT PARTICIPLE

schlafend

EXAMPLE PHRASES

Sie **schläft** immer noch. *She's still asleep.*
Heute Nacht **wirst** du bestimmt gut **schlafen**. *I'm sure you'll sleep well tonight.*
Er **schlief** während des Unterrichts. *He slept during lessons.*

schlagen (to hit)

strong, *formed with* **haben**

PRESENT

ich	**schlage**
du	**schlägst**
er/sie/es	**schlägt**
wir	**schlagen**
ihr	**schlagt**
sie/Sie	**schlagen**

PRESENT SUBJUNCTIVE

ich	**schlage**
du	**schlagest**
er/sie/es	**schlage**
wir	**schlagen**
ihr	**schlaget**
sie/Sie	**schlagen**

PERFECT

ich	**habe geschlagen**
du	**hast geschlagen**
er/sie/es	**hat geschlagen**
wir	**haben geschlagen**
ihr	**habt geschlagen**
sie/Sie	**haben geschlagen**

IMPERFECT

ich	**schlug**
du	**schlugst**
er/sie/es	**schlug**
wir	**schlugen**
ihr	**schlugt**
sie/Sie	**schlugen**

FUTURE

ich	**werde schlagen**
du	**wirst schlagen**
er/sie/es	**wird schlagen**
wir	**werden schlagen**
ihr	**werdet schlagen**
sie/Sie	**werden schlagen**

CONDITIONAL

ich	**würde schlagen**
du	**würdest schlagen**
er/sie/es	**würde schlagen**
wir	**würden schlagen**
ihr	**würdet schlagen**
sie/Sie	**würden schlagen**

IMPERATIVE

schlag(e)!/schlagen wir!/ schlagt!/schlagen Sie!

PAST PARTICIPLE

geschlagen

PRESENT PARTICIPLE

schlagend

EXAMPLE PHRASES

England **hat** Deutschland **geschlagen**. *England beat Germany.*
Ihr Herz **schlug** schneller. *Her heart beat faster.*
Die Uhr **schlägt** drei. *The clock strikes three.*

schneiden (to cut)

strong, *formed with* **haben**

PRESENT

ich	**schneide**
du	**schneidest**
er/sie/es	**schneidet**
wir	**schneiden**
ihr	**schneidet**
sie/Sie	**schneiden**

PRESENT SUBJUNCTIVE

ich	**schneide**
du	**schneidest**
er/sie/es	**schneide**
wir	**schneiden**
ihr	**schneidet**
sie/Sie	**schneiden**

PERFECT

ich	**habe geschnitten**
du	**hast geschnitten**
er/sie/es	**hat geschnitten**
wir	**haben geschnitten**
ihr	**habt geschnitten**
sie/Sie	**haben geschnitten**

IMPERFECT

ich	**schnitt**
du	**schnittst**
er/sie/es	**schnitt**
wir	**schnitten**
ihr	**schnittet**
sie/Sie	**schnitten**

FUTURE

ich	**werde schneiden**
du	**wirst schneiden**
er/sie/es	**wird schneiden**
wir	**werden schneiden**
ihr	**werdet schneiden**
sie/Sie	**werden schneiden**

CONDITIONAL

ich	**würde schneiden**
du	**würdest schneiden**
er/sie/es	**würde schneiden**
wir	**würden schneiden**
ihr	**würdet schneiden**
sie/Sie	**würden schneiden**

IMPERATIVE

schneid(e)!/schneiden wir!/ schneidet!/schneiden Sie!

PAST PARTICIPLE

geschnitten

PRESENT PARTICIPLE

schneidend

EXAMPLE PHRASES

Sie **schneidet** ihm die Haare. *She cuts his hair.*
Ich **habe** mir in den Finger **geschnitten**. *I've cut my finger.*
Sie **schnitt** die Tomaten in Scheiben. *She sliced the tomatoes.*

ich = I **du** = you **er** = he/it **sie** = she/it **es** = it/he/she **wir** = we **ihr** = you **sie** = they **Sie** = you

schreiben (to write)

strong, *formed with* **haben**

PRESENT

ich	**schreibe**
du	**schreibst**
er/sie/es	**schreibt**
wir	**schreiben**
ihr	**schreibt**
sie/Sie	**schreiben**

PRESENT SUBJUNCTIVE

ich	**schreibe**
du	**schreibest**
er/sie/es	**schreibe**
wir	**schreiben**
ihr	**schreibet**
sie/Sie	**schreiben**

PERFECT

ich	**habe geschrieben**
du	**hast geschrieben**
er/sie/es	**hat geschrieben**
wir	**haben geschrieben**
ihr	**habt geschrieben**
sie/Sie	**haben geschrieben**

IMPERFECT

ich	**schrieb**
du	**schriebst**
er/sie/es	**schrieb**
wir	**schrieben**
ihr	**schriebt**
sie/Sie	**schrieben**

FUTURE

ich	**werde schreiben**
du	**wirst schreiben**
er/sie/es	**wird schreiben**
wir	**werden schreiben**
ihr	**werdet schreiben**
sie/Sie	**werden schreiben**

CONDITIONAL

ich	**würde schreiben**
du	**würdest schreiben**
er/sie/es	**würde schreiben**
wir	**würden schreiben**
ihr	**würdet schreiben**
sie/Sie	**würden schreiben**

IMPERATIVE

**schreib(e)!/schreiben wir!/
schreibt!/schreiben Sie!**

PAST PARTICIPLE

geschrieben

PRESENT PARTICIPLE

schreibend

EXAMPLE PHRASES

Er **schrieb** das Wort an die Tafel. *He wrote the word on the blackboard.*
Wie **schreibst** du deinen Namen? *How do you spell your name?*
Sie **hat** mir einen Brief **geschrieben**. *She wrote me a letter.*

ich = I **du** = you **er** = he/it **sie** = she/it **es** = it/he/she **wir** = we **ihr** = you **sie** = they **Sie** = you

schreien (to shout)

strong, *formed with* **haben**

PRESENT

ich	**schreie**
du	**schreist**
er/sie/es	**schreit**
wir	**schreien**
ihr	**schreit**
sie/Sie	**schreien**

PRESENT SUBJUNCTIVE

ich	**schreie**
du	**schreiest**
er/sie/es	**schreie**
wir	**schreien**
ihr	**schreiet**
sie/Sie	**schreien**

PERFECT

ich	**habe geschrien**
du	**hast geschrien**
er/sie/es	**hat geschrien**
wir	**haben geschrien**
ihr	**habt geschrien**
sie/Sie	**haben geschrien**

IMPERFECT

ich	**schrie**
du	**schriest**
er/sie/es	**schrie**
wir	**schrien**
ihr	**schriet**
sie/Sie	**schrien**

FUTURE

ich	**werde schreien**
du	**wirst schreien**
er/sie/es	**wird schreien**
wir	**werden schreien**
ihr	**werdet schreien**
sie/Sie	**werden schreien**

CONDITIONAL

ich	**würde schreien**
du	**würdest schreien**
er/sie/es	**würde schreien**
wir	**würden schreien**
ihr	**würdet schreien**
sie/Sie	**würden schreien**

IMPERATIVE

schrei(e)!/schreien wir!/
schreit!/schreien Sie!

PAST PARTICIPLE

geschrie(e)n

PRESENT PARTICIPLE

schreiend

EXAMPLE PHRASES

Sie **schrie** vor Schmerzen. *She screamed with pain.*

Wir **haben geschrien**, er hat uns aber nicht gehört. *We shouted but he didn't hear us.*

Schreien Sie nicht so! *Don't shout!*

ich = I **du** = you **er** = he/it **sie** = she/it **es** = it/he/she **wir** = we **ihr** = you **sie** = they **Sie** = you

schwimmen (to swim)

strong, *formed with* **sein**

PRESENT

ich	**schwimme**
du	**schwimmst**
er/sie/es	**schwimmt**
wir	**schwimmen**
ihr	**schwimmt**
sie/Sie	**schwimmen**

PRESENT SUBJUNCTIVE

ich	**schwimme**
du	**schwimmest**
er/sie/es	**schwimme**
wir	**schwimmen**
ihr	**schwimmet**
sie/Sie	**schwimmen**

PERFECT

ich	**bin geschwommen**
du	**bist geschwommen**
er/sie/es	**ist geschwommen**
wir	**sind geschwommen**
ihr	**seid geschwommen**
sie/Sie	**sind geschwommen**

IMPERFECT

ich	**schwamm**
du	**schwammst**
er/sie/es	**schwamm**
wir	**schwammen**
ihr	**schwammt**
sie/Sie	**schwammen**

FUTURE

ich	**werde schwimmen**
du	**wirst schwimmen**
er/sie/es	**wird schwimmen**
wir	**werden schwimmen**
ihr	**werdet schwimmen**
sie/Sie	**werden schwimmen**

CONDITIONAL

ich	**würde schwimmen**
du	**würdest schwimmen**
er/sie/es	**würde schwimmen**
wir	**würden schwimmen**
ihr	**würdet schwimmen**
sie/Sie	**würden schwimmen**

IMPERATIVE

schwimm(e)!/schwimmen wir!/ schwimmt!/schwimmen Sie!

PAST PARTICIPLE

geschwommen

PRESENT PARTICIPLE

schwimmend

EXAMPLE PHRASES

Ich kann nicht **schwimmen**. *I can't swim.*
Er **ist** über den Fluss **geschwommen**. *He swam across the river.*
Wir **schwammen** im Geld. *We were rolling in money.*

sehen (to see)

strong, *formed with* **haben**

PRESENT

ich	**sehe**
du	**siehst**
er/sie/es	**sieht**
wir	**sehen**
ihr	**seht**
sie/Sie	**sehen**

PRESENT SUBJUNCTIVE

ich	**sehe**
du	**sehest**
er/sie/es	**sehe**
wir	**sehen**
ihr	**sehet**
sie/Sie	**sehen**

PERFECT

ich	**habe gesehen**
du	**hast gesehen**
er/sie/es	**hat gesehen**
wir	**haben gesehen**
ihr	**habt gesehen**
sie/Sie	**haben gesehen**

IMPERFECT

ich	**sah**
du	**sahst**
er/sie/es	**sah**
wir	**sahen**
ihr	**saht**
sie/Sie	**sahen**

FUTURE

ich	**werde sehen**
du	**wirst sehen**
er/sie/es	**wird sehen**
wir	**werden sehen**
ihr	**werdet sehen**
sie/Sie	**werden sehen**

CONDITIONAL

ich	**würde sehen**
du	**würdest sehen**
er/sie/es	**würde sehen**
wir	**würden sehen**
ihr	**würdet sehen**
sie/Sie	**würden sehen**

IMPERATIVE

sieh(e)!/sehen wir!/seht!/ sehen Sie!

PAST PARTICIPLE

gesehen

PRESENT PARTICIPLE

sehend

EXAMPLE PHRASES

Mein Vater **sieht** schlecht. *My father has bad eyesight.*
Ich **habe** diesen Film noch nicht **gesehen**. *I haven't seen this film yet.*
Er **sah** auf die Uhr. *He looked at his watch.*

sein (to be)

strong, *formed with* **sein**

PRESENT

ich	**bin**
du	**bist**
er/sie/es	**ist**
wir	**sind**
ihr	**seid**
sie/Sie	**sind**

PERFECT

ich	**bin gewesen**
du	**bist gewesen**
er/sie/es	**ist gewesen**
wir	**sind gewesen**
ihr	**seid gewesen**
sie/Sie	**sind gewesen**

FUTURE

ich	**werde sein**
du	**wirst sein**
er/sie/es	**wird sein**
wir	**werden sein**
ihr	**werdet sein**
sie/Sie	**werden sein**

IMPERATIVE

sei!/seien wir!/seid!/seien Sie!

PRESENT SUBJUNCTIVE

ich	**sei**
du	**sei(e)st**
er/sie/es	**sei**
wir	**seien**
ihr	**seiet**
sie/Sie	**seien**

IMPERFECT

ich	**war**
du	**warst**
er/sie/es	**war**
wir	**waren**
ihr	**wart**
sie/Sie	**waren**

CONDITIONAL

ich	**würde sein**
du	**würdest sein**
er/sie/es	**würde sein**
wir	**würden sein**
ihr	**würdet sein**
sie/Sie	**würden sein**

PAST PARTICIPLE

gewesen

PRESENT PARTICIPLE

seiend

EXAMPLE PHRASES

Er **ist** zehn Jahre alt. *He is ten years old.*
Wir **waren** gestern im Theater. *We were at the theatre yesterday.*
Mir **war** kalt. *I was cold.*

singen (to sing)

strong, *formed with* **haben**

PRESENT

ich	**singe**
du	**singst**
er/sie/es	**singt**
wir	**singen**
ihr	**singt**
sie/Sie	**singen**

PRESENT SUBJUNCTIVE

ich	**singe**
du	**singest**
er/sie/es	**singe**
wir	**singen**
ihr	**singet**
sie/Sie	**singen**

PERFECT

ich	**habe gesungen**
du	**hast gesungen**
er/sie/es	**hat gesungen**
wir	**haben gesungen**
ihr	**habt gesungen**
sie/Sie	**haben gesungen**

IMPERFECT

ich	**sang**
du	**sangst**
er/sie/es	**sang**
wir	**sangen**
ihr	**sangt**
sie/Sie	**sangen**

FUTURE

ich	**werde singen**
du	**wirst singen**
er/sie/es	**wird singen**
wir	**werden singen**
ihr	**werdet singen**
sie/Sie	**werden singen**

CONDITIONAL

ich	**würde singen**
du	**würdest singen**
er/sie/es	**würde singen**
wir	**würden singen**
ihr	**würdet singen**
sie/Sie	**würden singen**

IMPERATIVE

sing(e)!/singen wir!/singt!/ singen Sie!

PAST PARTICIPLE

gesungen

PRESENT PARTICIPLE

singend

EXAMPLE PHRASES

Sie **sang** das Kind in den Schlaf. *She sang the child to sleep.*
Er **singt** nicht gut. *He's a bad singer.*
Ich **habe** dieses Lied früher oft **gesungen**. *I used to sing this song a lot.*

ich = I **du** = you **er** = he/it **sie** = she/it **es** = it/he/she **wir** = we **ihr** = you **sie** = they **Sie** = you

sinken (to sink)

strong, *formed with* **sein**

PRESENT

ich	**sinke**
du	**sinkst**
er/sie/es	**sinkt**
wir	**sinken**
ihr	**sinkt**
sie/Sie	**sinken**

PRESENT SUBJUNCTIVE

ich	**sinke**
du	**sinkest**
er/sie/es	**sinke**
wir	**sinken**
ihr	**sinket**
sie/Sie	**sinken**

PERFECT

ich	**bin gesunken**
du	**bist gesunken**
er/sie/es	**ist gesunken**
wir	**sind gesunken**
ihr	**seid gesunken**
sie/Sie	**sind gesunken**

IMPERFECT

ich	**sank**
du	**sankst**
er/sie/es	**sank**
wir	**sanken**
ihr	**sankt**
sie/Sie	**sanken**

FUTURE

ich	**werde sinken**
du	**wirst sinken**
er/sie/es	**wird sinken**
wir	**werden sinken**
ihr	**werdet sinken**
sie/Sie	**werden sinken**

CONDITIONAL

ich	**würde sinken**
du	**würdest sinken**
er/sie/es	**würde sinken**
wir	**würden sinken**
ihr	**würdet sinken**
sie/Sie	**würden sinken**

IMPERATIVE

sink(e)!/sinken wir!/sinkt!/ sinken Sie!

PAST PARTICIPLE

gesunken

PRESENT PARTICIPLE

sinkend

EXAMPLE PHRASES

Wann **ist** die Titanic **gesunken**? *When did the Titanic sink?*
Er **sank** zu Boden. *He sank to the ground.*
Die Preise für Handys **sinken**. *Prices of mobile phones are falling.*

sitzen (to sit)

strong, *formed with* **haben**

PRESENT

ich	**sitze**
du	**sitzt**
er/sie/es	**sitzt**
wir	**sitzen**
ihr	**sitzt**
sie/Sie	**sitzen**

PRESENT SUBJUNCTIVE

ich	**sitze**
du	**sitzest**
er/sie/es	**sitze**
wir	**sitzen**
ihr	**sitzet**
sie/Sie	**sitzen**

PERFECT

ich	**habe gesessen**
du	**hast gesessen**
er/sie/es	**hat gesessen**
wir	**haben gesessen**
ihr	**habt gesessen**
sie/Sie	**haben gesessen**

IMPERFECT

ich	**saß**
du	**saßest**
er/sie/es	**saß**
wir	**saßen**
ihr	**saßt**
sie/Sie	**saßen**

FUTURE

ich	**werde sitzen**
du	**wirst sitzen**
er/sie/es	**wird sitzen**
wir	**werden sitzen**
ihr	**werdet sitzen**
sie/Sie	**werden sitzen**

CONDITIONAL

ich	**würde sitzen**
du	**würdest sitzen**
er/sie/es	**würde sitzen**
wir	**würden sitzen**
ihr	**würdet sitzen**
sie/Sie	**würden sitzen**

IMPERATIVE

sitz(e)!/sitzen wir!/sitzt!/ sitzen Sie!

PAST PARTICIPLE

gesessen

PRESENT PARTICIPLE

sitzend

EXAMPLE PHRASES

Er **saß** auf meinem Stuhl. *He was sitting on my chair.*
Deine Krawatte **sitzt** nicht richtig. *Your tie isn't straight.*
Ich **habe** zwei Jahre über dieser Arbeit **gesessen**. *I've spent two years on this piece of work.*

sollen (to be supposed to)

modal, *formed with* **haben**

PRESENT

ich	**soll**
du	**sollst**
er/sie/es	**soll**
wir	**sollen**
ihr	**sollt**
sie/Sie	**sollen**

PERFECT

ich	**habe gesollt/sollen**
du	**hast gesollt/sollen**
er/sie/es	**hat gesollt/sollen**
wir	**haben gesollt/sollen**
ihr	**habt gesollt/sollen**
sie/Sie	**haben gesollt/sollen**

FUTURE

ich	**werde sollen**
du	**wirst sollen**
er/sie/es	**wird sollen**
wir	**werden sollen**
ihr	**werdet sollen**
sie/Sie	**werden sollen**

PRESENT SUBJUNCTIVE

ich	**solle**
du	**sollest**
er/sie/es	**solle**
wir	**sollen**
ihr	**sollet**
sie/Sie	**sollen**

IMPERFECT

ich	**sollte**
du	**solltest**
er/sie/es	**sollte**
wir	**sollten**
ihr	**solltet**
sie/Sie	**sollten**

CONDITIONAL

ich	**würde sollen**
du	**würdest sollen**
er/sie/es	**würde sollen**
wir	**würden sollen**
ihr	**würdet sollen**
sie/Sie	**würden sollen**

PAST PARTICIPLE

gesollt/sollen*

PRESENT PARTICIPLE

sollend

**This form is used when combined with another infinitive.*

EXAMPLE PHRASES

Was **sollte** er machen? *What should he do?*
Das **sollst** du nicht. *You shouldn't do that.*
Ich **soll** um 5 Uhr dort sein. *I'm supposed to be there at 5 o'clock.*

ich = I **du** = you **er** = he/it **sie** = she/it **es** = it/he/she **wir** = we **ihr** = you **sie** = they **Sie** = you

sprechen (to speak)

strong, *formed with* **haben**

PRESENT

ich	**spreche**
du	**sprichst**
er/sie/es	**spricht**
wir	**sprechen**
ihr	**sprecht**
sie/Sie	**sprechen**

PERFECT

ich	**habe gesprochen**
du	**hast gesprochen**
er/sie/es	**hat gesprochen**
wir	**haben gesprochen**
ihr	**habt gesprochen**
sie/Sie	**haben gesprochen**

FUTURE

ich	**werde sprechen**
du	**wirst sprechen**
er/sie/es	**wird sprechen**
wir	**werden sprechen**
ihr	**werdet sprechen**
sie/Sie	**werden sprechen**

IMPERATIVE

sprich!/sprechen wir!/sprecht!/ sprechen Sie!

PRESENT SUBJUNCTIVE

ich	**spreche**
du	**sprechest**
er/sie/es	**spreche**
wir	**sprechen**
ihr	**sprechet**
sie/Sie	**sprechen**

IMPERFECT

ich	**sprach**
du	**sprachst**
er/sie/es	**sprach**
wir	**sprachen**
ihr	**spracht**
sie/Sie	**sprachen**

CONDITIONAL

ich	**würde sprechen**
du	**würdest sprechen**
er/sie/es	**würde sprechen**
wir	**würden sprechen**
ihr	**würdet sprechen**
sie/Sie	**würden sprechen**

PAST PARTICIPLE

gesprochen

PRESENT PARTICIPLE

sprechend

EXAMPLE PHRASES

Er **spricht** kein Italienisch. *He doesn't speak Italian.*
Ich **würde** dich gern privat **sprechen**. *I would like to speak to you privately.*
Hast du mit ihr **gesprochen**? *Have you spoken to her?*

springen (to jump)

strong, *formed with* **sein**

PRESENT

ich	**springe**
du	**springst**
er/sie/es	**springt**
wir	**springen**
ihr	**springt**
sie/Sie	**springen**

PRESENT SUBJUNCTIVE

ich	**springe**
du	**springest**
er/sie/es	**springe**
wir	**springen**
ihr	**springet**
sie/Sie	**springen**

PERFECT

ich	**bin gesprungen**
du	**bist gesprungen**
er/sie/es	**ist gesprungen**
wir	**sind gesprungen**
ihr	**seid gesprungen**
sie/Sie	**sind gesprungen**

IMPERFECT

ich	**sprang**
du	**sprangst**
er/sie/es	**sprang**
wir	**sprangen**
ihr	**sprangt**
sie/Sie	**sprangen**

FUTURE

ich	**werde springen**
du	**wirst springen**
er/sie/es	**wird springen**
wir	**werden springen**
ihr	**werdet springen**
sie/Sie	**werden springen**

CONDITIONAL

ich	**würde springen**
du	**würdest springen**
er/sie/es	**würde springen**
wir	**würden springen**
ihr	**würdet springen**
sie/Sie	**würden springen**

IMPERATIVE

spring(e)!/springen wir!/ springt!/springen Sie!

PAST PARTICIPLE

gesprungen

PRESENT PARTICIPLE

springend

EXAMPLE PHRASES

Er **sprang** über den Zaun. *He jumped over the fence.*
Der Zug **ist** aus dem Gleis **gesprungen**. *The train came off the rails.*
Ich **würde** ihm am liebsten an die Kehle **springen**. *I could strangle him.*

stehen (to stand)

strong, *formed with* **haben**

PRESENT

ich	**stehe**
du	**stehst**
er/sie/es	**steht**
wir	**stehen**
ihr	**steht**
sie/Sie	**stehen**

PRESENT SUBJUNCTIVE

ich	**stehe**
du	**stehest**
er/sie/es	**stehe**
wir	**stehen**
ihr	**stehet**
sie/Sie	**stehen**

PERFECT

ich	**habe gestanden**
du	**hast gestanden**
er/sie/es	**hat gestanden**
wir	**haben gestanden**
ihr	**habt gestanden**
sie/Sie	**haben gestanden**

IMPERFECT

ich	**stand**
du	**stand(e)st**
er/sie/es	**stand**
wir	**standen**
ihr	**standet**
sie/Sie	**standen**

FUTURE

ich	**werde stehen**
du	**wirst stehen**
er/sie/es	**wird stehen**
wir	**werden stehen**
ihr	**werdet stehen**
sie/Sie	**werden stehen**

CONDITIONAL

ich	**würde stehen**
du	**würdest stehen**
er/sie/es	**würde stehen**
wir	**würden stehen**
ihr	**würdet stehen**
sie/Sie	**würden stehen**

IMPERATIVE

steh(e)!/stehen wir!/steht!/ stehen Sie!

PAST PARTICIPLE

gestanden

PRESENT PARTICIPLE

stehend

EXAMPLE PHRASES

Wir **standen** an der Bushaltestelle. *We stood at the bus stop.*
Es **hat** in der Zeitung **gestanden**. *It was in the newspaper.*
Dieses Kleid **würde** dir gut **stehen**. *This dress would suit you.*

stehlen (to steal)

strong, *formed with* **haben**

PRESENT

ich	**stehle**
du	**stiehlst**
er/sie/es	**stiehlt**
wir	**stehlen**
ihr	**stehlt**
sie/Sie	**stehlen**

PRESENT SUBJUNCTIVE

ich	**stehle**
du	**stehlest**
er/sie/es	**stehle**
wir	**stehlen**
ihr	**stehlet**
sie/Sie	**stehlen**

PERFECT

ich	**habe gestohlen**
du	**hast gestohlen**
er/sie/es	**hat gestohlen**
wir	**haben gestohlen**
ihr	**habt gestohlen**
sie/Sie	**haben gestohlen**

IMPERFECT

ich	**stahl**
du	**stahlst**
er/sie/es	**stahl**
wir	**stahlen**
ihr	**stahlt**
sie/Sie	**stahlen**

FUTURE

ich	**werde stehlen**
du	**wirst stehlen**
er/sie/es	**wird stehlen**
wir	**werden stehlen**
ihr	**werdet stehlen**
sie/Sie	**werden stehlen**

CONDITIONAL

ich	**würde stehlen**
du	**würdest stehlen**
er/sie/es	**würde stehlen**
wir	**würden stehlen**
ihr	**würdet stehlen**
sie/Sie	**würden stehlen**

IMPERATIVE

stiehl!/stehlen wir!/stehlt!/ stehlen Sie!

PAST PARTICIPLE

gestohlen

PRESENT PARTICIPLE

stehlend

EXAMPLE PHRASES

Er **hat** das ganze Geld **gestohlen**. *He stole all the money.*
Er **stahl** sich aus dem Haus. *He stole out of the house.*
Du **stiehlst** uns doch nur die Zeit. *You're just wasting our time.*

steigen (to climb)

strong, *formed with* **sein**

PRESENT

ich	**steige**
du	**steigst**
er/sie/es	**steigt**
wir	**steigen**
ihr	**steigt**
sie/Sie	**steigen**

PRESENT SUBJUNCTIVE

ich	**steige**
du	**steigest**
er/sie/es	**steige**
wir	**steigen**
ihr	**steiget**
sie/Sie	**steigen**

PERFECT

ich	**bin gestiegen**
du	**bist gestiegen**
er/sie/es	**ist gestiegen**
wir	**sind gestiegen**
ihr	**seid gestiegen**
sie/Sie	**sind gestiegen**

IMPERFECT

ich	**stieg**
du	**stiegst**
er/sie/es	**stieg**
wir	**stiegen**
ihr	**stiegt**
sie/Sie	**stiegen**

FUTURE

ich	**werde steigen**
du	**wirst steigen**
er/sie/es	**wird steigen**
wir	**werden steigen**
ihr	**werdet steigen**
sie/Sie	**werden steigen**

CONDITIONAL

ich	**würde steigen**
du	**würdest steigen**
er/sie/es	**würde steigen**
wir	**würden steigen**
ihr	**würdet steigen**
sie/Sie	**würden steigen**

IMPERATIVE

steig(e)!/steigen wir!/steigt!/ steigen Sie!

PAST PARTICIPLE

gestiegen

PRESENT PARTICIPLE

steigend

EXAMPLE PHRASES

Die Temperatur **stieg** auf 28 Grad. *The temperature rose to 28 degrees.*
Sie **ist** auf die Leiter **gestiegen**. *She climbed up the ladder.*
Die Passagiere **stiegen** aus dem Flugzeug. *The passengers got off the plane.*

sterben (to die)

strong, *formed with* **sein**

PRESENT

ich	**sterbe**
du	**stirbst**
er/sie/es	**stirbt**
wir	**sterben**
ihr	**sterbt**
sie/Sie	**sterben**

PRESENT SUBJUNCTIVE

ich	**sterbe**
du	**sterbest**
er/sie/es	**sterbe**
wir	**sterben**
ihr	**sterbet**
sie/Sie	**sterben**

PERFECT

ich	**bin gestorben**
du	**bist gestorben**
er/sie/es	**ist gestorben**
wir	**sind gestorben**
ihr	**seid gestorben**
sie/Sie	**sind gestorben**

IMPERFECT

ich	**starb**
du	**starbst**
er/sie/es	**starb**
wir	**starben**
ihr	**starbt**
sie/Sie	**starben**

FUTURE

ich	**werde sterben**
du	**wirst sterben**
er/sie/es	**wird sterben**
wir	**werden sterben**
ihr	**werdet sterben**
sie/Sie	**werden sterben**

CONDITIONAL

ich	**würde sterben**
du	**würdest sterben**
er/sie/es	**würde sterben**
wir	**würden sterben**
ihr	**würdet sterben**
sie/Sie	**würden sterben**

IMPERATIVE

stirb!/sterben wir!/sterbt!/ sterben Sie!

PAST PARTICIPLE

gestorben

PRESENT PARTICIPLE

sterbend

EXAMPLE PHRASES

Er **starb** eines natürlichen Todes. *He died a natural death.*
Shakespeare **ist** 1616 **gestorben**. *Shakespeare died in 1616.*
Daran **wirst** du nicht **sterben**! *It won't kill you!*

ich = I **du** = you **er** = he/it **sie** = she/it **es** = it/he/she **wir** = we **ihr** = you **sie** = they **Sie** = you

studieren (to study)

strong, *formed with* **haben**

PRESENT

ich	**studiere**
du	**studierst**
er/sie/es	**studiert**
wir	**studieren**
ihr	**studiert**
sie/Sie	**studieren**

PERFECT

ich	**habe studiert**
du	**hast studiert**
er/sie/es	**hat studiert**
wir	**haben studiert**
ihr	**habt studiert**
sie/Sie	**haben studiert**

FUTURE

ich	**werde studieren**
du	**wirst studieren**
er/sie/es	**wird studieren**
wir	**werden studieren**
ihr	**werdet studieren**
sie/Sie	**werden studieren**

IMPERATIVE

studiere!/studieren wir!/ studiert!/studieren Sie!

PRESENT SUBJUNCTIVE

ich	**studiere**
du	**studierest**
er/sie/es	**studiere**
wir	**studieren**
ihr	**studieret**
sie/Sie	**studieren**

IMPERFECT

ich	**studierte**
du	**studiertest**
er/sie/es	**studierte**
wir	**studierten**
ihr	**studiertet**
sie/Sie	**studierten**

CONDITIONAL

ich	**würde studieren**
du	**würdest studieren**
er/sie/es	**würde studieren**
wir	**würden studieren**
ihr	**würdet studieren**
sie/Sie	**würden studieren**

PAST PARTICIPLE

studiert

PRESENT PARTICIPLE

studierend

EXAMPLE PHRASES

Sie möchte Biologie **studieren**. *She wants to study biology.*
Mein Bruder **studiert** Deutsch. *My brother is studying German.*
Er **hat** in Köln **studiert**. *He was a student at Cologne University.*

tragen (to wear; to carry)

strong, *formed with* **haben**

PRESENT

ich	**trage**
du	**trägst**
er/sie/es	**trägt**
wir	**tragen**
ihr	**tragt**
sie/Sie	**tragen**

PRESENT SUBJUNCTIVE

ich	**trage**
du	**tragest**
er/sie/es	**trage**
wir	**tragen**
ihr	**traget**
sie/Sie	**tragen**

PERFECT

ich	**habe getragen**
du	**hast getragen**
er/sie/es	**hat getragen**
wir	**haben getragen**
ihr	**habt getragen**
sie/Sie	**haben getragen**

IMPERFECT

ich	**trug**
du	**trugst**
er/sie/es	**trug**
wir	**trugen**
ihr	**trugt**
sie/Sie	**trugen**

FUTURE

ich	**werde tragen**
du	**wirst tragen**
er/sie/es	**wird tragen**
wir	**werden tragen**
ihr	**werdet tragen**
sie/Sie	**werden tragen**

CONDITIONAL

ich	**würde tragen**
du	**würdest tragen**
er/sie/es	**würde tragen**
wir	**würden tragen**
ihr	**würdet tragen**
sie/Sie	**würden tragen**

IMPERATIVE

trag(e)!/tragen wir!/tragt!/ tragen Sie!

PAST PARTICIPLE

getragen

PRESENT PARTICIPLE

tragend

EXAMPLE PHRASES

Ich **trug** ihren Koffer zum Bahnhof. *I carried her case to the station.*
Du **trägst** die ganze Verantwortung dafür. *You bear the full responsibility for it.*
Ich **würde** meine Haare gern länger **tragen**. *I'd like to wear my hair longer.*

treffen (to meet)

strong, *formed with* **haben**

PRESENT

ich	**treffe**
du	**triffst**
er/sie/es	**trifft**
wir	**treffen**
ihr	**trefft**
sie/Sie	**treffen**

PRESENT SUBJUNCTIVE

ich	**treffe**
du	**treffest**
er/sie/es	**treffe**
wir	**treffen**
ihr	**treffet**
sie/Sie	**treffen**

PERFECT

ich	**habe getroffen**
du	**hast getroffen**
er/sie/es	**hat getroffen**
wir	**haben getroffen**
ihr	**habt getroffen**
sie/Sie	**haben getroffen**

IMPERFECT

ich	**traf**
du	**trafst**
er/sie/es	**traf**
wir	**trafen**
ihr	**traft**
sie/Sie	**trafen**

FUTURE

ich	**werde treffen**
du	**wirst treffen**
er/sie/es	**wird treffen**
wir	**werden treffen**
ihr	**werdet treffen**
sie/Sie	**werden treffen**

CONDITIONAL

ich	**würde treffen**
du	**würdest treffen**
er/sie/es	**würde treffen**
wir	**würden treffen**
ihr	**würdet treffen**
sie/Sie	**würden treffen**

IMPERATIVE

triff!/treffen wir!/trefft!/ treffen Sie!

PAST PARTICIPLE

getroffen

PRESENT PARTICIPLE

treffend

EXAMPLE PHRASES

Sie **trifft** sich zweimal pro Woche mit ihm. *She meets with him twice a week.*
Der Ball **traf** ihn am Kopf. *The ball hit him on the head.*
Du **hast** das Ziel gut **getroffen**. *You hit the target well.*

treten (to kick; to step)

strong, *formed with* **haben/sein***

PRESENT

ich	**trete**
du	**trittst**
er/sie/es	**tritt**
wir	**treten**
ihr	**tretet**
sie/Sie	**treten**

PRESENT SUBJUNCTIVE

ich	**trete**
du	**tretest**
er/sie/es	**trete**
wir	**treten**
ihr	**tretet**
sie/Sie	**treten**

PERFECT

ich	**habe getreten**
du	**hast getreten**
er/sie/es	**hat getreten**
wir	**haben getreten**
ihr	**habt getreten**
sie/Sie	**haben getreten**

IMPERFECT

ich	**trat**
du	**trat(e)st**
er/sie/es	**trat**
wir	**traten**
ihr	**tratet**
sie/Sie	**traten**

FUTURE

ich	**werde treten**
du	**wirst treten**
er/sie/es	**wird treten**
wir	**werden treten**
ihr	**werdet treten**
sie/Sie	**werden treten**

CONDITIONAL

ich	**würde treten**
du	**würdest treten**
er/sie/es	**würde treten**
wir	**würden treten**
ihr	**würdet treten**
sie/Sie	**würden treten**

IMPERATIVE

tritt!/treten wir!/tretet!/ treten Sie!

PAST PARTICIPLE

getreten

PRESENT PARTICIPLE

tretend

EXAMPLE PHRASES

Er **hat** mich **getreten**. *He kicked me.*
Sie **trat** auf die Bremse. *She stepped on the brakes.*
Pass auf, wohin du **trittst**! *Watch your step!*
Er **ist** mir auf den Fuß **getreten**. *He stood on my foot.*

*When **treten** is used with no direct object, it is formed with **sein**.

trinken (to drink)

strong, *formed with* **haben**

PRESENT

ich	**trinke**
du	**trinkst**
er/sie/es	**trinkt**
wir	**trinken**
ihr	**trinkt**
sie/Sie	**trinken**

PRESENT SUBJUNCTIVE

ich	**trinke**
du	**trinkest**
er/sie/es	**trinke**
wir	**trinken**
ihr	**trinket**
sie/Sie	**trinken**

PERFECT

ich	**habe getrunken**
du	**hast getrunken**
er/sie/es	**hat getrunken**
wir	**haben getrunken**
ihr	**habt getrunken**
sie/Sie	**haben getrunken**

IMPERFECT

ich	**trank**
du	**trankst**
er/sie/es	**trank**
wir	**tranken**
ihr	**trankt**
sie/Sie	**tranken**

FUTURE

ich	**werde trinken**
du	**wirst trinken**
er/sie/es	**wird trinken**
wir	**werden trinken**
ihr	**werdet trinken**
sie/Sie	**werden trinken**

CONDITIONAL

ich	**würde trinken**
du	**würdest trinken**
er/sie/es	**würde trinken**
wir	**würden trinken**
ihr	**würdet trinken**
sie/Sie	**würden trinken**

IMPERATIVE

trink(e)!/trinken wir!/trinkt!/ trinken Sie!

PAST PARTICIPLE

getrunken

PRESENT PARTICIPLE

trinkend

EXAMPLE PHRASES

Er **trank** die ganze Flasche leer. *He drank the whole bottle.*
Ich **habe** zu viel **getrunken**. *I've had too much to drink.*
Wollen wir etwas **trinken** gehen? *Shall we go for a drink?*

ich = I **du** = you **er** = he/it **sie** = she/it **es** = it/he/she **wir** = we **ihr** = you **sie** = they **Sie** = you

tun (to do)

strong, *formed with* **haben**

PRESENT

ich	**tue**
du	**tust**
er/sie/es	**tut**
wir	**tun**
ihr	**tut**
sie/Sie	**tun**

PRESENT SUBJUNCTIVE

ich	**tue**
du	**tuest**
er/sie/es	**tue**
wir	**tuen**
ihr	**tuet**
sie/Sie	**tuen**

PERFECT

ich	**habe getan**
du	**hast getan**
er/sie/es	**hat getan**
wir	**haben getan**
ihr	**habt getan**
sie/Sie	**haben getan**

IMPERFECT

ich	**tat**
du	**tat(e)st**
er/sie/es	**tat**
wir	**taten**
ihr	**tatet**
sie/Sie	**taten**

FUTURE

ich	**werde tun**
du	**wirst tun**
er/sie/es	**wird tun**
wir	**werden tun**
ihr	**werdet tun**
sie/Sie	**werden tun**

CONDITIONAL

ich	**würde tun**
du	**würdest tun**
er/sie/es	**würde tun**
wir	**würden tun**
ihr	**würdet tun**
sie/Sie	**würden tun**

IMPERATIVE

tu(e)!/tun wir!/tut!/tun Sie!

PAST PARTICIPLE

getan

PRESENT PARTICIPLE

tuend

EXAMPLE PHRASES

Ich **werde** das auf keinen Fall **tun**. *There is no way I'll do that.*
So etwas **tut** man nicht! *That is just not done!*
Sie **tat**, als ob sie schliefe. *She pretended to be sleeping.*

sich überlegen (to consider)

weak, inseparable, reflexive, *formed with* **haben**

PRESENT

ich	**überlege mir**
du	**überlegst dir**
er/sie/es	**überlegt sich**
wir	**überlegen uns**
ihr	**überlegt euch**
sie/Sie	**überlegen sich**

PRESENT SUBJUNCTIVE

ich	**überlege mir**
du	**überlegest dir**
er/sie/es	**überlege sich**
wir	**überlegen uns**
ihr	**überleget euch**
sie/Sie	**überlegen sich**

PERFECT

ich	**habe mir überlegt**
du	**hast dir überlegt**
er/sie/es	**hat sich überlegt**
wir	**haben uns überlegt**
ihr	**habt euch überlegt**
sie/Sie	**haben sich überlegt**

IMPERFECT

ich	**überlegte mir**
du	**überlegtest dir**
er/sie/es	**überlegte sich**
wir	**überlegten uns**
ihr	**überlegtet euch**
sie/Sie	**überlegten sich**

FUTURE

ich	**werde mir überlegen**
du	**wirst dir überlegen**
er/sie/es	**wird sich überlegen**
wir	**werden uns überlegen**
ihr	**werdet euch überlegen**
sie/Sie	**werden sich überlegen**

CONDITIONAL

ich	**würde mir überlegen**
du	**würdest dir überlegen**
er/sie/es	**würde sich überlegen**
wir	**würden uns überlegen**
ihr	**würdet euch überlegen**
sie/Sie	**würden sich überlegen**

IMPERATIVE

überleg(e)dir!/überlegen wir uns!/ überlegt euch!/überlegen Sie sich!

PAST PARTICIPLE

überlegt

PRESENT PARTICIPLE

überlegend

EXAMPLE PHRASES

Ich **habe mir** schon **überlegt**, was ich machen werde. *I've already thought about what I'm going to do.*
Ich muss es **mir überlegen**. *I'll have to think about it.*
Würden Sie es **sich** noch einmal **überlegen**? *Would you reconsider?*

vergessen (to forget)

strong, inseparable, *formed with* **haben**

PRESENT

ich	**vergesse**
du	**vergisst**
er/sie/es	**vergisst**
wir	**vergessen**
ihr	**vergesst**
sie/Sie	**vergessen**

PRESENT SUBJUNCTIVE

ich	**vergesse**
du	**vergessest**
er/sie/es	**vergesse**
wir	**vergessen**
ihr	**vergesset**
sie/Sie	**vergessen**

PERFECT

ich	**habe vergessen**
du	**hast vergessen**
er/sie/es	**hat vergessen**
wir	**haben vergessen**
ihr	**habt vergessen**
sie/Sie	**haben vergessen**

IMPERFECT

ich	**vergaß**
du	**vergaßest**
er/sie/es	**vergaß**
wir	**vergaßen**
ihr	**vergaßt**
sie/Sie	**vergaßen**

FUTURE

ich	**werde vergessen**
du	**wirst vergessen**
er/sie/es	**wird vergessen**
wir	**werden vergessen**
ihr	**werdet vergessen**
sie/Sie	**werden vergessen**

CONDITIONAL

ich	**würde vergessen**
du	**würdest vergessen**
er/sie/es	**würde vergessen**
wir	**würden vergessen**
ihr	**würdet vergessen**
sie/Sie	**würden vergessen**

IMPERATIVE

vergiss!/vergessen wir!/ vergesst!/vergessen Sie!

PAST PARTICIPLE

vergessen

PRESENT PARTICIPLE

vergessend

EXAMPLE PHRASES

Ich **habe** seinen Namen **vergessen**. *I've forgotten his name.*
Sie **vergaß**, die Blumen zu gießen. *She forgot to water the flowers.*
Sie **vergisst** ständig ihren Laptop. *She always forgets to bring her laptop.*

ich = I **du** = you **er** = he/it **sie** = she/it **es** = it/he/she **wir** = we **ihr** = you **sie** = they **Sie** = you

verlangen (to demand)

weak, inseparable, *formed with* **haben**

PRESENT

ich	**verlange**
du	**verlangst**
er/sie/es	**verlangt**
wir	**verlangen**
ihr	**verlangt**
sie/Sie	**verlangen**

PRESENT SUBJUNCTIVE

ich	**verlange**
du	**verlangest**
er/sie/es	**verlange**
wir	**verlangen**
ihr	**verlanget**
sie/Sie	**verlangen**

PERFECT

ich	**habe verlangt**
du	**hast verlangt**
er/sie/es	**hat verlangt**
wir	**haben verlangt**
ihr	**habt verlangt**
sie/Sie	**haben verlangt**

IMPERFECT

ich	**verlangte**
du	**verlangtest**
er/sie/es	**verlangte**
wir	**verlangten**
ihr	**verlangtet**
sie/Sie	**verlangten**

FUTURE

ich	**werde verlangen**
du	**wirst verlangen**
er/sie/es	**wird verlangen**
wir	**werden verlangen**
ihr	**werdet verlangen**
sie/Sie	**werden verlangen**

CONDITIONAL

ich	**würde verlangen**
du	**würdest verlangen**
er/sie/es	**würde verlangen**
wir	**würden verlangen**
ihr	**würdet verlangen**
sie/Sie	**würden verlangen**

IMPERATIVE

verlang(e)!/verlangen wir!/ verlangt!/verlangen Sie!

PAST PARTICIPLE

verlangt

PRESENT PARTICIPLE

verlangend

EXAMPLE PHRASES

Unsere Lehrerin **verlangt** wirklich sehr viel von uns. *Our teacher demands an awful lot of us.*
Das kannst du nicht von mir **verlangen**. *You cannot ask that of me.*
Wie viel **hat** er dafür **verlangt**? *How much did he ask for it?*

verlieren (to lose)

strong, inseparable, *formed with* **haben**

PRESENT

ich	**verliere**
du	**verlierst**
er/sie/es	**verliert**
wir	**verlieren**
ihr	**verliert**
sie/Sie	**verlieren**

PRESENT SUBJUNCTIVE

ich	**verliere**
du	**verlierest**
er/sie/es	**verliere**
wir	**verlieren**
ihr	**verlieret**
sie/Sie	**verlieren**

PERFECT

ich	**habe verloren**
du	**hast verloren**
er/sie/es	**hat verloren**
wir	**haben verloren**
ihr	**habt verloren**
sie/Sie	**haben verloren**

IMPERFECT

ich	**verlor**
du	**verlorst**
er/sie/es	**verlor**
wir	**verloren**
ihr	**verlort**
sie/Sie	**verloren**

FUTURE

ich	**werde verlieren**
du	**wirst verlieren**
er/sie/es	**wird verlieren**
wir	**werden verlieren**
ihr	**werdet verlieren**
sie/Sie	**werden verlieren**

CONDITIONAL

ich	**würde verlieren**
du	**würdest verlieren**
er/sie/es	**würde verlieren**
wir	**würden verlieren**
ihr	**würdet verlieren**
sie/Sie	**würden verlieren**

IMPERATIVE

verlier(e)!/verlieren wir!/ verliert!/verlieren Sie!

PAST PARTICIPLE

verloren

PRESENT PARTICIPLE

verlierend

EXAMPLE PHRASES

Wenn du **verlierst**, musst du mir 10 Euro zahlen. *If you lose, you'll have to pay me 10 euros.*

Wir **haben** drei Spiele hintereinander **verloren**. *We lost three matches in a row.*

Er **verlor** kein Wort darüber. *He didn't say a word about it.*

verschwinden (to disappear)

strong, inseparable,
formed with **sein**

PRESENT

ich	**verschwinde**
du	**verschwindest**
er/sie/es	**verschwindet**
wir	**verschwinden**
ihr	**verschwindet**
sie/Sie	**verschwinden**

PRESENT SUBJUNCTIVE

ich	**verschwinde**
du	**verschwindest**
er/sie/es	**verschwinde**
wir	**verschwinden**
ihr	**verschwindet**
sie/Sie	**verschwinden**

PERFECT

ich	**bin verschwunden**
du	**bist verschwunden**
er/sie/es	**ist verschwunden**
wir	**sind verschwunden**
ihr	**seid verschwunden**
sie/Sie	**sind verschwunden**

IMPERFECT

ich	**verschwand**
du	**verschwand(e)st**
er/sie/es	**verschwand**
wir	**verschwanden**
ihr	**verschwandet**
sie/Sie	**verschwanden**

FUTURE

ich	**werde verschwinden**
du	**wirst verschwinden**
er/sie/es	**wird verschwinden**
wir	**werden verschwinden**
ihr	**werdet verschwinden**
sie/Sie	**werden verschwinden**

CONDITIONAL

ich	**würde verschwinden**
du	**würdest verschwinden**
er/sie/es	**würde verschwinden**
wir	**würden verschwinden**
ihr	**würdet verschwinden**
sie/Sie	**würden verschwinden**

IMPERATIVE

verschwind(e)!/verschwinden wir!/ verschwindet!/verschwinden Sie!

PAST PARTICIPLE

verschwunden

PRESENT PARTICIPLE

verschwindend

EXAMPLE PHRASES

Sie **verschwanden** in der Dunkelheit. *They disappeared into the darkness.*
Der Zauberer ließ das Kaninchen **verschwinden**. *The magician made the rabbit disappear.*
Er **ist** seit Sonntag **verschwunden**. *He has been missing since Sunday.*

wachsen (to grow)

strong, *formed with* **sein**

PRESENT

ich	**wachse**
du	**wächst**
er/sie/es	**wächst**
wir	**wachsen**
ihr	**wachst**
sie/Sie	**wachsen**

PRESENT SUBJUNCTIVE

ich	**wachse**
du	**wachsest**
er/sie/es	**wachse**
wir	**wachsen**
ihr	**wachset**
sie/Sie	**wachsen**

PERFECT

ich	**bin gewachsen**
du	**bist gewachsen**
er/sie/es	**ist gewachsen**
wir	**sind gewachsen**
ihr	**seid gewachsen**
sie/Sie	**sind gewachsen**

IMPERFECT

ich	**wuchs**
du	**wuchsest**
er/sie/es	**wuchs**
wir	**wuchsen**
ihr	**wuchst**
sie/Sie	**wuchsen**

FUTURE

ich	**werde wachsen**
du	**wirst wachsen**
er/sie/es	**wird wachsen**
wir	**werden wachsen**
ihr	**werdet wachsen**
sie/Sie	**werden wachsen**

CONDITIONAL

ich	**würde wachsen**
du	**würdest wachsen**
er/sie/es	**würde wachsen**
wir	**würden wachsen**
ihr	**würdet wachsen**
sie/Sie	**würden wachsen**

IMPERATIVE

wachs(e)!/wachsen wir!/ wachst!/wachsen Sie!

PAST PARTICIPLE

gewachsen

PRESENT PARTICIPLE

wachsend

EXAMPLE PHRASES

Der Baum **wächst** nicht mehr. *The tree has stopped growing.*
Er ließ sich einen Bart **wachsen**. *He grew a beard.*
Ich **bin** im letzten Jahr 10 Zentimeter **gewachsen**. *I've grown 10 centimetres in the past year.*

wandern (to roam; to go walking)

weak, *formed with* **sein**

PRESENT

ich	**wand(e)re**
du	**wanderst**
er/sie/es	**wandert**
wir	**wandern**
ihr	**wandert**
sie/Sie	**wandern**

PRESENT SUBJUNCTIVE

ich	**wand(e)re**
du	**wand(e)rest**
er/sie/es	**wand(e)re**
wir	**wandern**
ihr	**wandert**
sie/Sie	**wandern**

PERFECT

ich	**bin gewandert**
du	**bist gewandert**
er/sie/es	**ist gewandert**
wir	**sind gewandert**
ihr	**seid gewandert**
sie/Sie	**sind gewandert**

IMPERFECT

ich	**wanderte**
du	**wandertest**
er/sie/es	**wanderte**
wir	**wanderten**
ihr	**wandertet**
sie/Sie	**wanderten**

FUTURE

ich	**werde wandern**
du	**wirst wandern**
er/sie/es	**wird wandern**
wir	**werden wandern**
ihr	**werdet wandern**
sie/Sie	**werden wandern**

CONDITIONAL

ich	**würde wandern**
du	**würdest wandern**
er/sie/es	**würde wandern**
wir	**würden wandern**
ihr	**würdet wandern**
sie/Sie	**würden wandern**

IMPERATIVE

wandre!/wandern wir!/ wandert!/wandern Sie!

PAST PARTICIPLE

gewandert

PRESENT PARTICIPLE

wandernd

EXAMPLE PHRASES

Im Schwarzwald kann man gut **wandern**. *The Black Forest is good for walking.*
Wir **sind** am Wochenende **gewandert**. *We went hiking at the weekend.*
Seine Gedanken **wanderten** zurück in die Vergangenheit. *His thoughts strayed back to the past.*

waschen (to wash)

strong, *formed with* **haben**

PRESENT

ich	**wasche**
du	**wäschst**
er/sie/es	**wäscht**
wir	**waschen**
ihr	**wascht**
sie/Sie	**waschen**

PRESENT SUBJUNCTIVE

ich	**wasche**
du	**waschest**
er/sie/es	**wasche**
wir	**waschen**
ihr	**waschet**
sie/Sie	**waschen**

PERFECT

ich	**habe gewaschen**
du	**hast gewaschen**
er/sie/es	**hat gewaschen**
wir	**haben gewaschen**
ihr	**habt gewaschen**
sie/Sie	**haben gewaschen**

IMPERFECT

ich	**wusch**
du	**wuschest**
er/sie/es	**wusch**
wir	**wuschen**
ihr	**wuscht**
sie/Sie	**wuschen**

FUTURE

ich	**werde waschen**
du	**wirst waschen**
er/sie/es	**wird waschen**
wir	**werden waschen**
ihr	**werdet waschen**
sie/Sie	**werden waschen**

CONDITIONAL

ich	**würde waschen**
du	**würdest waschen**
er/sie/es	**würde waschen**
wir	**würden waschen**
ihr	**würdet waschen**
sie/Sie	**würden waschen**

IMPERATIVE

wasch(e)!/waschen wir!/ wascht!/waschen Sie!

PAST PARTICIPLE

gewaschen

PRESENT PARTICIPLE

waschend

EXAMPLE PHRASES

Ich **habe** mir die Hände **gewaschen**. *I washed my hands.*
Er **wäschst** sich jeden Tag. *He washes every day.*
Die Katze **wusch** sich in der Sonne. *The cat was washing itself in the sunshine.*

werben (to recruit; to advertise)

strong, *formed with* **haben**

PRESENT

ich	**werbe**
du	**wirbst**
er/sie/es	**wirbt**
wir	**werben**
ihr	**werbt**
sie/Sie	**werben**

PRESENT SUBJUNCTIVE

ich	**werbe**
du	**werbest**
er/sie/es	**werbe**
wir	**werben**
ihr	**werbet**
sie/Sie	**werben**

PERFECT

ich	**habe geworben**
du	**hast geworben**
er/sie/es	**hat geworben**
wir	**haben geworben**
ihr	**habt geworben**
sie/Sie	**haben geworben**

IMPERFECT

ich	**warb**
du	**warbst**
er/sie/es	**warb**
wir	**warben**
ihr	**warbt**
sie/Sie	**warben**

FUTURE

ich	**werde werben**
du	**wirst werben**
er/sie/es	**wird werben**
wir	**werden werben**
ihr	**werdet werben**
sie/Sie	**werden werben**

CONDITIONAL

ich	**würde werben**
du	**würdest werben**
er/sie/es	**würde werben**
wir	**würden werben**
ihr	**würdet werben**
sie/Sie	**würden werben**

IMPERATIVE

wirb!/werben wir!/werbt!/ werben Sie!

PAST PARTICIPLE

geworben

PRESENT PARTICIPLE

werbend

EXAMPLE PHRASES

Die Partei **wirbt** zur Zeit Mitglieder. *The party is currently recruiting members.*

Unsere Firma muss um neue Kunden **werben**. *Our company has to attract new customers.*

Im Fernsehen **wird** zu viel **geworben**. *There's too much advertising on TV.*

werden (to become)

strong, *formed with* **sein**

PRESENT

ich	**werde**
du	**wirst**
er/sie/es	**wird**
wir	**werden**
ihr	**werdet**
sie/Sie	**werden**

PRESENT SUBJUNCTIVE

ich	**werde**
du	**werdest**
er/sie/es	**werde**
wir	**werden**
ihr	**werdet**
sie/Sie	**werden**

PERFECT

ich	**bin geworden**
du	**bist geworden**
er/sie/es	**ist geworden**
wir	**sind geworden**
ihr	**seid geworden**
sie/Sie	**sind geworden**

IMPERFECT

ich	**wurde**
du	**wurdest**
er/sie/es	**wurde**
wir	**wurden**
ihr	**wurdet**
sie/Sie	**wurden**

FUTURE

ich	**werde werden**
du	**wirst werden**
er/sie/es	**wird werden**
wir	**werden werden**
ihr	**werdet werden**
sie/Sie	**werden werden**

CONDITIONAL

ich	**würde werden**
du	**würdest werden**
er/sie/es	**würde werden**
wir	**würden werden**
ihr	**würdet werden**
sie/Sie	**würden werden**

IMPERATIVE

werde!/werden wir!/werdet!/ werden Sie!

PAST PARTICIPLE

geworden

PRESENT PARTICIPLE

werdend

EXAMPLE PHRASES

Mir **wird** schlecht. *I feel ill.*
Ich will Lehrerin **werden**. *I want to be a teacher.*
Der Kuchen **ist** gut **geworden**. *The cake turned out well.*

ich = I **du** = you **er** = he/it **sie** = she/it **es** = it/he/she **wir** = we **ihr** = you **sie** = they **Sie** = you

werfen (to throw)

strong, *formed with* **haben**

PRESENT

ich	**werfe**
du	**wirfst**
er/sie/es	**wirft**
wir	**werfen**
ihr	**werft**
sie/Sie	**werfen**

PRESENT SUBJUNCTIVE

ich	**werfe**
du	**werfest**
er/sie/es	**werfe**
wir	**werfen**
ihr	**werfet**
sie/Sie	**werfen**

PERFECT

ich	**habe geworfen**
du	**hast geworfen**
er/sie/es	**hat geworfen**
wir	**haben geworfen**
ihr	**habt geworfen**
sie/Sie	**haben geworfen**

IMPERFECT

ich	**warf**
du	**warfst**
er/sie/es	**warf**
wir	**warfen**
ihr	**warft**
sie/Sie	**warfen**

FUTURE

ich	**werde werfen**
du	**wirst werfen**
er/sie/es	**wird werfen**
wir	**werden werfen**
ihr	**werdet werfen**
sie/Sie	**werden werfen**

CONDITIONAL

ich	**würde werfen**
du	**würdest werfen**
er/sie/es	**würde werfen**
wir	**würden werfen**
ihr	**würdet werfen**
sie/Sie	**würden werfen**

IMPERATIVE

wirf!/werfen wir!/werft!/ werfen Sie!

PAST PARTICIPLE

geworfen

PRESENT PARTICIPLE

werfend

EXAMPLE PHRASES

Er **warf** den Ball über den Zaun. *He threw the ball over the fence.*
Sie **wirft** mit Geld um sich. *She is throwing her money around.*
Der Chef **hat** ihn aus der Firma **geworfen**. *The boss has kicked him out of the company.*

wissen (to know)

mixed, *formed with* **haben**

PRESENT

ich	**weiß**
du	**weißt**
er/sie/es	**weiß**
wir	**wissen**
ihr	**wisst**
sie/Sie	**wissen**

PRESENT SUBJUNCTIVE

ich	**wisse**
du	**wissest**
er/sie/es	**wisse**
wir	**wissen**
ihr	**wisset**
sie/Sie	**wissen**

PERFECT

ich	**habe gewusst**
du	**hast gewusst**
er/sie/es	**hat gewusst**
wir	**haben gewusst**
ihr	**habt gewusst**
sie/Sie	**haben gewusst**

IMPERFECT

ich	**wusste**
du	**wusstest**
er/sie/es	**wusste**
wir	**wussten**
ihr	**wusstet**
sie/Sie	**wussten**

FUTURE

ich	**werde wissen**
du	**wirst wissen**
er/sie/es	**wird wissen**
wir	**werden wissen**
ihr	**werdet wissen**
sie/Sie	**werden wissen**

CONDITIONAL

ich	**würde wissen**
du	**würdest wissen**
er/sie/es	**würde wissen**
wir	**würden wissen**
ihr	**würdet wissen**
sie/Sie	**würden wissen**

IMPERATIVE

wisse!/wissen wir!/wisset!/ wissen Sie!

PAST PARTICIPLE

gewusst

PRESENT PARTICIPLE

wissend

EXAMPLE PHRASES

Ich **weiß** nicht. *I don't know.*
Er **hat** nichts davon **gewusst**. *He didn't know anything about it.*
Sie **wussten**, wo das Kino war. *They knew where the cinema was.*

ich = I **du** = you **er** = he/it **sie** = she/it **es** = it/he/she **wir** = we **ihr** = you **sie** = they **Sie** = you

wollen (to want)

modal, *formed with* **haben**

PRESENT

ich	**will**
du	**willst**
er/sie/es	**will**
wir	**wollen**
ihr	**wollt**
sie/Sie	**wollen**

PRESENT SUBJUNCTIVE

ich	**wolle**
du	**wollest**
er/sie/es	**wolle**
wir	**wollen**
ihr	**wollet**
sie/Sie	**wollen**

PERFECT

ich	**habe gewollt/wollen**
du	**hast gewollt/wollen**
er/sie/es	**hat gewollt/wollen**
wir	**haben gewollt/wollen**
ihr	**habt gewollt/wollen**
sie/Sie	**haben gewollt/wollen**

IMPERFECT

ich	**wollte**
du	**wolltest**
er/sie/es	**wollte**
wir	**wollten**
ihr	**wolltet**
sie/Sie	**wollten**

FUTURE

ich	**werde wollen**
du	**wirst wollen**
er/sie/es	**wird wollen**
wir	**werden wollen**
ihr	**werdet wollen**
sie/Sie	**werden wollen**

CONDITIONAL

ich	**würde wollen**
du	**würdest wollen**
er/sie/es	**würde wollen**
wir	**würden wollen**
ihr	**würdet wollen**
sie/Sie	**würden wollen**

IMPERATIVE

wolle!/wollen wir!/wollt!/ wollen Sie!

PAST PARTICIPLE

gewollt/wollen*

PRESENT PARTICIPLE

wollend

**This form is used when combined with another infinitive.*

EXAMPLE PHRASES

Er **will** nach London gehen. *He wants to go to London.*
Das **habe** ich nicht **gewollt**. *I didn't want this to happen.*
Sie **wollten** nur mehr Geld. *All they wanted was more money.*

zerstören (to destroy)

weak, inseparable, *formed with* **haben**

PRESENT

ich	**zerstöre**
du	**zerstörst**
er/sie/es	**zerstört**
wir	**zerstören**
ihr	**zerstört**
sie/Sie	**zerstören**

PRESENT SUBJUNCTIVE

ich	**zerstöre**
du	**zerstörest**
er/sie/es	**zerstöre**
wir	**zerstören**
ihr	**zerstöret**
sie/Sie	**zerstören**

PERFECT

ich	**habe zerstört**
du	**hast zerstört**
er/sie/es	**hat zerstört**
wir	**haben zerstört**
ihr	**habt zerstört**
sie/Sie	**haben zerstört**

IMPERFECT

ich	**zerstörte**
du	**zerstörtest**
er/sie/es	**zerstörte**
wir	**zerstörten**
ihr	**zerstörtet**
sie/Sie	**zerstörten**

FUTURE

ich	**werde zerstören**
du	**wirst zerstören**
er/sie/es	**wird zerstören**
wir	**werden zerstören**
ihr	**werdet zerstören**
sie/Sie	**werden zerstören**

CONDITIONAL

ich	**würde zerstören**
du	**würdest zerstören**
er/sie/es	**würde zerstören**
wir	**würden zerstören**
ihr	**würdet zerstören**
sie/Sie	**würden zerstören**

IMPERATIVE

zerstör(e)!/zerstören wir!/ zerstört!/zerstören Sie!

PAST PARTICIPLE

zerstört

PRESENT PARTICIPLE

zerstörend

EXAMPLE PHRASES

Die ganzen Abgase **zerstören** die Ozonschicht. *All the fumes are destroying the ozone layer.*
Er **hat** ihr Selbstvertrauen **zerstört**. *He has destroyed her self-confidence.*
Er **zerstörte** ihre Ehe. *He wrecked their marriage.*

ziehen (to go; to pull)

strong, *formed with* **sein/haben***

PRESENT

ich	**ziehe**
du	**ziehst**
er/sie/es	**zieht**
wir	**ziehen**
ihr	**zieht**
sie/Sie	**ziehen**

PERFECT

ich	**bin gezogen**
du	**bist gezogen**
er/sie/es	**ist gezogen**
wir	**sind gezogen**
ihr	**seid gezogen**
sie/Sie	**sind gezogen**

FUTURE

ich	**werde ziehen**
du	**wirst ziehen**
er/sie/es	**wird ziehen**
wir	**werden ziehen**
ihr	**werdet ziehen**
sie/Sie	**werden ziehen**

IMPERATIVE

zieh(e)!/ziehen wir!/zieht!/ ziehen Sie!

PRESENT SUBJUNCTIVE

ich	**ziehe**
du	**ziehest**
er/sie/es	**ziehe**
wir	**ziehen**
ihr	**ziehet**
sie/Sie	**ziehen**

IMPERFECT

ich	**zog**
du	**zogst**
er/sie/es	**zog**
wir	**zogen**
ihr	**zogt**
sie/Sie	**zogen**

CONDITIONAL

ich	**würde ziehen**
du	**würdest ziehen**
er/sie/es	**würde ziehen**
wir	**würden ziehen**
ihr	**würdet ziehen**
sie/Sie	**würden ziehen**

PAST PARTICIPLE

gezogen

PRESENT PARTICIPLE

ziehend

EXAMPLE PHRASES

Seine Familie **ist** nach München **gezogen**. *His family has moved to Munich.*
In diesem Zimmer **zieht** es. *There's a draught in this room.*
Sie **hat** mich am Ärmel **gezogen**. *She pulled at my sleeve.*

*When **ziehen** is used with a direct object, it is formed with **haben**.

ich = I **du** = you **er** = he/it **sie** = she/it **es** = it/he/she **wir** = we **ihr** = you **sie** = they **Sie** = you

zwingen (to force)

strong, *formed with* **haben**

PRESENT

ich	**zwinge**
du	**zwingst**
er/sie/es	**zwingt**
wir	**zwingen**
ihr	**zwingt**
sie/Sie	**zwingen**

PRESENT SUBJUNCTIVE

ich	**zwinge**
du	**zwingest**
er/sie/es	**zwinge**
wir	**zwingen**
ihr	**zwinget**
sie/Sie	**zwingen**

PERFECT

ich	**habe gezwungen**
du	**hast gezwungen**
er/sie/es	**hat gezwungen**
wir	**haben gezwungen**
ihr	**habt gezwungen**
sie/Sie	**haben gezwungen**

IMPERFECT

ich	**zwang**
du	**zwangst**
er/sie/es	**zwang**
wir	**zwangen**
ihr	**zwangt**
sie/Sie	**zwangen**

FUTURE

ich	**werde zwingen**
du	**wirst zwingen**
er/sie/es	**wird zwingen**
wir	**werden zwingen**
ihr	**werdet zwingen**
sie/Sie	**werden zwingen**

CONDITIONAL

ich	**würde zwingen**
du	**würdest zwingen**
er/sie/es	**würde zwingen**
wir	**würden zwingen**
ihr	**würdet zwingen**
sie/Sie	**würden zwingen**

IMPERATIVE

zwing(e)!/zwingen wir!/
zwingt!/zwingen Sie!

PAST PARTICIPLE

gezwungen

PRESENT PARTICIPLE

zwingend

EXAMPLE PHRASES

Er **hat** ihn **gezwungen**, das zu tun. *He forced him to do it.*
Sie **zwangen** uns, den Vertrag zu unterschreiben. *They forced us to sign the contract.*
Ich kann dich nicht **zwingen**. *I can't force you.*

How to use the Verb Index

The verbs in bold are the model verbs which you will find in the Verb Tables. All the other verbs follow one of these patterns, so the number next to each verb indicates which pattern fits this particular verb. For example, **begleiten** *(to accompany) follows the same pattern as* **arbeiten** *(to work), number 3 in the Verb Tables.*

All the verbs are in alphabetical order. For reflexive verbs like **sich setzen** *(to sit down) look under* **setzen**, *not under* **sich**.

With the exception of reflexive verbs which are always formed with **haben**, *most verbs have the same auxiliary (***sein** *or* **haben***) as their model verb. If this is different, it is shown in the Verb Index. Certain verbs can be formed with both* **haben** *and* **sein** *and there is a note about this at the relevant verb table.*

Some verbs in the Verb Index have a dividing line through them to show that the verb is separable, for example, **durch|setzen**.

➪ *For more information on* ***separable*** *and* ***inseparable*** *verbs, see page 109.*

Verb Index

Verb Index